AF323525

MUSIC AS A SCIENCE OF MANKIND IN EIGHTEENTH-CENTURY BRITAIN

Music as a Science of Mankind in Eighteenth-Century Britain

MARIA SEMI
University of Bologna, Italy

Translated by
TIMOTHY KEATES

ASHGATE

Published by
Ashgate Publishing Limited
Wey Court East
Union Road
Farnham
Surrey, GU9 7PT
England

Ashgate Publishing Company
Suite 420
101 Cherry Street
Burlington
VT 05401-4405
USA

www.ashgate.com

British Library Cataloguing in Publication Data
Semi, Maria.
Music as a science of mankind in eighteenth-century Britain.
1. Music and philosophy--Great Britain--History--18th century. 2. Musical perception--Great Britain--History--18th century. 3. Musicology--Great Britain--History--18th century. 4. Great Britain--Intellectual life--18th century.
I. Title
780'.01-dc22

Library of Congress Cataloging-in-Publication Data
Semi, Maria.
Music as a science of mankind in eighteenth-century Britain / Maria Semi.
     p. cm.
Includes bibliographical references and index.
ISBN 978-1-4094-2868-8 (hardcover : alk. paper)--ISBN 978-1-4094-2869-5 (ebook)
1. Musicology--Great Britain--History--18th century. 2. Music--Philosophy and aesthetics--History--18th century. 3. Music theory--History--18th century. I. Title.

ML3797.2.G7S45 2011
780.72'041--dc23

2011026575

ISBN 9781409428688 (hbk)
ISBN 9781409428695 (ebk)

Printed and bound in Great Britain by the
MPG Books Group, UK.

Contents

List of figures   vii
Acknowledgments   ix

Introduction   1

PART I   The contribution of music to the 'Science of Man'

1   An ethical pleasure? Music and the education of man   27
    Art at the tea-table: Joseph Addison, the pleasures of the
    imagination and listening as a social virtue   27
    Interior listening and political harmony: Lord Shaftesbury   31
    The critic at the opera: John Dennis, music-hating moralist   37
    Addison and Steele: critique and practice of music   46
    Conclusions   54

2   Anthropologies and psychologies of listening   57
    Music and 'natural sympathy'   62
    Sympathetic emotions: vocal and instrumental music according to
    Lord Kames   71
    A 'mechanical' musical sympathy: Daniel Webb   77
    Musical expression   83
    Mimesis and imitation in music: Aristotle and the Moderns in the
    comparison of Thomas Twining   89
    The beauty of the 'system': the new musical listening of
    Adam Smith   93
    Conclusions   102

**PART II   An intellectual background for British musical theories
and histories**

3   Musical knowledge and human knowledge   109
    Alexander Malcolm: *A Treatise of Musick, Speculative, Practical
    and Historical* (Edinburgh, 1721)   109
    Musical sound in a Lockeian mind: Alexander Malcolm's
    speculative music   111

Music and the human mind: a new goal for the music of
the Moderns   115
John Frederick Lampe: *The Art of Musick* (London, 1740)   118
Charles Avison: *An Essay on Musical Expression* (London, 1752)   121
The foundations of the art of music: the philosophical background
of Charles Avison   123
Expression and imitation   124
Musical perfection as the ideal combination of knowledge, deed
and action   128
Conclusions   130

4   Music and history   131
Historical Pyrrhonism and antiquarian research: the music of the
Ancients in Burney and Hawkins.   133
A forgotten 'Science of Music': the musicology conceived by
Sir John Hawkins   137
'Sonata' replies to Fontenelle: Charles Burney's *Essay on Musical
Criticism*   142
'Unluckily for Purcell!': Charles Burney and the progressive fate
of musical material   144
Sir John Hawkins and the non-progressive nature of taste   147
The histories of music: cultural collocation of a literary genre   151
Conclusions   156

Bibliography   159
Index   179

List of figures

I.1   Wright of Derby, *An Experiment on a Bird in the Air Pump*,
c. 1767-68. By courtesy of the National Gallery (London).   5

1.1   Anthony, Third Earl of Shaftesbury, *Characteristics of Men,
Manners, Opinions, Times* (London, J. Darby, 1714²),
frontispiece (detail).   34

4.1   Sir Francis Bacon, General distribution of human knowledge
– Memory   154

4.2   Sir Francis Bacon, General distribution of human knowledge
– Imagination   154

4.3   Sir Francis Bacon, General distribution of human knowledge
– Reason   155

Acknowledgments

My work on this project began with a doctoral dissertation at the University of Bologna in Italy, a study that greatly benefited from the guidance of Tom Dixon, Paolo Gozza and Antonio Serravezza. I also wish to express my gratitude to Lorenzo Bianconi, who at that stage read and commented on some chapters. Invaluable advice came from Penelope Gouk, who read some parts of the book and supported my proposal from the very beginning.

I gratefully acknowledge the assistance of the staff of the library of the Dipartimento di Musica e Spettacolo (University of Bologna), in particular Angela Capelli, who granted me the possibility of unlimited book borrowing. The resources of the British Library have been of inestimable value to me throughout the work. My thanks go also to the National Gallery, which granted me permission to use a picture from their collection. Readers for Ashgate Publishing made many helpful suggestions. To Timothy Keates I owe a particular debt of gratitude for translating the whole work from Italian into English. Financial support came mostly from the University of Bologna, with a PhD scholarship at the beginning of my studies on this subject, and subsequently with a research Fellowship. A final, special, thank you goes again to Paolo Gozza, who with endless kindness and considerable patience encouraged me along this uneven path.

Maria Semi
Bologna, Italy

Introduction

> The images of men's wits and knowledges remain in books, exempted from the wrong of time, and capable of perpetual renovation. Neither are they fitly to be called images, because they generate still, and cast their seeds in the minds of others [...]
>
> SIR FRANCIS BACON, *Of the Proficience and Advancement of Learning*

The eighteenth-century 'Science of Man' can be characterized as an attempt to conceive of mankind – in its physical, psychological and social dimensions – as a privileged object of investigation. From the wealth of studies ranging through the seventeenth and eighteenth centuries, starting with Bacon in England and Descartes in France, it can be seen how in the aim to construct knowledge the emphasis is not merely to investigate the external world but also to probe the perceptual and cognitive processes that govern the human mind. A change of perspective occurs in the vision of the external world: no longer merely a matter of projecting the view 'outside' in order to enquire into phenomena, but rather to understand what relation there may be between the phenomena themselves (for example, the vibration of air) and the effect produced by these phenomena when perceived (sound). Knowledge becomes a complex network, full of ramifications, that explores individual disciplines of study and their interconnections and takes man as its basis. As witness, for example, the construction of encyclopaedia of knowledge where knowledge is arranged starting from the distinction between the various mental faculties. Such a conception can be seen in Sir Francis Bacon's tree of knowledge in *Of the Proficience and Advancement of Learning* (1605), where the individual contexts of study are deployed on the basis of the particular human faculty brought into play. Memory, reason and imagination represent three different ways of observing and studying the surrounding world, and in the citadel of the Baconian mind these faculties play the role of archive (memory), court of justice (reason) and theatre (imagination). An interesting result of this way of organizing knowledge is that one and the same object of study may beget different kinds of knowledge, according to the faculty by which it is examined: by this means, each of the many paths to be taken engenders a different sort of knowledge. The same event that will be assessed in the court of justice may give rise to a play in the theatre, and its narration can be preserved in the city archives. Each of the three 'sites' of knowledge has its own way of reading and interpreting reality.

The faculties, on the one hand, and the senses, on the other, are the two poles on which the construction of the new knowledge hinges. As already noted by Ernst Cassirer, each sense is equipped with a specific structure of its own, and no single sense is credited with a privileged access to reality.[1] From this point of view, the remarks on the sense of sight following the formulation of the well-known 'problem of Molyneux' are emblematic. As is known, Molyneux in a letter to John Locke of 1688 wondered whether a person born blind, who had learnt to distinguish certain geometrical figures by touch and had then recovered sight, would be able to recognize the same figures merely by seeing them. The empirical response to the question came in 1728 after the physician William Cheselden successfully operated on a patient blind from birth and restored his sight. As Locke and Berkeley had already predicted, the patient was unable immediately to identify and distinguish the figures, thus demonstrating that the perception conveyed by the senses and the representation of it formed in our mind are two different things. The relation of a person with the surrounding world is altered by these discoveries. In order to know the world it is no longer sufficient to direct one's gaze towards the exterior: that same gaze must be aimed at man's interior, at the place where representation and thought are shaped. This is not a 'metaphysical' observation but, rather, the critical scrutiny brilliantly described by Starobinski in his *Le voile de Poppée*:[2]

> Yet criticism, having condemned deceptive appearances, is not incapable of turning on itself. If a little reflection takes us away from the sensible world, a more demanding philosophy brings us back [...]. Skepticism first warns us against universal deception, then leads us very gently to the idea of recommencing knowledge with a wisdom that, under the protection of the *reflexive* gaze, trusts in the senses and in the world the senses reveal.

This reflected gaze,[3] which after condemning appearances restores trust in the senses, and proceeds in the glorious attempt to describe man as he really is, embodies one of the characteristic traits of British philosophical-literary culture of the seventeenth and eighteenth centuries. It goes beyond the kind of self-knowledge promoted by the inscription at the temple of Delphi – spiritual knowledge – and beyond the search for ideal man: Diogenes will not return to wander among people, lantern in hand, saying 'I seek man'. The investigations of Locke, Hutcheson, Hume, Reid and others are no longer bent on the quest for a divine ideal, nor for the exceptional or the strange, nor yet – in the case of authors dealing with literature and the arts – for natures of 'genius'. The characteristics of genius are sought and its nature described. In this context genius is not madness or intemperance, it can be comprehended and explained; as Sir Joshua Reynolds told

---

[1]   Ernst Cassirer, *The Philosophy of the Enlightenment* (Princeton, 1951).

[2]   Jean Starobinski, *The Living Eye*, trans. A. Goldhammer (Cambridge, MA, and London, 1989), pp. 5-6.

[3]   For a recent study of empricism as a method for researching the origin and foundation of knowledge, and the status of 'reflection', see André Charrak, *Empirisme et théorie de la connaissance. Réflexion et fondement des sciences au XVIIIe siècle* (Paris, 2009).

his students at the Royal Academy in 1774: 'What we now call Genius, begins, not where rules, abstractedly taken, end; but where known vulgar and trite rules have no longer any place. It must of necessity be, that even works of Genius, like every other effect, as they must have their cause, must likewise have their rules'.[4] Every effect must have a cause and in order to know causes it is necessary to know how the common man perceives the surrounding world, forms an idea of it and thence elaborates new forms and enriches his environment. All science, all knowledge must assist the philosopher to proceed in this direction.

This attention to the perception of the ambient world, and its relation with the subject, for that matter, underpins not only works of philosophy or artistic and literary criticism. Literature itself unmistakably testifies to the eighteenth century's interest in man and especially the private sphere, the sphere of feelings, as witnessed by the advent of the novel. In a study of the cultural ambience in which this new literary genre appears, Paul J. Hunter identifies some characteristic traits of the novel, among them the verisimilitude by which[5]

> the people who exist and the things that transpire in novels are recognizable as behaving and occurring in believable human ways, and readers are given the sense that things happen in the fictional world according to laws that are essentially like those governing the everyday world they themselves experience.

Namely, the mise-en-scène of a fully conscious subjectivity, and empathy. The attention to feeling, which is characteristic of this literature, is doubly linked to the all-important study of man and will indeed influence the conception of historical study and how history should be written: in this period it ceases to be a mere narrative of political events and expands its vision to comprehend customs, arts, religion, trade. David Hume, for example, in a letter to his friend William Mure writes that 'the finest quality of an historian is to be true and impartial; the next to be interesting. If you do not say, that I have done both parties justice; and if Mrs Mure be not sorry for poor King Charles, I shall burn my papers, and return to philosophy.' As Mark Salber Phillips (to whom I am indebted for this consideration

---

[4]   Sir Joshua Reynolds, *Discourses on Art,* ed. Robert R. Wark (New Haven and London, 1997), p. 97.

[5]   Paul J. Hunter, *Before Novels. The Cultural Contexts of Eighteenth-Century English Fiction* (New York and London, 1990), p. 24. Some very interesting considerations about the need for verisimilitude in eighteenth-century literature can be found in Reinhart Koselleck's study on the topos *'historia magistra vitae'*, where he interpretates this need as a symptom of a new widespread historical awareness of reality (see Reinhart Koselleck, *Futures Past: on the Semantics of Historical Time*, trans. Keith Tribe (New York, 2004); see also 'Geschichte, Historie' in *Geschichtliche Grundbegriffe. Historisches Lexikon zur politisch-sozialen Sprache in Deutschland* (Stuttgart, 1975)).

of Hume) notes,[6] the Scottish philosopher and author of the important *History of England from the Invasion of Julius Caesar to the Revolution in 1688* and *History of Great Britain*, is concerned here with the *emotive effect* of his narrative: in order to be 'interesting' he must arouse the reader's 'sympathy' – one of the key concepts of the period. History, too, must be able to call the affects into play.

A similar attention to the emotional reactions of the person observing the surrounding world is well represented in painting: for example, in the work of Joseph Wright of Derby, in the series dedicated to *The Blacksmith's Shop*, depicting a forge with smiths at work watched by women and children,[7] and in the paintings of scientific experiments performed in private houses. I have in mind particularly the two paintings *A Philosopher Giving a Lecture on the Orrery* and *An Experiment on a Bird in the Air Pump* (Figure I.1) whose real subject is the different emotional responses of the spectators to the experiments – curiosity, fear, meditation, being clearly shown on their faces.

Every detail of the painting aims to illustrate and arouse a feeling. The figure of the natural philosopher, who is eccentrically dressed and only half of whose face is illuminated, is ambiguous and still carries an aura of mystery associated with the magician; the girls on the right contemplate with anguish the fate of their little bird, whose expected death appears to have cast the man seated beside them into grave meditation – he has by now averted his gaze from the experiment. In contrast, the spectators on the left seem intellectually engrossed by the demonstration of the vacuum pump, whereas the two young figures standing look rather as though they are seizing the opportunity of togetherness for exchange of a more intimate nature. Moreover, the scene is illuminated partly from a hidden source of the scientist's mysterious equipment, and partly by the diaphanous, somewhat disturbing light of a moon half-concealed among the clouds. In the multitudinous variety of possible emotional effects elicited by the situation in the persons depicted a spectator can scarcely help exercising the faculty that enables the experience of identification, the 'sympathy' with which Adam Smith was to be so concerned in the *Theory of Moral Sentiments*.

---

[6]   In this connection, see the ample and interesting study by Mark Salber Phillips, *Society and Sentiment. Genres of Historical Writing in Britain, 1740-1820* (Princeton, NJ, 2000).

[7]   On the function of feminine representation in the work of Wright see the article by Susan L. Siegfried, 'Engaging the Audience: Sexual Economies of Vision in Joseph Wright', *Representations*, 68 (1999): pp. 34-58, who remarks on the series of the *Blacksmith's Shop*: 'No doubt the blacksmith and forge subjects referred to contemporary ideas about labor, but they were not just moral lessons directed at man. They were also designed, and still function, to elicit immediate emotional responses from an audience engaged above all in viewing pictures, which the paintings do by playing out a gendered thematic of viewing that depends upon the feminine' (ibid., p. 39).

Figure I.1   Wright of Derby, *An Experiment on a Bird in the Air Pump*, c. 1767-68. By courtesy of the National Gallery, London

As emphasized by Peter Jones, editor of a programmatically titled work (*The Science of Man in the Scottish Enlightenment*), the secondary literature has often addressed individual aspects of the study of human nature in the eighteenth century, yet 'the scope of their enquiries has been neglected by modern scholars, no doubt in part because later ages parcelled up and allocated their questions to different professional disciplines'.[8] The keynote in all eighteenth-century research is that scientific and philosophical investigation, in every field, must never lose sight of its own objective: mankind, its welfare and its happiness. Knowledge appears not as an end in itself but as the means to attain an improvement of the human condition. Moreover, the study of the type of approach of philosophical literature to the Science of Man is made all the harder for the contemporary scholar by the fact that, as Alexander Broadie writes, 'although it is of course possible to distinguish different disciplines or fields investigated during the Scottish Enlightenment, no attempt was made in practice to keep the separate disciplines in their separate boxes. A holistic approach was characteristic of the literati [...].'[9] Of course, in addressing these sources one may risk losing oneself in the details of the individual disciplines and forgetting that each one belongs in a broader project, from which it acquires its own significance.

So what was this project? In British society of the eighteenth century, the study of man, his faculties and his beliefs is not an end in itself. The knowledge of man and his potentials must serve to improve him and make it easier for him to attain the aim of every individual: the achievement of happiness. At this point, philosophy sets itself a well-defined target. In a brilliant work of the 1980s, *La philosophie comme méthode de vie* – developed from an inaugural lecture and subsequent courses at the Collège de France – Pierre Hadot lays stress on the distinction between *philosophy* and *philosophical discourse*; the first involving 'the philosophical way of life', the second 'a theoretical and abstract activity'. In Hadot's view, the demarcation between these two spheres of philosophy faded in the Middle Ages and, in particular, with the institution of the university; he points out how Christian spirituality adopted certain characteristics of ancient philosophy, especially with regard to the practice of *spiritual exercises*. And he goes on to explain how the teachers in the universities were professionals who trained other professionals, not just men aiming to train men. He identifies the birth of a new philosophy between the sixteenth and eighteenth centuries, developing with Descartes, Spinoza, Malebranche and Leibnitz outside the university, differing from mediaeval scholasticism but placing itself in the same terrain: *philosophical discourse*. To be sure, modern philosophy may not fully regain the aspect that Hadot holds to be characteristic of ancient philosophy – namely that 'in ancient philosophy, it was not only Chrysippus or Epicurus who, just because they had

---

[8]   Peter Jones (ed.), *The Science of Man in the Scottish Enlightenment*, (Edinburgh, 1989), p. 1.

[9]   Alexander Broadie (ed.), *The Cambridge Companion to the Scottish Enlightenment* (Cambridge, 2003), p. 5.

developed a philosophical discourse, were considered philosophers. Rather, every person who lived according to the precepts of Chrysippus or Epicurus was every bit as much of a philosopher as they.'[10] But it is equally true that the 'philosophical discourse' developed by the British philosophers of mind and moralists seeks to be 'effective', to influence reality and the human condition. Emblematic of this interpretation of philosophy is the figure of Antony Ashley Cooper, Third Earl of Shaftesbury, close to the Ancients, reader of Epictetus and Marcus Aurelius, author of spiritual exercises and writings, in particular on morals and the beautiful. In his personal notebooks, not destined for publication and compiled on the model of the *Askemata* (exercises) of the Stoics, Shaftesbury gives an unequivocal definition of what 'philosophy' means for him:[11]

> If I have a right idea of *life* now at this moment, that I think slightly of it, and resolve with myself that it may easily be laid down on any honourable occasion of service to my friends or country, teach me how I shall remain in this opinion; what it is that changes; and how this disturbance happens; by what innovation, what composition, what intervention of other ideas. If this be the subject of the *philosophical art*, I readily apply to it and study it. If there be nothing of this in the case I have no occasion for the sort of learning, and am no more desirous of knowing how I form or compound those ideas which are distinguished by words, than I have of knowing how and by what motions of my mouth I form those articulate sounds, which I can full as well pronounce and use without any such science or speculation.

The knowledge of the formation of ideas, then – and remember that Shaftesbury was taught by John Locke – is useful only if placed in the service of life. For that matter, the activities of the numerous Clubs in the British eighteenth century were devoted to the idea of 'improvement', whether in the field of morals or that of the mechanical arts,[12] as was a great deal of publicist literature, the most successful example being undoubtedly that of the *Spectator*. As Salber Phillips writes:[13]

> concern for manners was a key place where a variety of moral discourses – classical republicanism, Addisonian politeness, sentimentalism – intersected with a number of philosophical or learned ones. Thus the idea of manners and its various extensions served as a common currency linking the themes of law,

---

[10]   Pierre Hadot, *Philosophy as a Way of Life, Spiritual Exercises from Socrates to Foucault*, ed. A. I. Davidson (Oxford, 1995), pp. 264-276: 272.

[11]   Benjamin Rand (ed.), *The Life, Unpublished Letters, and Philosophical Regimen of Antony, Earl of Shaftesbury* (London and New York, 1900), p. 268.

[12]   In this connection see the historical study by Davis D. McElroy, *Scotland's Age of Improvement. A Survey of Eighteenth-Century Literary Clubs and Societies* (Washington, 1969).

[13]   M. S. Phillips, *Society and Sentiment*, p. 147.

history, or ethnographic travel with other, more overtly moral languages of the times.

A further instance of the importance ascribed to the 'way of life' in the eighteenth century is the abundance of and interest evinced by biography, with the aim of teaching correct living by means of examples. Note, in this connection, how Oliver Goldsmith's description of 'the man of taste' in *The Present State of Polite Learning* characterizes him as an intermediary 'between the world and the cell, between learning and common sense' that 'teaches the vulgar on what part of a character to lay the emphasis of praise':[14]

> by the means of polite learning alone, the patriot and the hero, *the man who praiseth virtue and he who practises it*, who fights successfully for his country or who dies in its defence, becomes immortal.

Here, Goldsmith's ideal of 'polite learning' clearly refers to biographical study which – as though echoing what Hadot says of ancient philosophy – proposes as model not only the person who celebrates virtue but also the one who practises it. Biography is a genre that can serve as a bridge between the cell – of the philosopher as of the theologian – and the world, supplying clear examples.[15] We reiterate, then, that the aim that underpins the majority of the literary, philosophical and historiographic production of the period and decrees that it shall be effective is the desire to educate and improve mankind, and this goal can only be achieved by studying man's faculties and possibilities, whether of man as individual or man in society.

With regard to the title of our work, how does speculation on music enter this context? In what way does the art of sounds participate in and contribute to this project? Between the seventeenth and eighteenth centuries the reflection on music underwent an important transition. For this period witnessed the passage from a system centred on the paradigm of the liberal arts – divided into *trivium* and *quadrivium*, where music belonged in the latter grouping (together with mathematics, geometry and astronomy) – to the new 'modern system of the arts', where music came to be dealt with alongside poetry, painting and sculpture.[16]

---

[14]   Oliver Goldsmith, *An Enquiry into the Present State of Polite Learning in Europe* (London, 1774²), p. 83 (my italics).

[15]   A further example of this way of intending biographies can be found in the works of Roger North. On this topic see the recent work of Jamie C. Kassler, *The Honourable Roger North, 1651-1734. On Life, Morality, Law and Tradition* (Farnham and Burlington, 2009), esp. pp. 77-99.

[16]   See Paul Oskar Kristeller, 'The Modern System of the Arts: A Study in the History of Aesthetics I & II', *Journal of the History of Ideas*, 12 (1951), pp. 496-527; 13 (1952), pp. 17-46; reprinted in Kristeller, *Renaissance Thought and the Arts: Collected Essays* (Princeton, NJ, 1990).

This transition was to influence the very concept of music, whose significance was transformed: as witness the need – already present in Bacon – to find a new name for that particular study of music whose focus is on 'sound' (and that, even with appreciable changes, remains linked to the *quadrivium* tradition), leading to the birth of *acoustic* science. During this period of transition, the two systems coexisted, generating a quantity of studies in which music is considered within both the ancient and the modern systems.

The heritage of the quadrivial studies, the space allocated to music in Plato and Aristotle, the mention of music in the Holy Scriptures and the patristic writings – suffice it to recall Saint Augustine – gave the art of sounds a fairly definite status and contexts for discussion. One question in particular that linked those contexts, and which has never ceased to be raised, concerns the nature of musical pleasure. The study of this problem could spill over into mathematical discussion (musical pleasure is linked with the nature of the mathematical relations that constitute consonances), discussion of morals (is the pleasure virtuous or not?) and of religion (does musical pleasure elevate the soul to God or is it confined to the senses?). None of these contexts disappears in the British eighteenth century; rather, the dimension of mathematics is accompanied and increasingly replaced by those of physics, acoustics, mechanics, in the attempt to find the place occupied by musical pleasure in man's body, how music may affect the fibres and nerves and thence generate emotions. In addition, the moral question becomes a subject for discussion and a tool for judgement by one of the new literary figures of the century – namely, the critic who, by expressing his own opinion, aims to direct that of others and seeks rational, as far as possible 'certain', arguments in the assessment of works.[17] In reflections on music the discussions of critics will concentrate on two themes in particular: the morality (doubtful...) of the musical work and whether instrumental music can have any moral value.

That the quantitative, mathematical dimension in evaluation of the arts continued to be held legitimate between the seventeenth and eighteenth centuries is indirectly witnessed by the frequency with which Tristram Shandy, in Sterne's novel, attacks the way of judging art by this criterion. Sterne's withering irony plays with his readers' expectations, he subverts and ultimately invalidates the status of the traditional concepts associated with what he intends to criticize: from a rapid reading of the main passages on judgement of arts and music, then, we can infer some of the commonplaces in the criticism of the period. Among those of interest here, the first worthy of mention does not actually concern music but is a judgement the narrator passes on his own work and is significant from at least two points of view: his ridicule of 'quantification' of merit, and his mention of all the

---

[17]   To what extent the question of musical pleasure was at the centre of attention between the seventeenth and eighteenth centuries is underlined also by Jamie C. Kassler in her introduction to the edition of *Roger North's The Musicall Grammarian 1728*, ed. J. C. Kassler and M. Chan (Cambridge, 1990), pp. 5-11.

classical criteria of aesthetic evaluation to be found in treatises on painting, music and poetry.[18]

> The design, your Lordship sees, is good, the colouring trasparent, – the drawing not amiss; – or to speak more like a man of science, – and measure my piece in the painter's scale, divided into 20, – I believe, my Lord, the out-lines will turn out as 12, – the composition as 9, – the colouring as 6, – the expression 13 and a half, – and the design, – if I may be allowed, my Lord, to understand my own *design*, and supposing absolute perfection in designing, to be as 20, – I think it cannot well fall short of 19. Besides all this, – there is keeping in it, and the dark strokes in the Hobby-Horse, (which is a secondary figure, and a kind of background to the whole) give great force to the principal lights in your own figure, and make it come off wonderfully; – and besides, there is an air of originality in the *tout ensemble.*

We read how the 'man of science' judges by numbers and the criteria he uses are design, composition, colouring, expression and originality. We shall continue to encounter these tools of evaluation frequently in our study; in particular, expression will play a leading role in the discussions on music. Further on in the story, Tristram returns to the attack on the 'measure' – the *mot juste* indeed – of evaluation of certain critics, miming the dialogue between a critic and a person who requests his judgement: the critic has been to see the famous actor Garrick perform, and in his opinion Garrick has made an ill-advised pause between a noun and an adjective 'three seconds and three fifths by a stop-watch, my Lord, each time!'. At which point his poor interlocutor seeks further understanding and asks him:[19]

> But, in suspending his voice – was the sense suspended likewise? Did no expression of attitude or countenance fill up the chasm? – Was the eye silent? Did you narrowly look? – I look'd only at the stop-watch, my Lord – Excellent observer! And what of this new book the whole world makes such a rout about? – Oh! 'tis out of all plum, my Lord, – quite an irregular thing! – not one of the angles at the four corners was a right angle. – I had my rule and compasses &c. my Lord, in my pocket. – Excellent critic! [...] – And did you step in, to take a look at the grand picture, in your way back. – 'Tis a melancholy daub! my Lord; not one principle of the *pyramid* in any one group! – and what a price! – for there is nothing of the colouring of *Titian*, – the expression of *Rubens*, – the grace of *Raphael*, – the purity of *Dominichino*, – the *corregiescity* of *Correggio*, – the learning of *Poussin*, – the airs of *Guido*, – the taste of the *Carachi's* – or the contour of *Angelo.*

---

[18]   Laurence Sterne, *The Life and Opinions of Tristram Shandy, Gentleman,* ed. M. and J. New (London, 1997), p. 12.

[19]   Ibid., p. 160.

This account is, of course, a caricature but it puts its finger on a defect in the critic: by his analogy the objectivity of rule and compass too easily turns into objective judgement. Sterne excoriates the lack of emotional participation of such geometrical assessment and the absolute nature of its sentence. As against that, the literature of the period supplies examples that seem the perfect embodiment of the kind of aesthetic judgement that Tristram abhors. In 1780, for instance, the reverend William Jones published *Letters from a Tutor to his Pupils*, one of them 'On Taste'. Without going into Jones's system in detail, suffice it to say that he tries to reduce judgement on beauty to a harmonious relation between three elements of the work of art, the model of which would be perfect musical agreement, composed of the key note, its third and its fifth; in painting and sculpture this principle is resolved in the balanced rapport among the planes or the figures themselves, leading the author to write: 'I suspect that the celebrated statue of the Laocoon, however excellent in other respects, strikes every eye with more pleasure because it consists of three figures, all contributing to the same effect. [...] In oratory, does not experience teach us, that the association of three ideas satisfies the mind, as the union of three sounds satisfies the ear?'[20] After reading the passages from Sterne we can hardly repress an ironic smile at Jones, but the theories on beauty developed through the eighteenth century in the attempt to retrace it to one or a few principles, as Jones does here, represent a corollary of that faith in the existence of a standard of taste so typical of the period.

In *Tristram Shandy*, music or the musical lexicon are often employed by the author to depict (sometimes literally) the passions by which the characters are moved. As we know, every time Uncle Toby Shandy is perturbed and does not know how to react he begins to whistle 'Lillabullero', thus expressing his unease by filling the air with a trivial tune. Again, in rendering the anger on his father's face, Tristram explains that his complexion was reddened a full octave above its natural colour. The connection between music and passions – doubly linked with the question of morality – is undoubtedly the subject most discussed in the literature we shall deal with, and it is interesting to note how Sterne chose musical parlance to describe his characters' changes of mood.

Religion provided an important context in which the connection between music, passions and morals was developed, as witnessed by the quantity of sermons devoted to music, often occasioned by the celebration of Saint Cecilia's Day or by the inauguration of a new church organ. As Ruth Smith recalls:[21]

> sermons, biblical commentaries and works on religion formed a major, possibly
> the largest, part of the nation's reading-matter. The comments of churchmen
> form the bulk of contemporary music criticism, reaching a much wider audience

---

[20] William Jones, *Letters from a Tutor to his Pupils* (London, 1780), pp. 77-78; 81.

[21] Ruth Smith, *Handel's Oratorios and Eighteenth-Century Thought* (Cambridge, 1995), p. 83; for a first survey of the sermons dedicated to music, see the bibliography on pp. 438-441.

than the writings of professional musicians, and they were not confined to church music; they assessed the effects of all kinds of music.

The above-mentioned William Jones has left us a sermon dealing with 'The Nature and Excellence of Music' given in 1787 at the installation of a new organ at Nayland. His text testifies to the high quality of this literature, which unfortunately we have not space to study here in the depth it deserves. Jones directs his congregation to 'a rational consideration of the nature and uses of music [...]. For this art is a great and worthy object to the understanding of man.'[22] In evidencing the qualities of music and its utility for devotional purposes he does not confine himself to citing examples from Holy Scripture but expatiates on the laws of music theory and the philosophy of sound, explaining how there exists a 'sympathetic feeling' between the fibres of our body and musical sounds, and dwells on another of the traditional topoi that we shall go on to examine – namely, the relation between music and text 'when words convey to the mind the same sense as the music does, and dispose us to the same affection, then the effect of music is greatest',[23] a position repeatedly encountered in the writings to be dealt with below. Again, in a sermon of 1726 by Thomas Bisse, chancellor of the diocese of Hereford, music and harmony are powerfully exalted as 'the chief among the delights ordained for the sons of men'.[24] Indeed, the preacher asserts that man's two main organs, hand and ear, can be seen to have been provided for the purpose of music, in the first place, since their perfection is achieved and manifested in relation to music. Hearing, inasmuch as it is not the mere faculty itself that makes us feel pleasure, but a genuine 'listening' that we reserve for music, and in this pleasure we experience the manifestation of the aim for which the ear was conceived. The hand, since while the myriad even noble activities we perform by means of this organ, such as writing, require only a modest, easily attained ability, whereas in playing a musical instrument the hand acquires an agility and rapidity not to be compared with any other activity, and therein reaches its own 'perfection'.

After sketching the importance of the link between music and morality as witnessed in critical and devotional literature, and the possibilities it offers for discussing the nature of musical pleasure and the relation between music and text, something must be said on the rapport between the studies of philosophy of mind – highlighted at the outset of this chapter – and the writings on music. The emphasis given in the British tradition to perception, sensations, emotions – terms that were established in this period in the very tradition we are dealing

---

[22]   William Jones, *The Nature and Excellence of Music. A Sermon Preached at the Opening of a New Organ, in the Parish Church of Nayland in Suffolk; on Sunday, July the 29th, 1787* (London, 1787), p. 3.

[23]   Ibid., p. 7.

[24]   Thomas Bisse, *Musick the Delight of the Sons of Men. A Sermon Preached at the Cathedral Church of Hereford, at the Anniversary Meeting of the Three Choirs, Gloucester, Worcester, Hereford, September 7, 1726* (London, 1726), p. 22.

with[25] – led philosophers to a deep interest in the arts, as stimulating the senses of sight and hearing in a very particular way and producing really remarkable 'effects', alterations of feeling. The attempt to explain *how* we come to experience the sentiment of beauty, what is *taste*, what is the nature of the pleasure we feel in the perception of art – all these challenges are of particular interest for theories that aimed to account for the working of man as a whole, and thus of his feelings and opinions. Philosophers like Hutcheson, Hume, Smith and Reid – to cite only the best-known – provided a determining contribution to the discussions on the arts, in some cases including remarks on music. The latter are important not only for their intrinsic value but also because, together with the discussions of natural philosophy, they supply a model to approach the debates on music pursued in other contexts. For example, in the sermon by William Jones quoted above music is discussed in this same perspective, but the identical categories and frame of reference are also employed in writings on musical theory, as in the well-known *Essay on Musical Expression* by Charles Avison and lesser-known texts, and in the two important histories of music by Charles Burney and Sir John Hawkins.

The secondary literature in the musicological area that addresses the British tradition of writing on music between the seventeenth and eighteenth centuries does indeed reflect the dichotomy that has arisen in thinking about music following the advent of the modern system of the arts. Thus we find a polarization in two main channels: on the one hand, the studies that deal with music within the speculations of natural philosophy (comprising fields now separate such as physics, acoustics, chemistry, biology, and so on); and, on the other hand, the studies in the philosophical-aesthetic context.

Among the first of these we note the research of Penelope Gouk, who has reconstructed the discussions on acoustics appearing in the *Philosophical Transactions* – the bulletin of the Royal Society of London – and has investigated the relation between medicine and music.[26] We are also indebted to Jamie C. Kassler, who has not only devoted specific study to authors like Hobbes, Hooke and William Jones, and has edited, with Mary Chan, Roger North's writings on music, but has also prepared a vast catalogue in two volumes comprising the British sources (from 1713 to 1830) dealing with or containing discussions on music.[27]

---

[25]   On this point, see the interesting volume by Thomas Dixon, *From Passions to Emotions. The Creation of a Secular Psychological Category* (New York, 2003).

[26]   See in particular Gouk's 'Acoustics in the early Royal Society, 1660-1680', *Notes and Records of the Royal Society*, 36 (1982): pp. 155-175; 'Some English Theories of Hearing in the Seventeenth Century: before and after Descartes', in C. Burnett, M. Fend and P. Gouk (eds), *The Second Sense: Studies in Hearing and Musical Judgment from Antiquity to the Seventeenth Century* (London, 1991), pp. 95-113; and *Music, Science and Natural Magic in Seventeenth-Century England* (New Haven and London, 1999).

[27]   Jamie C. Kassler, *The Science of Music in Britain, 1714-1830: A Catalogue of Writings, Lectures and Inventions* (2 vols, New York and London, 1979).

With regard to the aesthetic-philosophical context, however, in spite of some interesting studies, nothing of similar scope has been produced. In the 1940s and 1950s, Herbert Schueller published some articles on the discussion of music within the tradition of 'British Criticism', focusing on the concepts of 'imitation' and 'expression', the conjunction between music and the other arts, and the positive and negative assessments of the pleasure conveyed by music. Schueller examined an enormous quantity of sources, realizing that real music criticism in Britain appeared not only in the *Spectator*, but also in poems, essays and biographies.[28] His studies may be said to have paved the way for a new field of research, but this has yet to be developed in a systematic manner. An important study on the English musical aesthetics of the eighteenth century is Nikolaus de Palézieux's *Die Lehre vom Ausdruck in der englischen Musikästhetik des 18. Jahrhunderts,*[29] of which insufficient notice has been taken. This work has the virtue of making detailed examination of the transformation of the concept of 'musical expression' from 'Musikbegriff' to 'ästhetische Kategorie', but in so doing narrows the range of investigation, leading the author to confine his examination to a specific topic in the British tradition without seeking to set it in a more precise context.

The concepts of 'imitation' and 'expression' have been treated by a much better-known author, John Neubauer. In his essay *The Emancipation of Music from Language*, he examines the relevant French, German and English writings in order to trace how in the eighteenth century 'a new understanding of the arts emerged, and the struggle to legitimize instrumental music became the first, decisive battle about nonrepresentational art'.[30] But his investigation of the tradition of 'British Criticism'[31] has a rather different orientation. Neubauer is concerned to highlight the inadequacy of the concept of expression in freeing music from the mimetic paradigm. As against the positive assessment of the application of the idea of expression put forward by scholars like Roger Scruton and Peter Kivy, his enquiry into the British tradition aims to show how expression is scarcely detached from the concept of imitation. Though it may not be incorrect to see the terms 'expression' and 'imitation' as linked, Neubauer's analysis of authors such as Avison, Beattie, Twining and Smith is so summary as to misunderstand them at several points, failing to place them in the context of the theories advanced by them and considering only the passages in their writings bearing on the mimetic principle.

---

[28]   Herbert M. Schueller, 'The Use and Decorum of Music as Described in British Literature, 1700 to 1780', *Journal of the History of Ideas*, 13/1 (1952), pp. 73-93: 74 (for references to Schueller's other articles see the Bibliography.

[29]   Nikolaus de Palézieux, *Die Lehre vom Ausdruck in der englischen Musikästhetik des 18. Jahrhunderts* (Hamburg: 1981).

[30]   John Neubauer, *The Emancipation of Music from Language. Departure from Mimesis in Eighteenth-Century Aesthetics* (New Haven and London, 1986), p. 2.

[31]   Ibid., pp. 152-157.

The most recent musicological contribution to the literature we will deal with is, as far as I know, the 2009 monograph by Pierre Dubois.[32] This essay is centred on the concept of 'musical mystery', the expression by which he designates the questions regarding how music works and what causes its effects. One of Dubois's aims is to show how the category of the sublime made it possible to 'plumb' the mystery of music in virtue of the transformation of an analytic-aesthetic discourse, stemming from the spirit of the Enlightenment, into a poetic of expression, of sensibility that heralds Romanticism.[33]

Although my study and that of Dubois draw almost entirely on the same sources, they diverge somewhat in their intentions. Mine refers almost exclusively to the tradition he defines as 'analytic aesthetic discourse' and excludes reflections on the sublime; for it is not part of my programme to trace the path that leads to the ideas subsequently developed in Romantic thought.

I should specify that the lack of secondary literature I mention does not apply to the studies devoted to individual authors or texts in eighteenth-century Britain. As will become clear from the references to the secondary literature in the chapters that follow and as a glance at the bibliography shows, there is no dearth of secondary literature. Numerous articles and studies of aesthetics have dealt with the figures of Hutcheson (including P. Kivy, C. DeWitt Thorpe, E. Michael, E. Migliorini, L. Turco), Rev. William Jones (J. C. Kassler), Thomas Reid (L. E. Brown, P. Kivy, D. Townsend) James Beattie (K. Kloth, C. Jones, N. Phillipson), John Gregory (P. Gouk), James Harris (J. Malek, R. Dunhill, C. Probyn) or Adam Smith (W. Seidel, J. Malek) among others. The more serious lack is of broad-based studies linking the discussions of music with other spheres of the intellectual world within which it belonged.

The prime objective of my work is to 'open' the musicological discourse on music to the philosophical and historiographic discussions of the period. For example, to evidentiate how the advent of music history by Hawkins and Burney should not be dealt with merely from the point of view of the musical-aesthetic ideas and debates of the time, but must also be considered in the light of the profound changes in the discussion of history-writing and aesthetics in general. This type of approach is, in my view, what distinguishes the works by Gouk and Kassler among the studies cited, the book by Ruth Smith on the Handelian oratorio, or the illuminating study by William Weber dedicated to the birth of the

---

[32]   Pierre Dubois, *La conquête du mystère musical en Grande-Bretagne au siècle des Lumières* (Lyon, 2009). Unfortunately, this contribution came to my notice only after I had finished my study. Thanks are due to Xavier Bisaro.

[33]   Ibid., p. 27: 'En effet, la conquête du mystère musical peut se comprendre comme la transformation d'un discours esthétique analytique qui prend ses origines dans l'esprit des Lumières en une poétique de l'expression, de la sensibilité et du sentiment annonciatrice du romantisme'.

idea of 'classic' in music in eighteenth-century Britain.[34] In the studies just cited the sociological enquiry, the history of science, and the intellectual, philosophical and religious context combine to illuminate how the vision of music in the societies under investigation is related to the ideas developed in the aforesaid fields. Studies confined within the strict bounds of musicology risk losing sight of crucial contexts for understanding the significance ascribed to music in the periods and societies of interest.

The eighteenth century is familiarly viewed as the period that witnessed the birth of *aesthetics*: the term received its 'baptism' at the hands of Alexander G. Baumgarten in 1735 and was thereafter 'confirmed' with the publication in 1750 of the volume by Georg Friedrich Meier titled Ästhetik, containing a systematization of the lessons on aesthetics by Baumgarten himself – whose pupil Meier was – not to mention the *Aesthetica* by Baumgarten published in 1750-58.[35] A distinctive feature in the secondary literature on aesthetics is the attempt to discover in the eighteenth century not only the birth of this discipline but also its 'detachment' from the areas with which it was historically linked (from morality, first and foremost).[36] This search for autonomy, however, has led scholars to be drastically selective in the subjects and categories they deal with and has thus engendered a very partial view of the debate on the arts; whereas setting the aesthetic reflections within a broader cultural framework could further enrich them and enable better understanding of their significance and range. Specifically, in the secondary musicological-aesthetic literature there is an attempt at a further form of autonomization, whose roots are, once again, located in the eighteenth century: namely, the emancipation of music from the text and, with this, the theoretical justification of the independence of instrumental music. Here, too, although the subject deserves attention, discussion and research tend to be confined to a handful of concepts. In this case in particular, as suggested above, the focus is on the categories of 'imitation' and 'expression', emphasizing the need to abandon the mimetic paradigm in order to enable the independent affirmation of instrumental music, at theoretical level.

An interesting example of this type of approach, where the sources are sifted in search of everything that conduces to the dual autonomy of music (from an aim external to it and from the word) is provided by the well-known study by Lydia Goehr devoted to the establishment of the 'work' as regulative principle

---

[34]   William Weber, *The Rise of Musical Classics in Eighteenth-Century England: A Study in Canon, Ritual, and Ideology* (Oxford, 1992).

[35]   The term 'baptism' is used by Leonardo Amoroso, editor of the volume *Il battesimo dell'estetica: scritti di Alexander G. Baumgarten, Immanuel Kant* (Pisa, 1993), where passages from the *Meditationes philosophicae de nonnullis ad poema pertinentibus* (1735) are cited.

[36]   See, for example, Serge Trottein (ed.), *L'ésthétique naît-elle au XVIIIe siècle?* (Paris, 2000).

between the end of the eighteenth and the beginning of the nineteenth centuries.[37] Over and above the importance and value of the thesis expounded, studies of this kind, which supply a large quantity of citations taken quite out of their proper context, run the risk of slanting the interpretation of the sources more than is warranted.[38]

If the British school of thought on music remains little investigated, this is also because it lends itself poorly to this dual search for autonomy. This is the cue, then, to introduce some elements that may evidentiate the specificity of British thinking on music in the eighteenth century, in order to highlight how it needs to be set within a much wider cultural framework if it is to be fully understood. The present work will consider the mutual rapport between philosophical speculation and musical speculation. In Part I, we shall examine the philosophical sources and focus on the nature and value of the philosophers' contribution to thought on music. In Part II, we shall deal with musical sources (treatises, histories of music), in order to provide evidence for their relation with the philosophical culture previously examined. It is important to underline how this enquiry brings out a healthy relation between the various contexts of knowledge – a relation not based on the modern contraposition between 'autonomy' and 'heteronomy': the examples cited illustrate, rather, a genuine regime of 'intellectual exchange'.

In particular, we intend to argue that in the tradition here investigated there is a special link between the development of specific philosophies of mind – like that expounded by Locke and, subsequently, Hume – and the elaboration of determinate modes of thinking about music. Two authors of the Scottish Enlightenment provide the clearest illustration of this connection: first, Lord Kames (1696-1782), author of the highly regarded and influential *Elements of Criticism* (1762) – as well as of a history of humanity (*Sketches of the History of Man*, 1776); second, Adam Smith (1723-1790), best known for *The Theory of Moral Sentiments* (1765) and *An Inquiry into the Nature and Causes of the Wealth of Nations* (1776), considered to be the foundation stone of political economy, whose essay *Of the Nature of that imitation which takes Place in what are called the Imitative Arts* we shall examine. These two authors,[39] as will be seen in detail in the sections devoted to them, enquire into the particular nature of the pleasure conveyed by musical sound and develop explanations possible only within the dynamic conception of mind elaborated by David Hume in his *Treatise on Human Nature* (1739), in which the temporal dimension of consciousness and human thought come to occupy

---

[37]   Lydia Goehr, *The Imaginary Museum of Musical Works. An Essay in the Philosophy of Music* (Oxford, 1992).

[38]   For the debate on Goehr's text, see in particular Harry White, '"If It's Baroque, Don't Fix It": Reflections on Lydia Goehr's "Work Concept" and the Historical Integrity of Musical Composition', *Acta Musicologica*, 69 (1997), pp. 94-104; and Willem Eraw, 'Canon Formation : Some More Reflections on Lydia Goehr's Imaginary Museum of Musical Works', *Acta Musicologica*, 70 (1998), pp. 109-115.

[39]   See below, Chapter 2, pp. 71-77 and 93-102.

a central place. In Hume's model, thought is made up of a continuous 'train of thoughts', acting in accord with rules determined first and foremost by the relation between perception, memory and imagination. Music, an art that unfolds in time and that, as with thought, features an unceasing motion but is governed by laws, lends itself to interpretation on the basis of the analogy with the mental processes described by Hume.

The dimension of time is obviously a leading factor in discussion of music and has also supplied a vehicle for comparing music with oratory and appropriating some rhetorical terminology for the musical context. Mark Evan Bonds in his study of the concept of musical 'form' reads the use of the metaphor of music as an oration employed in the eighteenth century, and its link with the time dimension as a real characteristic of the period that differentiates it from the subsequent one:[40]

> Whereas the eighteenth century's metaphor emphasized the temporal nature of the work in performance and viewed form primarily from the perspective of a listening audience, the preferred metaphor of the nineteenth and twentieth centuries [the musical work as an organism] has been more spatial in perspective, in that it considers the work and its constituent units as a simultaneously integrated whole.

While Bonds's study is largely based on German and French sources, we may add that the British tradition not only validates his thesis but consolidates and expands it, linking the construction of rhetorical discourse and that of musical form to a common source: the rules by which human thought is constituted and structured.

At the same time, as the philosophy of mind provided new tools for thinking about music, so music supplied philosophy with useful models. On the one hand, as we shall see in a passage from Hume, music turned out to be of service in describing time itself, facilitating the creation of a mental representation of the latter. On the other hand, the acoustic-musical phenomenon of sympathetic vibration enabled philosophers and physicians to work out theories of a mechanical kind aiming to explain how sound, by means of vibration, may act on man's body – and hence on his feelings. Thus music supplied natural philosophers with a fine instrument for investigating complex aspects of the working of the human machine (as will be exemplified from Daniel Webb's *Observations on the Correspondence between Poetry and Music* of 1769).[41]

The reflection on the concepts of imitation and expression is not without relevance for the foregoing. As mentioned above, the secondary literature abounds in discussion of these two concepts, focusing attention prevalently on the sources of an 'aesthetic' nature. In particular, there exists a specific kind of sources in which the mimetic principle is always brought into play – namely, the comparison

---

[40]   Mark Evan Bonds, *Wordless Rhetoric. Musical Form and the Metaphor of the Oration* (Cambridge, MA, and London, 1991), p. 4.

[41]   See below, Chapter 2, pp. 77-83.

among the arts. In dealing with this literature we shall be at pains to highlight at least two factors: first and foremost, in line with the interpretation of Stephen Halliwell,[42] we shall provide evidence for the debt to antiquity, displayed on almost every page by the relevant authors. Secondly, attention will focus on the particular way – a distinctive characteristic of the British tradition – in which the discourse on the aesthetic categories of 'imitation' and 'expression' comes to intermesh with the analysis of the faculties and workings of the human mind. What appears especially significant to this end is that, alongside the two categories bearing on the semantic context of *mimesis*, the British sources contemplate the existence of a third principle – sympathy – which will play an important role in the theories of Francis Hutcheson, Lord Kames and Sir William Jones.

The second part of this work, in examining sources from the musical context, will show how the heads of the discussion previously traced are integrated in the tissue of the thinking on music and further developed in this framework. By way of example, we focus on the *Essay on Musical Expression* (1753) by the Newcastle composer and organist Charles Avison, who re-elaborates certain arguments of James Harris in the *Discourse on Music, Painting and Poetry* (1744) in the attempt to supply some principles for assessing works of music.

While the first three chapters of our work provide a picture of the many productive exchanges between philosophy and music, the fourth and last chapter adds a further element to the discussion, setting the reflection on music in its historical perspective. As with the previous aesthetic reflections, here, too, our aim is to place the music-history discussion in a wider context. The histories of music by Sir John Hawkins and Charles Burney are well known and, especially in Burney's case, have been much commented on; nonetheless, we still lack broad-spectrum studies that interpret their connection with the reflections that permeate history-writing between the seventeenth and eighteenth centuries. The secondary literature contains only two works that attempt to deal with the history of musical historiography, both dating back to the 1960s: *Philosophies of Music History* (1962) by Warren Dwight Allen and the more detailed *Geschichte und Musikgeschichte* (1967) by Werner Friedrich Kümmel. While readers seeking to orient themselves in the musical-historiographical genre will find plenty of food for thought in these works, those who aim to focus on the peculiarity of the historiographical work of Hawkins and Burney are likely to be disappointed; for both books devote scant attention to the two English historians. In the course of our work we shall attempt to read the two *Histories of Music* in the light of the historiographical debates that led to the creation of a new model of history, making

---

[42] Stephen Halliwell, *The Aesthetics of Mimesis. Ancient Texts and Modern Problems* (Princeton and Oxford, 2002). On the reflections about the idea of 'mimesis' in eighteenth-century England see also the pioneering, albeit now somewhat dated, study by John W. Draper, 'Aristotelian "mimesis" in Eighteenth Century England', *Publications of the Modern Language Association of America*, 36/3 (1921), pp. 372-400.

special use of the studies that Arnaldo Momigliano[43] dedicated to the figures of the historian and the antiquarian, as well as providing evidence for the role played in them by aesthetic categories – such as 'taste' – and by the personal visions of historical progress held by Hawkins and Burney.

It is hoped that the reflections set forth in this work may pave the way towards outlining an overall picture of the cultural contexts within which eighteenth-century Britain found scope for thinking about music. We also intend to shed light on how these reflections, as a whole – developing around conceptual nuclei constantly underpinning this literature – gave rise to a genuine 'Science of Music': a complex and articulated vision of the discipline that was later to be known as 'musicology' or *Musikwissenschaft*.

Although many of the principal 'obligatory categories' of eighteenth-century aesthetic literature are dealt with here, and many – like the sublime or genius – are neglected, the perspective in which they are studied is not precisely that of contemporary studies of musical aesthetics. Our aim has always been to link these thematics with the original context to which they belong – namely, a philosophy of man (mental, moral and natural), an *anthropology*. As will become evident, this study does not comprehend all the reflections on music in eighteenth-century Britain and makes no claim to be exhaustive. The chapters that follow deal with specific themes, giving a chronological account of the theories that seemed most significant in relation to the topic as a whole. In this way we have sought to provide a reading and a multiple view of the subject itself – music. We began by sketching the Baconian idea of the citadel of the mind, in which reason, memory and imagination perform the functions of judicial court, archive and theatre and, according to their several instruments, reflect reality and the ambient world in different ways. The writer hopes that this study may act in a like manner: music is here examined through different lenses that produce narrations of various kinds but also compose a unified picture. The intention is to restore an idea of meaning that music, as a form of culture, assumed in eighteenth-century Britain, and of the intellectual landscape in which it was located, conceived and listened to.

By way of introduction and to begin the book, the best way of presenting the subject would seem to be to recount the interpretation of two musical myths reported in Sir Francis Bacon's *De sapientia veterum*, where music, philosophy and pleasure are marvellously linked together. The myths are those of Orpheus and of the Sirens. In *Orpheus sive Philosophia*, Bacon narrates Orpheus's unlucky descent into the underworld, and how, made melancholy, he withdrew into solitude where, with the same sweetness of song and lyre, he first attracted to him every species of animal,[44] proceeding thence to move even the inanimate elements, until

---

43   See Arnaldo Momigliano, 'Ancient History and the Antiquarian', *Journal of the Warburg and Courtauld Institutes*, 13 (1950), pp. 285-315; reprinted in *Contributo allo studio degli studi classici* (Rome, 1955), pp. 67-106.

44   Sir Francis Bacon, *The Wisedome of the Ancients*, trans. Sir Arthur George (London, 1619), pp. 56-57: 'From that time Orpheus, falling into a deepe melancholy [...] bequeathed

at last another sound, that of the Bacchantes blowing a loud and hideous blast on the horn, came to obscure the melody of Orpheus, who was subsequently torn to pieces by them. In Bacon's interpretation, the melodies played by the divine music represent two types of philosophy: the melody that served to descend into the underworld stands for *natural philosophy* that seeks to preserve and restore corruptible things. This is possible only through 'the due and exquisite temper of nature, as by the melody and delicate touch of an instrument'.[45] But the task is a particularly arduous one and often destined to fail:[46]

> therefore philosophy, hardly able to produce so excellent an effect, in a pensive humour (and that without cause) busies herselfe about human objects, and by perswasion and eloquence, insinuating the love of vertue, equitie, and concord in the minds of men, draws multitudes of people to a society, makes them subject to lawes, obedient to government, and forgetfull of their unbridled affections, whilst they give heare to precepts, and submit themselves to discipline.

Natural philosophy therefore leads on to *moral* philosophy, whose end is the virtue of customs, the law, the harmonization of life in society. Not by chance does Bacon choose music to represent philosophy. In addition to the outstanding precedent of Plato's Socrates, Bacon is familiar with the entire corpus of ancient narratives that exalt music's power over the emotions – in particular its capacity to temper the spirits, which render it a perfect art to represent the aims of moral philosophy. Moreover, the physical dimension of sound can be summoned to represent a natural philosophy engaged in 'preserving the corruptible', also because sound, as a phenomenon that occurs in time, is itself labile. It is regulated by the laws of acoustics, and thus 'preserved' by the means of invariable laws that natural philosophy may investigate, but is nonetheless destined to extinction, as sound is bound to fade away.

Many of the narratives of the Ancients tell of music's capacity not only to temper the spirits but also to arouse the emotions and to disturb. In this connection, Bacon recounts the myth of the Sirens, whose song 'neither was [...] plaine and single, but consisting of such variety of melodious tunes, so fitting and delighting the eares that heard them'.[47] How, then, in this case to reconcile this image of music with the seductive music of the Sirens that leads to perdition? Well, Bacon tells of how tradition has handed down two ways to resist the Sirens' song: the first is the stratagem of Ulysses, who had himself chained to the mast of his ship; the second was that of Orpheus who, with clear voice, sang the praises of the gods on his lyre, overcame the voices of the Sirens and escaped all danger. Music, in this

---

himselfe to a solitary life in the deserts, where by the same melody of his voice and harpe, hee first drew all manner of wild beastes unto him'.

45   Ibid., p. 58.

46   Ibid.

47   Ibid., p 168.

case, is summoned to represent pleasures – the Sirens' song – and the regulation of them, in the figure of Orpheus.

In introducing the dimension of music in the British project for a new 'Science of Man', we mentioned how the question of pleasure was one of the most frequently discussed topics with regard to music. Here we see that Bacon recognizes the attractive side of the art of sounds and makes it the prototype itself of pleasure; but he also indicates how the power of regulating the affects that has always been acknowledged to music may lead to the analogy between music and moral philosophy and theology. In considering melodious sound, however, there remains a fundamental ambiguity: it may be dangerous if we fall prey to it, or salvific if we make use of its harmonizing capacity. The danger ultimately springs from considering sound as absolute, from allowing ourselves to be bewitched and captured by it. If, instead, we confront it from a different perspective, with the mediation of a second type of music, representing theology, we can listen to that melody without fear.

All the thematics we will deal with are expressed in a nutshell in Bacon's readings of the ancient myths above-mentioned. Bacon felt that those myths represented the 'sacred reliquies or abstracted ayres' of the wisdom of the Ancients, but his reinterpretation of them is also redolent of the age that read them. The analogies and metaphors are always significant. If Bacon elected to compare the three elements music-pleasure-philosophy by means of metaphor, this means that in the culture of his time those elements must have been linked in some significant way. My hope is that the pages that follow will illustrate how this linkage is perpetuated and discussed in the same cultural context through the eighteenth century.

PART I
The contribution of music to the 'Science of Man'

The first part of this study investigates the reflections on music by some of the most representative philosophers and men of letters of the eighteenth century. Many of the writings we shall encounter are not exclusively devoted to discussion of the art of sound; their starting point is not usually a description of the functioning of music per se. Rather, they set out from the need to explain certain phenomena regarding human nature – in particular, they are interested in the nature of pleasure – and appeal to music, as to other arts or manifestations of human ingenuity, in the search for answers to their questions.

One of these concerns the train of thought that I think can be identified as the stimulus to the enquiries we will presently describe: the search for *eudaimonia*.[1] In what way mankind can happily live its own inner life and that of society is a question that underpins the reflections of the thinkers we shall deal with. If the ultimate aim of life is the achievement of happiness, or pleasure, which embodies the faculty of making men happy, it becomes a fundamental element in the life of mankind: 'the importance of any truth is nothing else than its moment, or efficacy to make men happy, or to give them the greatest and most lasting pleasure'[2] writes Francis Hutcheson in the preface to his *Inquiry into the Original of our Ideas of Beauty and Virtue* (1725). Of course, not all pleasures lead mankind to 'real' happiness. At which point we encounter a second important principle: in order that men should learn which are the pleasures to pursue and which to shun, they must receive an *education*. This makes it possible for the pleasure to be matched with the aim proposed: in the attainment of *eudaimonia* the end does not justify the means. Hence it is of the greatest importance to distinguish between virtuous pleasures and those conducive to vice.

---

[1]   This term is preferable to 'happiness' as it seems more pregnant and closer to the concept I try to define here. For further reference on this topic, see *Die Frage nach der Glück*, ed. G. Bien (Stuttgart and Bad Cannstatt, 1978) and R. Mauzi, *L'idée du bonheur dans la littérature et pensée française au XVIIe siècle* (Paris, 1994).

[2]   Francis Hutcheson, *An Inquiry into the Original of our Ideas of Beauty and Virtue*, in *Collected Works of Francis Hutcheson*, ed. B. Fabian, 7 vols (Hildesheim, 1971), vol. I, p. iii.

The age-old tradition by which music was endowed with active influence on human emotions provided philosophers with a rich heritage of reflections on the relation between music and pleasure, and on the use and functions of music in a social context. Music, then, was investigated in this context with the purpose of defining the nature of the pleasure it conveys and how a better use can be made of it. The question is whether it acts on the senses, the imagination or the intellect; whether it promotes social values or isolates man. In which connection, it must be emphasized how this particular reflection stems from precise *ethical* and *moral* demands.

We shall see how two ways of addressing the question take shape, according to whether the educative value of music is ascribed to a characteristic intrinsic to music, or to a content conveyed by it. Instances of the former occur in the reflections on the art of sound in the works of Shaftesbury and Hutcheson. The thought of both authors hinges on a particular concept of musical tradition: harmony. This concept – as we shall see in what follows – has the advantage of considering music from a formal standpoint, bypassing the problem of whether some possible meaning should be ascribed to music. The concept of harmony, as promoting an ideal of equilibrium, may find fertile application in the moral context and thus enables music to be collocated among the sources of 'ethical' pleasure. As witness to the second way of understanding the pleasure conveyed by music – that is, when the attribution (or not) of an educative value to music depends on the content - we will first refer to the debate on the performance of Italian opera on the London stages in the late seventeenth and early eighteenth centuries, especially in the writings of Joseph Addison and John Dennis.

An important aspect of these writings, that run from the end of the seventeenth century to the beginning of the eighteenth, has to do with the manifest link between the choice of one of the two ways aforementioned of conceiving musical pleasure and the each author's idea of how music acts upon persons. In order to ascribe an educative function to music, where it is held that music influences sense alone it will be necessary to add a text that provides evidence for the moral dimension. Our authors, therefore, frequently choose to discuss vocal music. In contrast, when it is acknowledged that musical sound 'acts upon' and 'interacts with' the cognitive processes of the human spirit, instrumental music, too – in virtue of its own structural and formal aspects – becomes an object of interest and enquiry.

The eighteenth-century search for a principle common to the arts, and for the principle underpinning musical communication, is influenced by studies on the philosophy of mind. In Chapter 2 we shall consider the main categories used to account for the action of music (in particular, imitation, expression and sympathy) and evidence how the choice of one rather than another is often swayed by the application of theories of the functioning of mind or, more generally, of perception; we shall also underline how the choice of the principle of imitation, expression or sympathy affects the authors' decision to give a positive assessment of vocal music alone or to include instrumental music.

What cannot go unremarked in all these reflections is the enormous attention devoted to the senses and perception, which gave birth to the vast cultural movement known as British empiricism. Sensation and perception, the otherness that comes into contact with the subject and the latter's response to it, the modality of the relation between the subject and the world – all these are fundamental themes that involve philosophical thought and crucially influence the theories elaborated to give account of the relation between mankind and the arts. Seen in this light, Locke's theory of mind – even if he dedicated no elaborate reflections to the world of art – is of inescapable importance for all the theories we shall explicate. Addison had already notified his readers that:[3]

> Mr Lock's *Essay on Human Understanding* would be thought a very odd book for a man to make himself master of, who would get a reputation by critical writings; though at the same time it is very certain, that an author who has not learned the art of distinguishing between words and things, and of ranging his thoughts, and setting them in proper lights, whatever notions he may have, will lose himself in confusion and obscurity.

In order for our argument to proceed, I feel it important to emphasize how Locke's epistemology elevates to a cardinal principle of knowledge the procedures activated by perception in our mind. Although he is not concerned with criticism of the arts, his point of view is 'aesthetic' in the literal sense[4] since his standpoint is that of feeling. The distinction between the point of view of the artificer and of the person who judges – and therefore starts out from the horizon of perception – is treated expressly as a theme in a discourse on the faculty of 'discernment' in chapter XI of book II of the *Essay on Human Understanding*, where Locke dwells on the distinction between the modus operandi of *Wit* and *Judgement*, and develops an argument that recalls the passage from Addison cited above:[5]

> Men who have a great deal of wit, and prompt memories, have not always the clearest judgment, or deepest reason. For *wit* lying most in the assemblage of ideas, and putting those together with quickness and variety, wherein can be found any resemblance or congruity, thereby to make up pleasant pictures,

---

³ *The Works of the Right Honourable Joseph Addison*, ed. R. Hurd (London, 1889), vol. III, p. 196 (*Spectator*, 291).

⁴ From the Greek verb *aisthanomai*, to perceive.

⁵ John Locke, *An Essay concerning Human Understanding*, ed. P. H. Nidditch (Oxford, 1975), p. 156 (II, XI, 2). This distinction frequently arose in the subsequent debates: for example, Burke refers expressly to the passage in the second, expanded edition of the *Philosophical Enquiry into the Origin of Our Ideas of the Sublime and Beautiful* (1759) and Sterne makes polemical reference to it in *Tristram Shandy*. On the distinction between wit and judgment in the eighteenth century, see Roger D. Lund, 'Wit, Judgment, and the Misprisions of Similitude', *Journal of the History of Ideas*, 65/1 (2004), pp. 53-74.

agreeable visions in the fancy: *judgment*, on the contrary, lies quite on the other side, in separating carefully, one from another, ideas, wherein can be found the least difference [...]. This is a way of proceeding quite contrary to metaphor and allusion, wherein, for the most part, lies that entertainment and pleasantry of wit, which strikes so lively on the fancy, and therefore so acceptable to all people; because its beauty appears at first sight, and there is required no labour of thought, to examine what truth or reason there is in it.

Wit, which clearly evokes the figure of the artist, is therefore the element that associates ideas with each other in order that they be agreeable, and Judgement – that is, the critic – is summoned to discern the 'truth or reason' concealed in that association, with the task of bringing clarity and order to thought. Wit and judgement are not oriented to the same end: the one must strike the imagination of 'people' (the users), the other must understand the process that has enabled the imagination to be struck. As Locke adds shortly after, 'it is a kind of affront to go about to examine it [the combinations of the wit], by the severe rules of truth, and good reason'.[6] Wit and judgement proceed by different paths;[7] while Locke is concerned with indicating a correct path for judgement, Addison's aim is to lead his readers to correct judgement, to endow them with 'good taste'.[8]

---

[6]   Ibid.

[7]   The relation between wit and judgement is well expressed by Pope's pregnant couplet: 'For wit and judgment often are at strife, / Though meant each other's aid, like man and wife' (*Essay on Criticism*, ll. 82-83).

[8]   On the rise and fortunes of the notion of 'good taste', see George Dickie, *The Century of Taste: The Philosophical Odyssey of Taste in the Eighteenth Century* (Oxford, 1996); on Locke and Addison, see Jerome Stolnitz, 'Locke and the Categories of Value in Eighteenth-Century British Aesthetic Theory', *Philosophy*, 38 (1963), pp. 40-51, and K. MacLean, *John Locke and English Literature of the 18th Century* (New Haven, 1936).

Chapter 1
An ethical pleasure? Music and the education of man

> Nec vero sine philosophorum disciplina genus et speciem cuiusque rei cernere neque eam definiendo explicare nec tribuere in partis possumus nec iudicare quae vera quae falsa sint.
>
> Cicero, *De Oratore*

Art at the tea-table: Joseph Addison, the pleasures of the imagination and listening as a social virtue

The pages of the *Spectator*, and even more of the *Tatler*, are replete with reflections on art and literature. Among the series that have worn best with the passage of time we must undoubtedly include those devoted to the *Pleasures of the Imagination*.[1] In brief but dense pages, these issues of the magazine summarize Addison's thinking on art. According to him, the 'pleasures of the imagination' proceed 'from such objects as are before our eyes' (primary pleasures) or that 'flow from the idea of visible objects'[2] (secondary pleasures). The imagination is described as a faculty pre-eminently connected with the sense of sight; it plays with the ideas stored in the mind and is able to 'enlarge, compound, and vary them at her own pleasure'[3], and the 'idea' is described, in turn, as a form of visual representation, linked to an image. Such a conception of the imagination and the pleasures it may convey would appear to leave little room for reflections on music and, indeed, only in no. 416, of 27 June 1712, do we find that art given any fuller treatment. This number of the periodical supplies a sort of hierarchy among the arts, classifying them according to their greater or lesser capacity for representation. Thus sculpture is awarded pride of place, since 'let one who is born blind take an image in his hands, and trace out with his fingers the different furrows and impressions of the chissel, and he will easily conceive how the shape of a man, or beast, may be represented

---

[1]   See *Spectator*, numbers 411-421, published from 21 June to 3 July 1712. On Addison's aesthetic theory, see William H. Youngren, 'Addison and the Birth of Eighteenth-century Aesthetics', *Modern Philology*, 79 (1981-82), pp. 267-83; on his theory of imagination, see Clarence DeWitt Thorpe, 'Addison's Theory of Imagination as "Perceptive Response"', *Papers of the Michigan Academy of Science, Arts and Letters*, 21 (1936), pp. 509-530.

[2]   J. Addison, *The Works*, vol. III, p. 394 (*Spectator*, 411).

[3]   Ibid., p. 411 (*Spectator*, 416).

by it';[4] then come painting, poetry and, lastly, music. But let us follow Addison's argument more closely:[5]

> It would be yet more strange, to represent visible objects by sounds that have no ideas annexed to them, and to make something like description in music. Yet it is certain, there may be confused, imperfect notions of this nature raised in the imagination by an artificial composition of notes; and we find that great masters in the art are able, sometimes, to set their hearers in the heat and hurry of a battle, to overcast their minds with melancholy scenes and apprehensions of deaths and funerals, or to lull them into pleasing dreams of groves and Elysiums.

Addison makes no secret of his interest in the arts according to their descriptive capacity. And here we encounter a principle that will crop up repeatedly, the mimetic principle, at once the bane and the delight of every discussion of music in the eighteenth century. Whenever the mimetic capacity is taken as criterion for a hierarchy of the arts, music finds itself at a disadvantage.[6] In Addison's hierarchy, the art of sounds is saved *in extremis* thanks to the very ancient tradition that acknowledges its ability to represent determinate states of mind: hence, even though it can never assist a person devoid of sight to form a visual image of an event, it can create the 'ardour' or the 'sweetness' of it.

Yet, if we leave behind this celebrated series of the *Spectator* and rove about in the individual numbers of the review, we can see how the sensation of music's marginality conveyed by reading of the 'Pleasures of the Imagination' does not correspond to the space allotted to this art in the periodical as a whole.

The majority of Addison's articles on music are concerned with opera. We shall deal only briefly with it here, and opera in London will receive fuller treatment later on. But note that in the four issues of the *Spectator* entirely devoted to this subject (nos. 5, 18, 29 and 31) the author's overriding concern is to provide evidence for the link between music and word. In particular, Addison dwells on the problem posed by the performance of Italian operas sung in Italian – hence not understood by most of the public – and on the difficulties that may arise from a translation of the Italian libretto that takes account only of the English version without attending to the music with which the text is connected. The subject of the relation between music and text also emerges in a later article on sacred music,[7] where we see

---

[4]   Ibid.

[5]   Ibid., p. 412.

[6]   See, for example, the well-known text by Charles Batteux, *Les Beaux Arts réduits à un même principe* (Paris, 1746). As we shall see later, it is noteworthy, how music – especially as from the 1740s and often together with dance – is made the subject of an ad hoc discourse, in which the expressive principle is set alongside the mimetic one (as was also the case in Batteux). On this topic, see J. Neubauer, *The Emancipation of Music from Language*.

[7]   *Spectator*, 405.

how in Addison the dignity and seriousness of music depend exclusively on the significance it assumes in virtue of its union with the word. The article begins by hoping that sacred music will soon benefit from the same effort and attention accorded to the improvement of opera. In the author's opinion, composers should feel particularly summoned to this task in consideration of the fact that there are no texts in English more compelling and laden with pathos than the Holy Scriptures. Addison insists on the fact that in the text of the Bible the English language would manage to appropriate to itself certain stylistic characters of the Hebrew original, from which it would draw 'innumerable elegancies and improvements'.[8] Music's task, then, is to enhance the action of the word on the mind:[9]

> Since we have therefore such a treasury of words, so beautiful in themselves, and so proper for the air in music, I cannot but wonder that persons of distinction should give so little attention and encouragement to that kind of music, which would have its foundation in reason, and which would improve our virtue in proportion as it raised our delight. The passions that are excited by ordinary compositions, generally flow from such silly and absurd occasions, that a man is ashamed to reflect upon them seriously: but the fear, the love, the sorrow, the indignation that are awakened in the mind by the hymns and anthems, make the heart better, and proceed from such causes as are altogether reasonable and praiseworthy. Pleasure and duty go hand in hand, and the greater our satisfaction is, the greater is our religion.

Although Addison is writing these lines in the same period as when he published the articles on the *Pleasures of the Imagination*, in describing the effect of music linked with a sacred text he makes no reference to the faculty of imagination but, rather, to reason. Music composed to a biblical text would find 'its foundation in reason' since it would invite us to reflect on moral themes and the feelings aroused would be at the service of virtue.[10]

Music, when thus applied, raises noble hints in the mind of the hearer, and fills it with great conceptions. It strengthens devotion, and advances praise into rapture. It lengthens out every act of worship, and produces more lasting and permanent impressions in the mind, that those which accompany any transient form of words that are uttered in the ordinary method of religious worship. However, Addison does not attempt to explain why music may enhance the effects of a poetical text.[11]

---

[8]   J. Addison, *The Works*, vol. III, p. 383 (*Spectator*, no. 405).

[9]   Ibid., vol. III, p. 384. As Ruth Smith notes, 'Addison is, as usual in the *Spectator*, making an elegant synthesis of current ideas; he is original here only in being the first to draw them all together and in the comprehensiveness of his survey' (R. Smith, *Handel's Oratorios and Eighteenth-Century Thought*, p. 159.

[10]   J. Addison, *The Works*, vol. III, p. 385.

[11]   As far as I know, the first writer in English to give a detailed explanation of this capacity is James Harris in his 1744 *Essay on music, painting and poetry* (in *Three Treatises*,

Another article by Addison (*Tatler*, 1 April 1710) gives jocular testimony of the traditional union of music and *ethos*, imagining an association between specific musical instruments and the different typologies that make up 'the several conversable parts of mankind'[12] – that is, the kinds of 'talkers' who populated and enlivened London's myriad clubs and coffee houses. With his characteristic verve, Addison constructs some ingenious associations to give a satirical version of the metaphor of man as a musical instrument.[13] The first character to be discussed is the drum: dominator of public assemblies, it fills the spaces with its rattling sound, imposes itself easily on the ignorant and deceives young ladies into mistaking its joyous company for a manifestation of cleverness. Addison passes judgement on this character in his concluding remark: 'I need not observe, that the emptiness of the drum very much contributes to its noise'.[14] Another delightful member of the company is the trumpet, which can only play a few notes but, for as long as it manages to stay in tune, is particularly agreeable and is a necessary item at court and in all the calm discussions among gentlemen. A more popular version of it is the bagpipe-man, who 'will entertain you from morning to night with the repetition of a few notes, which are played over and over, with the perpetual humming of a drone running underneath them'.[15] Addison's judgement of himself as a 'musical instrument' is worth reading in full:[16]

> For my own part, I must confess, I was a drum for many years; nay, and a very noisy one, till having polished myself a little in good company, I threw as much of the trumpet into my conversation as was possible for a man of an impetuous temper [...]. I have since very much endeavoured at the sweetness of the lute; but in spite of all my resolutions, I must confess with great confusion, that I find myself daily degenerating into a bagpipe; whether it be the effect of my old age, or of the company I keep, I know not. All that I can do, is to keep a watch over my conversation, and to silence the drone as soon as I find it begin to hum in my discourse, being determined rather to hear the notes of others, than to play out of time, and encroach upon their parts in the concert by the noise of so tiresome an instrument.

Not only is each kind of talker associated with an instrument, whose musical characteristics reflect his style of speech, but the concert of the instruments becomes a way of conceiving society and describing its fundamental virtues. To this end, *listening* assumes particular importance. The man of taste must learn to

---

London, 1744), see below pp. 62-71.

[12]   J. Addison, *The Works*, vol. II, p. 115 (*Tatler*, 153).

[13]   For a study of this metaphor in the English scientific context, see Jamie C. Kassler, *Inner Music: Hobbes, Hooke and North on Internal Character* (London, 1995).

[14]   J. Addison, *The Works*, vol. II, p. 116 (*Tatler*, 153).

[15]   Ibid., p. 117.

[16]   Ibid., p. 118 et seq.

listen to himself and others; by listening to himself he will learn to judge himself, to understand which 'musical instrument' he corresponds to, and possibly to seek to match his behaviour with the 'instrument' – that is, with the position in society – to which he aspires. Secondly, by listening to others he will learn to be in tune and not go 'out of time', not be untimely. Thus Addison views listening as a useful virtue for man as a social being, a virtue that serves to regulate with taste his own behaviour in society, as projected outwards. Listening, then, is aimed at forming *politeness*.

Interior listening and political harmony: Lord Shaftesbury

Listening (interior) is undoubtedly a fundamental element also in the thought of Anthony Ashley Cooper, Third Earl of Shaftesbury, who identified in the practice of philosophical dialogue (or the soliloquy) a device like a mirror for reflecting mind and character.[17] The soliloquy has the peculiar character of being a *sounding mirror*, a form of echo. By its very nature, then, it cannot but be truthful since it reproduces in an audible way an echo of our thought and feeling; and the objective dimension that renders it distinct from the subject enables it to act on the subject himself with greater force:[18]

> our thoughts have generally such an obscure implicit language that it is the hardest thing in the world to make them speak out distinctly. For this reason, the right method is to give them voice and accent. And this, in our default, is what the moralists and philosophers endeavour to do, to our hand, when, as is usual, they hold us out a kind of *vocal* looking-glass, draw sound out of our breasts and instruct us to personate ourselves in the plainest manner.

Shaftesbury's reflection on art treads a very different path from that of Addison. Although the third Earl studied under John Locke, his mode of arguing and writing diverge from those of his master, for Shaftesbury's immediate references hark back to the dialogues of Plato, to the English Neoplatonists of the seventeenth century[19] and to the late Stoics Epictetus and Marcus Aurelius.

---

[17]　On the ancient practice of soliloquy and spiritual exercises, see P. Hadot, *Philosophy as a Way of Life*.

[18]　Lord Shaftesbury, *Soliloquy, or Advice to an Author,* in *Characteristics of Men, Manners, Opinions, Times*, ed. L. Klein (Cambridge, 1999), pp. 70-162: 78.

[19]　As well as the two classic studies by Ernst Cassirer, *The Platonic Renaissance in England*, trans. J. P. Pettegrove (London, 1953) and the section devoted to Shaftesbury in *The Philosophy of the Enlightenment*, trans J. P. Pettegrove (Princeton, 1951), and the standard monograph by R. L. Brett, *The Third Earl of Shaftesbury* (London, 1951), see the recent study by Andrea Gatti, *'Il gentile Platone d'Europa'. Quattro saggi su Lord Shaftesbury* (Udine, 2000), and G. Carabelli and P. Zanardi (eds), *Il Gentleman filosofo,*

One of Shaftesbury's best-known writings, *The Moralists* (1709), contains the basic points of his theory of the Beautiful.[20] Here, I shall confine myself to dealing with two aspects of this theory: the importance assumed in it by the concept of *harmony* and the nature of aesthetic judgement. In his philosophy, harmony represents the very basis of the universe, of nature and of man's relationship with these, and supplies a proof of the existence of a Mind governing the cosmos. In the cosmologies that lay stress on the connection of the elements and the need to *fit* oneself to the universal rhythm in order to live in conformity with nature and place oneself *in tune* with the universe, a musical vision of the world is expressed, its main concept being that of harmony:[21] Shaftesbury belongs squarely in that tradition. According to him[22]

> Nothing surely is more strongly imprinted on our minds or more closely interwoven with our souls than the idea or sense of order and proportion. Hence all the force of numbers and those powerful arts founded on their management and use! What a difference there is between harmony and discord, cadency and convulsion! [...] Now, as this difference is immediately perceived by a plain internal sensation, so there is withal in reason this account of it: that whatever things have order, the same have unity of design and concur in one, are parts constituent of one whole or are, in themselves, entire systems. [...] What else is even a tune or symphony or any excellent piece of music than a certain system of proportioned sounds?

The consciousness of the unity of the world and the sympathy that obtains between things has the fundamental role of enabling one who contemplates physical beauty not to lose himself in it. The enthusiast able to listen to his own interior harmony will be capable of relating the immediate forms of Beauty to the supreme power from which they all stem – the Divine Artificer – and will thus succeed in capturing all the more fully the sense of his own belonging to the

---

nuovi saggi su Shaftesbury (Padua, 2003). On Shaftesbury's relation to the classics, see Alfred O. Aldridge, 'Shaftesbury and the Classics', in Karl Bosl (ed.), *Gesellschaft, Kultur, Literatur: Rezeption und Originalität im Wachsen einer europäischen Literatur und Geistigkeit* (Stuttgart, 1975), pp. 241-258.

[20]   On Shaftesbury's aesthetic theory see Dabney Townsend, 'Shaftesbury's Aesthetic Theory', *The Journal of Aesthetics and Art Criticism*, 41/2 (1982), pp. 205-213.

[21]   For an in-depth study of the Pythagorean stamp of this thought and its legacy as far as seventeenth-century England, see S. K. Heninger, Jr., *Touches of Sweet Harmony. Pythagorean Cosmology and Renaissance Poetics* (San Marino, CA, 1974); while, for a historical-semantic study of the terminology that harks back to the concept of harmony and temperament, see Leo Spitzer, *Classical and Christian Ideas of World Harmony*, ed. A. Granville Hatcher (Baltimore and London, 1963).

[22]   Lord Shaftesbury, *The Moralists, a Philosophical Rhapsody*, in *Characteristics*, p. 273 et seq.

cosmos: the sense of harmony saves man from isolation. The sense that enables these *concenti* of harmony to be perceived is a sense *within* man. It must be cultivated if it is to bear fruit: 'labour and pains are required and time to cultivate a natural genius ever so apt and forward'.[23] Man attains to self-perfection and, *inter alia*, realization of the perfection that surrounds him in virtue of the study and knowledge of (listening to) himself, the importance of which was mentioned above. But the natural presence of this sense is an absolutely necessary condition and is also defined by Shaftesbury as an *instinct* or *pre-conception*:[24] by means of its action 'no sooner the eye opens upon figures, the ear to sounds, then straight the beautiful results and grace and harmony are known and acknowledged'.[25] Its existence is not in contradiction with natural taste, since it represents, in reality, only a 'capacity' to perceive the Beautiful – and, together with this, the Good and the True with which it is indissolubly linked – without determining the object that arouses this feeling in us. In other words, it could be said that the interior sense constitutes the a priori of taste: in order that an individual taste may be developed, the individual must possess the capacity to experience beauty. Add to which, by the same token, that the fact that the Beautiful is made to rest on the concept of harmony implies that it has an objective nature, since harmony consists in relationships among different parts that constitute a whole and is thus a 'measurable' or quantifiable phenomenon. This has a further consequence: if harmony represents the foundation of everything that is, and therefore also of beauty, in order to be able to judge beauty one must learn to recognize harmony. The rule of taste is founded in harmony, and the knowledge of it must be pursued by rational means. The use of the 'sounding mirror' represents the first step on the road to this knowledge.

In Shaftesbury, this 'interior' dimension of the sense of the Beautiful and his insistence on the importance of self-knowledge are intimately linked with his closeness to Stoic thought. In this connection, recall that, according to Epictetus, there are two orders of things: those that depend on us – over which we therefore have power – and those that do not, i.e. external objects. Man's welfare does not

---

23   Ibid., p. 320.

24   *The Moralists*, in *Characteristics*, p. 326. Shaftesbury takes the idea of the existence of a *pre-conception* from Epictetus. In the *Diatribes*, Epictetus affirms the existence of pre-notions (*prolepseis*) that afford a rule of thumb regarding the rationality or irrationality of an action, but without being sufficient to ensure uniformity of judgement applied to particular cases: 'it is for this reason especially that we need education, so as to learn how, in conformity with nature, to adapt to specific instances our preconceived idea of what is rational and what is irrational' (Epictetus, *The Discourses, as reported by Arrian, the Manual, and Fragments*, trans. W. A. Oldfather (London and Cambridge, MA, 1959-1961), p. 17 [Disc., I, 2, 6]). The education here referred to – as specified in *Disc.*, I, 22, 9 – is philosophical education, that must teach us 'to apply the natural preconceptions to particular cases, each to the other in conformity with nature' (ibid., p. 145).

25   Ibid.

rest in the external objects but in his own interior, and on it depends the happiness of mankind. In order to judge rightly and recognize virtue, man must therefore have a correct opinion with regard to his own feelings. This mode of understanding the human spirit and its relation with the external world is wonderfully pictured by Shaftesbury in his choice of the emblem and the motto for the frontispiece of the *Characteristics of Men, Manners, Opinions, Times* (1711) (Figure 1.1). The central figure of the emblem, against the background of a rocky seascape, is a ray of sunlight reflected by a bowl full of water, and around the emblem the motto *panta hypolepsis* ('all is assumption').

Figure 1.1   Anthony, Third Earl of Shaftesbury, *Characteristics of Men, Manners, Opinions, Times* (London: J. Darby, 1714[2]), frontispiece (detail)

This image could be said to sum up the significance and the status of knowledge according to Shaftesbury. The references of the emblem are to Epictetus, on the one hand, and to Marcus Aurelius, one the other. In Epictetus we find the description of the emblem:[26]

---

[26]   Epictetus, *The Discourses*, II, p. 35 (*Disc.*, III, 3, 20-22).

> The soul is something like a bowl of water, and the external impressions
> something like the ray of light that falls upon the water. Now when the water
> is disturbed, it looks as though the ray of light is disturbed too, but it is not
> disturbed. And so, therefore, when a man has an attack of vertigo, it is not the
> arts and the virtues that are thrown into confusion, but the spirit in which they
> exist; and when this grows steady again, so do they too.

The motto refers to a sentence of Marcus Aurelius, the perfect corollary
to which is represented by the above-cited passage from Epictetus: 'all is
assumption', continuing with 'and the assumption lies in your hands'. Faced
with any representation and before performing an action, man must examine and
reflect on the situation and then decide whether or not to give his *assent* to the
representation. This is the meaning of Marcus Aurelius' statement regarding the
value of *assumption*: it lies in our hands because it represents our relation with
external objects and is the result of a *choice* of ours. Thus the 'ray of light' is the
external element, the representation we face, whereas the way in which the water
in the bowl reflects that ray is 'ourselves', our actions, our decisions.[27]

In *Soliloquy, or Advice to an Author* (1710) – where the aspiring man of letters
is instructed as to which models he should follow and how he should behave –
Shaftesbury dwells at length on the political conditions that enable the arts to
develop, and on the figure of the critic.[28] Something further must be said on
these points, since the connection between political liberty and how far the arts
developed will be important for the evaluation of the Italian opera which will be
dealt with in the next chapter. In Shaftesbury's view, the arts can only be developed
in free communities, in which the rulers recognize the need to learn to *persuade*
the listeners, employing 'the most soft and inviting numbers […] to charm the
public ear and to incline the heart by the agreeableness of expression', such that[29]

> almost all the ancient masters of this sort were said to have been musicians. And
> tradition, which soon grew fabulous, could not better represent the first founders
> or establishers of these larger societies than as real songsters who, by the power
> of their voice and lyre, could charm the wildest beasts and draw the rude forests
> and rocks into the form of fairest cities. Nor can it be doubted that the same
> artists who so industriously applied themselves to study the numbers of speech

---

[27]　To the entirely visual metaphor handed down from Antiquity Shaftesbury adds the
auditive one. The visual mirror, the bowl, is subject to turmoil, a puff of wind will ruffle the
water, and the sense of sight, projected entirely outwards, is an easy prey to hallucination.
In contrast, the sounding mirror – the form of dialogue described in the *Soliloquy* – enables
greater concentration, allows a form of projection towards the interior of man and affords a
more comfortable way of reasoning. The succour provided to man by the sounding mirror
restores calm to the troubled water in the bowl.

[28]　In particular in Part II, section II (*The Discourses*, pp. 103-117).

[29]　Shaftesbury, *Soliloquy*, in *Characteristics*, p. 106.

must have made proportionable improvements on the study of mere sounds and harmony, which, of itself, must have considerably contributed towards the softening the rude manners and harsh temper of their new people.

By founding itself on the numbers of harmony, music succeeded in becoming a symbol of the capacity to give order to the situation, and in virtue of its own agreeableness was used to fortify those arts of discourse that served for the exercise of power. According to Shaftesbury, the pre-eminence of the arts in free societies and the high esteem in which artists were held in ancient times sharpened the competition among them, and this led to a gradual refinement in the arts and in their partakers:[30]

> these [the arts] they would the better enjoy, the more they refined their taste and cultivated their ear. For to all music there must be an ear proportionable. There must be an art of hearing found before the performing arts can have their due effect or anything exquisite in the kind be felt or comprehended.

As already said with regard to the internal sounding mirror, which represents the first and necessary step on the path to knowledge, external listening is also a first, indispensable stage in order for the representative arts to be developed. This process of refinement and the need to educate the public in listening were the reasons, according to Shaftesbury, for the advent of the figure of the 'critic', whose task was to 'interpret' the creations of artists and to point to what was correct and excellent in them. He sees the critic as absolutely necessary also to the artist, since respect for competent judgement will spur the latter to do his best:[31]

> What is there which an expert musician more earnestly desires than to perform his part in the presence of those who are knowing of his art? It is to the ear alone he applies himself – the critical, the nice ear. Let his hearers be of what character they please, be they naturally austere, morose or rigid – no matter, so they are critics, able to censure, remark and sound every accord and symphony.

The birth and perfection of the arts are thus connected with the existence of a state where liberty is present – Shaftesbury describes at length the state of the arts in Ancient Greece and, especially, in the Athens of Pericles – and this liberty will be manifest in both the production of the artist and that of the critic, who will not have to fear censorship. All this will ultimately come about only through education to listening, which can engender that form of critical listening of which interior listening is the prototype.

---

[30] Ibid., p. 108.

[31] Ibid., p. 105.

The critic at the opera: John Dennis, music-hating moralist

In the England of the last decade of the seventeenth century and the first decade of the eighteenth a great debate on theatre and opera developed.[32] In particular, after 1705, the year when an opera in the Italian style, *Arsinoe*, sung throughout, was first performed, the Italian opera became the target of criticism. As from the debut in 1708 of Nicola Grimaldi – called 'Nicolini' in England – the castrati became all the rage with the public and the debate grew even fiercer. It may therefore be useful to deal at some length with this diatribe in order to see what was at stake and what positions were taken by the authors discussed above. To appreciate fully the sense of the criticisms levelled at opera at the start of the eighteenth century we will need to take a step backward and consider a polemic regarding the utility of the theatre which, in the 1690s, had mainly involved three writers: Thomas Rymer, who in 1693 – but the date is not certain – published *A Short View of Tragedy; It's Original, Excellency, and Corruption*; Jeremy Collier, who in 1698 published *A Short View of the Immorality, and Profaneness of the English Stage*; and John Dennis, who in the same year replied to the detractors of the stage with *The Usefulness of the Stage*, but who had already taken sides against Rymer in 1693 with a dialogue titled *The Impartial Critick*.[33]

In the *Short View* Rymer reflects on the association between the development of the arts and political liberty – which, as we saw, is also present in Shaftesbury – and interprets the rise of opera and its success in France as evidence of the corruption in that country. One of the models from which English men of letters and philosophers drew the idea of a connection between political liberty and a flourishing state of the arts was Horace. Whether in Rymer, or in Shaftesbury, or in the *Spectator*, we find frequent quotation of a passage from the *Epistle to Augustus*, where Horace outlines a sort of history of the Latin stage; he follows its transformations against the background of parallel political events up to the end of the Punic Wars, marking that moment as the apogee but also the beginning of the decline of the Roman theatre. His criticism is aimed at the

---

[32]   On this debate and its treatment in the English periodicals see Henrik Knif, *Gentlemen and Spectators. Studies in Journals, Opera and the Social Scene in Late Stuart London* (Helsinki, 1995).

[33]   As stated by John Morillo: 'Despite Edward Niles Hooker's magisterial *Critical Works of John Dennis* (1939-43), Dennis (1657-1734) has barely avoided the trash heap of history' (Morillo, 'John Dennis: Enthusiastic Passions, Cultural Memory, and Literary Theory', *Eighteenth-Century Studies*, 34/1 (2000), pp. 21-41); however, for Dennis's contribution to aesthetic and critique, see Jeffrey Barnouw, 'Of the Sublime: To John Dennis', *Comparative Literature*, 35/1 (1983), pp. 21-42. On his works for the stage, see Kathryn Lowerre, 'Dramatick Opera and the Theatrical Reform: Dennis's *Rinaldo and Armida* and Motteux's *The Island Princess*', *Theatre Notebook*, 59 (2005), pp. 23-40, and her *Music and Musicians on the London Stage, 1695-1705* (Farnham and Burlington, 2009), esp. pp. 96-119.

modern tendency of playwrights to kow-tow to their public, to pander to their coarse tastes, as with prizefighting or bear-baiting, and he imagines a revived Democritus witnessing the decline of the theatre: 'he'd have [Democritus] enough reason for mirth, just watching the people gape at their favourite new monster, a giraffe or a nice white elephant',[34] or imagines an actor entering on the stage to be applauded for the 'Taranto purple' of his costume even before he has opened his mouth. Horace, then, ascribes the decline of the theatre to the fact that its pleasures have become vaguer and frivolous, passing from the sense of hearing to that of mere sight:[35]

> iam migravit ab aure voluptas
> omnis ad incertos oculos et gaudia vana.

These lines of Horace were to be frequently quoted by the authors we are examining here, but would not always be used to defend the same arguments. In most cases, as in Rymer, Dennis and Addison, the quotation from Horace would be employed in support of their condemnation of the stage machinery and gaudy décor of the productions, but also to criticize the work in music, ignoring the positive assessment of the sense of hearing clearly implied in Horace's words. More faithful to Horace was Shaftesbury, who spared opera 'as music', even while he continued to oppose the abuse of stage machinery. Both he and Dennis, at least at the outset, addressed the problem of the combination of theatre and music, starting from the conception of the role played by the chorus in Ancient Greek tragedy.

As noted above, *The Impartial Critick*[36] is a reply by Dennis to Rymer's text, written in dialogue form. In particular, Dennis questions Rymer's contention that the rules of Greek drama can be fully applied to contemporary English theatre: in some cases, to be sure, they may still be valid and useful – for example, in the chaste manner of dealing with the passion of love – but in others they may turn out confusing and incompatible. Dennis insists at length on the fact that Greek drama was intimately connected with religion and Greek political institutions – once again we encounter the link between art and politics – and many situations

---

[34]   'Si foret in terris, rideret Democritus, seu diversum confusa genus panthera camelo sive elephas albus vulgi convertet ora' (*The Satires and Epistles of Horace: A Modern English Verse Translation*, trans. Smith Palmer Bovie (Chicago, 2002 [1959]), p. 256 (vv. 194-196)).

[35]   Ibid., vv. 187-188: 'Pleasure has switched her allegiance from the ear to the eye'. Note that Aristotle, too, in the *Poetics* more than once emphasizes the primacy of hearing over sight in regard to stage performances (see 50a, 12-15; 50b, 15-20; 53b, 3-8).

[36]   Its full title is *The Impartial Critick: or, some Observations upon a Late Book, entituled, A Short View of Tragedy, written by Mr Rymer*. For the works of Dennis, we rely on the volumes edited by Edward Niles Hooker, *The Critical Works of John Dennis*, 2 vols (Baltimore, 1939) [hereafter indicated as CW].

typical of these tragedies would therefore be ill-suited to contemporary customs, beginning with the use of the chorus. The latter, he explains, certainly had a great effect on the Athenians, but today[37]

> it is neither probable, nor natural, that the chorus, who represent the interested spectators of a tragical action, should sing and dance upon such terrible or moving events, as necessarily arrive in every tragedy. And I wonder that Mr Rymer should cry up a chorus, in the very same book in which he cries down the Opera: for no man can give any reason, why an Opera is an extravagant thing; but I will, by retorting the same reason, prove a chorus extravagant too.

The fourth of Dennis's dialogues deals with the problem of the chorus, the utility of which he denies. He dwells on the well-known passage of Aristotle which states that 'tragedy is the imitation of a good action which is complete and of a certain length, by means of *language made pleasing*' which 'through pity and fear [...] achieves the purgation (catharsis) of such emotions'. Strangely, however, Dennis takes no account of the subsequent passage where Aristotle affirms: 'By 'language made pleasing' I mean language which has melody, rhythm and music'.[38] Dennis, then, 'forgets' (or ignores) the imitative dimension Aristotle acknowledges to music and states that if the imitation of an action is the principal aspect of tragedy, clearly this can be effected by the episode alone, without needing intervention by the chorus. Towards the end of the dialogue Dennis states his own idea of the catharsis wrought by the tragedy and its relation to music, and the theory he expounds – albeit only briefly sketched – is not without surprises. For, according to him, music impedes the cathartic function that the flux of passions would otherwise effect in the spectator:[39]

> he who makes use of a chorus in tragedy, seems to me, to do like a physitian, who prescribing a dose for the evacuation of peccant humors, should afterwards order restringents to be taken in the midst of its operation [...]. For the design of the chorus is to give good advice, to preach up morality, to extol virtue, to praise or pray to the gods [...]. Now I would fain know, how an audience that is extreamly disturbed with terror, or with compassion, can be capable of harkning to good advice [...].

Hence, Dennis argues, if the aim of tragedy is to arouse violent passions, with the purpose of purging the spectators of them in their daily life, the music connected with the function of the chorus acts in the opposite direction and actually hinders catharsis. For that matter, he adds shortly after, if the plot of the tragedy

---

[37]   J. Dennis, *The Impartial Critick*, in *CW*, vol. I, p. 11.

[38]   Aristotle, *Poetics* in *Aristotle on Poetry and Style*, trans. G.M.A. Grube (New York, 1958), p. 11.

[39]   J. Dennis, *The Impartial Critick*, in *CW*, vol. I, p. 33.

is well devised – on the model of the *fabula recte morata* of Horace – there will be no need for intervention from outside, like that of the chorus, to comment on the morality of an action: the spectator will be enabled to judge for himself.[40] This argument tending to negate the utility of the chorus suggests that moral comment combined with music has too much influence on the intellect, without affecting the feelings. But since the task of tragedy is catharsis, an instrument that fails to arouse those feelings of which drama must purge us is inadequate.

Of relevance here is another work by Dennis, *The Usefulness of the Stage* (1698). In this essay the author illustrates the functions he ascribes to the theatre, and an examination of them will help us to understand the condemnation of Italian opera he was to deliver ten years later. In his view, 'the stage in general is useful to the happiness of mankind, to the welfare of government, and the advancement of religion'.[41] He explains how the primary task of a human being is the attainment of happiness and how this is connected with the pursuit of pleasure. Now, pleasure cannot be sought by rational means – indeed, reason seems to be a hindrance to the sentiment of pleasure:[42]

> For to be pleas'd, a man must come out of his ordinary state; now nothing in this life can bring him out of it, but passion alone, which reason pretends to combat. Nothing but passion, in effect, can please us, which every one may know by experience: for when any man is pleas'd, he may find by reflection, that at the same time he is mov'd. The pleasure that any man meets with oftenest, is the pleasure of sense.

As we can see, this is the same argument that led to his condemnation of the use of the chorus in modern drama: the theatre must take us 'out of ourselves', and this is effected by the passions, not by reason. What acts against arousal of the passions runs counter to the function of drama. However, Dennis adds, it is important to bear in mind that, if reason is not the *cause* of pleasure, one cannot expect to attain pleasure by going against it. The passions aroused by drama must be of such a kind 'as to take reason along with them', since 'no passion can move in a full consent with the will, unless at the same time it be approv'd of by the understanding'.[43]

The essay contains only one short passage bearing on music, in the section dedicated to showing that the theatre is useful for government. In this section Dennis attempts to refute the thesis of the work he attacks, namely *A Short View of the Immorality, and Profaneness of the English Stage* by Jeremy Collier, according to which – as Dennis sees it – the theatre conduces to ruin of the state by incitement to vengeance and pride. Dennis, on the contrary, stresses how important

---

40   Ibid., p. 35.

41   J. Dennis, *The Usefulness of the Stage*, in *CW*, vol. I, p. 147.

42   Ibid., p. 149.

43   Ibid., p. 150.

stage performances may be in promoting the values that underpin the State, and in support of his thesis adduces a well-known passage regarding music in the *Histories* of Polybius, reading from the version of André Dacier who translated Aristotle's *Poetics*. The passage – often cited in the subsequent translation into English as evidence of the power of music in the improvement of manners (for example, in Charles Avison and Lord Kames) – tells of the habits of the dwellers in Arcadia, whose virtues 'proceeded principally from the love which they had for musick'. Polybius contrasts them with the Cynethians, famous for their crimes, whose rough temper was ascribed to their neglect of the art of music. Uniquely, in the current of thought we are dealing with, Dennis's comment on this passage is not used to evidence the educative function of music, but rather to demonstrate the civic usefulness of the theatre alone:[44]

> and if Polybius [...] speaks this in the behalf of musick [...]: what may we not justly affirm of tragedy, of which musick is but a little ornament; and which as far transcends it, as the reasoning speech of a man, excels the brutes inarticulate voice, which never has any meaning.

Here is a second condemnation of music: in the chorus it fails to find redemption because the chorus appeals to reason and seeks to soothe the passions by countering the aim of tragic drama, but even considered in itself music appears of scant value because, like the inarticulate utterance of primitive people, it has no meaning.

Although Collier's weighty treatise makes little reference to musical matters, we find some remarks that lead to the same conclusion as Dennis's – namely, condemnation of music – at which Collier arrives by an opposite route: recognition of music's impact on the human spirit leads him to be chary of it. After plentiful quotation from the patristic writers in support of his contention that the theatre is responsible for corrupting manners, he tries to forestall the eventual objection that the fathers of the Church condemned the theatre of their own time – above all, dance and pantomime – but how could their kind of spectacle be likened to the contemporary sort? So, why condemn the latter on the basis of the former? At which point, Collier dwells on the use of music and begins by saying that the music of the moderns is probably not to be blamed. Nay[45]

> 'twere to be wish'd, that either the plays were better or the musick worse. I'm sorry to see art so meanly prostituted: atheism ought to have nothing charming in its retinue. 'Tis a great pity debauchery should have the assistance of a fine hand to whet the appetite, and play it down.

---

[44]   Ibid., p. 165.

[45]   Jeremy Collier, *A Short view of the Profaneness and Immorality of the English Stage, with the Several Defences of the same. In Answer to Mr Congreve, Dr Drake, etc.* (London, 1730); anastatic reprint (Hildesheim, 1969), p. 182.

Though music in itself, as he reiterates shortly after, knows no vice, its compulsion to serve the needs of the drama being performed turns it into a formidable weapon of corruption. Hence Collier's contention that 'music is almost dangerous as gunpowders'[46]. And Collier follows this up by quoting from the standard 'authorities' on the subject – the use of harmonies in the *Republic* of Plato and the case of Timotheus, expelled from Sparta for having altered the number of strings on the lyre. His conclusion is that, if the English 'have any advantage in their instrumental musick, they lose it in their vocal. Their songs are often rampantly lewd, and irreligious to a flaming excess. Here you have the very spirit and essence of vice drawn off strong scented, and thrown into a little compass.'[47] While denying any intention of censuring pleasant and innocent pastimes, he wittily insists that people, if they wish to combat melancholy, should take care 'not to [...] shake off their spleen, and their reason together'.[48] Thus, albeit in completely different perspectives, the only thing in common among the detractors and promoters of the theatre afore-mentioned is their condemnation of the use of music.

We are now ready to deal directly with the critique of Italian opera made by John Dennis. From the outset he contends that his blame regards only 'those operas which are entirely musical',[49] whose overriding fault is to encourage sensual pleasure to such a point as to deter the cultivation of the pleasures of reason, which are harder to attain. In Dennis's view, the effects of Italian opera can be observed in the contemporary population of Italy – 'neither virtuous, nor wise, nor valiant'[50] – which by now has nothing in common with the Ancient Romans beyond the soil and the climate. Dennis's terror is that England may succumb to the fate that overtook Rome according to Horace's well-known lines:[51]

> Graecia capta ferum victorem cepit
> et artes intulit agresti Latio

But what Horace regarded as a positive change, here becomes a negative element:[52]

> I presume to oppose a popular and prevailing caprice, and to defend the English
> stage, which together with our English liberties has descended to us from our

---

[46]   Ibid., p. 183.

[47]   Ibid., p. 183 et seq.

[48]   Ibid., p. 251.

[49]   John Dennis, *An Essay on the Opera's after the Italian Manner, which are about to be establish'd on the English Stage: with some Reflections upon the Damage which they may bring to the Publick*, in CW, vol. I, p. 382.

[50]   Ibid., p. 384.

[51]   Horace, *Satires*, vv. 156-157: 'Conquered Greece took captive her savage conqueror and brought her arts into rustic Latium'.

[52]   J. Dennis, *An Essay on the Opera's...*, in *CW*, vol. I, p. 385.

ancestors; [...] that while the English arms are every where victorious abroad, the English arts may not be vanquish'd and oppress'd at home by the invasion of foreign luxury.

In this essay Dennis is at pains to emphasize his own sensitivity to music: not for him to appear unmusical.[53] Nonetheless, he insists that music appeals to sense rather than reason and, given that in opera music tends to prevail over poetry, the resulting spectacle cannot but act upon the sensual pleasure of the spectator. The greatest risk, however, is that, if the spectators become accustomed to these 'facile pleasures', they will no longer be able to appreciate the arts that demand a greater effort; and young writers, no longer supported by a public, will find no stimulus to exercise their talent in drama or poetry. In short, the enormous power enjoyed by music would lead to the decay of every art whose language appeals to the intellect. Dennis adds that he does not understand how music can be said to imbue the soul with feelings of a social and positive kind; in confining the effect of music to the senses alone, he precludes any possible impact it may have on the soul. Indeed, he sees it as tending to isolate the individual from society, encouraging him to focus on himself, on his own sphere of sensitivity, so that it remains an individual experience, unable to be shared. The final outcome of this process is the loss of one's own liberty, a form of slavery induced by not cultivating the more 'taxing' arts that appeal to reason:[54]

> These unspeakable advantages has lofty poetry over empty sounds and harmonious trifles; which, as the pleasure that they give us is a sensual delight, utterly independent of reason, must do something directly opposite to this: since 'tis natural to sense to bring a man home to himself, and confine him there, as 'tis natural to reason to expand the soul, if I may have leave to use the expression, and throw it out upon the publick. And as soft and delicious musick, by soothing the senses, and making a man too much in love with himself, makes him too little fond of the publick; so by emasculating and dissolving the mind, it shakes the very foundation of fortitude, and so is destructive of the publick spirit. [...] After what has been said, I appeal to any lover of this country, if poetry, which begets a publick spirit, ought to be banish'd for musick which destroys it, which as it corrupts mankind, has a natural tendency to the inslaving them.

For that matter, the music that Dennis criticizes is the music that comes from a people so much in decline, in his view, that 'they quickly grew to write such

---

[53]	As James Hutton very convincingly demonstrates in the essay 'Some English Poems in Praise of Music', the unmusical man is associated with malevolence, unreliability, devilry, (in Rita Guerlac (ed.), *Essays on Renaissance Poetry* (Ithaca and London, 1980), pp. 17-73).

[54]	J. Dennis, *An Essay on the Opera's*, in *CW*, vol. I, p. 389.

sense, that sound deserv'd to be preferr'd to it'.[55] At which point we can hardly acquit Dennis of writing in nationalistic, xenophobic vein. In a period of constant warfare for the safeguard of his own State and the balance of power in Europe, and in a culture so imbued with the idea of a specific connection between the degree of development of the arts and the degree of political liberty, a person like Dennis must have been not a little dismayed to witness the success of a foreign artistic genre on Albion's soil. In *An Essay upon Publick Spirit* (1711) he returns to the subject of Italian opera and doubles the dose. The critique based on the contrast between British virtues and pernicious Italian qualities – 'why [...] prefer Italian sound to British sense, Italian nonsense to British reason, the blockheads of Italy to their own countrymen, who have wit; and the luxury, and effeminacy of the most profligate portion of the globe to the British virtue?'[56] – is combined with a topic that was already vaguely suggested in the previous essays and here becomes explicit: homophobia. The traditional censures of a musical genre that conduces to effeminacy are here much less general, much more targeted. Dennis belabours the reader with statements about the hedonism that reigns in Italy and the twittering voices of the castrati arriving in England – adducing, like Addison, Nicolini, beloved of the London public – but at a certain point, unable to contain himself, he alludes obscurely to what so disturbs him in those men with so particular a voice:[57]

> The ladies [...] seem to mistake their interest a little in encouraging opera's; for the more the men are enervated and emasculated by the softness of the Italian musick, the less they will care for them, and the more for one another. There are some certain pleasures which are mortal enemies to their pleasures, that past the Alps about the same time with the opera.

We now leave Dennis and move on to what, as far as I know, is Shaftesbury's only reference to opera. Previously, I mentioned that in one of his writings he quotes the lines of Horace deploring the growing importance of the visual aspect of the theatre of his time:[58] this comes in a letter sent in February 1709 by Shaftesbury to Pierre Coste – translator of the works of Locke into French – who had sent him the celebrated work by François Raguenet, *Paralèle des Italiens et des François, en ce qui regarde la musique et les opéra* (Paris, 1702). In his comment on Raguenet, Shaftesbury declared that while for the most part he admired the work, he was disconcerted by a couple of propositions expressed in the *Parallèle*. One of these concerns Italian recitative, in judging which Raguenet displays poor taste.

---

55   Ibid., p. 391.

56   John Dennis, *An Essay upon Publick Spirit* (London, 1711), in *CW*, vol. II, p. 395.

57   Ibid., p. 396.

58   Scholars are indebted to the article by Thomas McGeary, 'Shaftesbury on Opera, Spectacle and Liberty', *Music & Letters*, 74 (1993), pp. 530-541, for having brought this text of Shaftesbury to their attention. It is reproduced in the appendix to the article (pp. 539-541).

Raguenet claims 'qu'il est trop simple, trop uni',[59] whereas Shaftesbury prefers to exalt this simplicity since the Italians 'would for this very reason be in a fair way of restoring the antient tragedy (the true opera) with its chorus, and all the charms depending on that antient and plain method'.[60] Shaftesbury is the only one of the authors I have dealt with who, in quoting the lines of the *Epistle to Augustus*, confines his criticism to the use of stage machinery and is at one with Horace in approving of the use of that *voluptas* that is conveyed through the sense of hearing. As we saw above in the section devoted to Shaftesbury, he attributes enormous importance to the development of the arts, since their condition testifies to the presence of political liberty. In particular, he evidences how education to listening is the necessary condition for the birth of the critic who, in turn, is indispensable for the arts to progress. But there is another text of Shaftesbury's in which the development of musical art, especially, is connected to an idea of expression of political liberty, *A Letter concerning Design*, included in the third part of *Characteristics of Men, Manners, Opinions, Times* (1714), in its second, posthumous edition. We read:[61]

> I can myself remember the time, when, in respect of music, our reigning taste was in many degrees inferior to the French. The long reign of luxury and pleasure under King Charles II and the foreign helps and studied advantages given to music in a following reign, could not raise our genius the least in this respect. But when the spirit of the nation was grown more free, though engaged at that time in the fiercest war, and with the most doubtful forces; we no sooner began to turn ourselves toward music, and inquire what Italy in particular produced, than in an instant we outstripped our neighbours the French, entered into a genius far beyond theirs, and raised ourselves an ear and judgment not inferior to the best now in the world.

As we see, Shaftesbury always tends to link the development of music alongside the sense of hearing and, with it, that of critical capabilities, judgement. Shortly after, in the same letter, he adds:[62]

> when the free spirit of a nation turns itself this way, judgments are formed; critics arise; the public eye and ear improve; a right taste prevails, and in a manner forces its way. Nothing is so improving, nothing so natural, so congenial to the liberal arts, as that reigning liberty and high spirit of a people, which, from

---

[59] François Raguenet, *Paralèle des Italiens et des François, en ce qui regarde la musique et les opéra* (Geneva, 1976), p. 73.

[60] In T. McGeary, 'Shaftesbury on Opera, Spectacle and Liberty', p. 540.

[61] Lord Shaftesbury, *Characteristicks of Men, Manners, Opinions, Times*, ed. Douglas den Uyl (Indianapolis, 2001), vol. III, p. 399.

[62] Ibid., p. 403.

the habit of judging in the highest matters for themselves, makes them freely judge of other subjects [...].

Music, then, is inseparably linked with the ideal of a political liberty that, in Shaftesbury's view, marks a crucial step in the progress of a nation. In particular, from his letter to Pierre Coste we deduce that, of all the musical genres, opera is the one closest to Ancient Greek tragedy. Another reason for interest in Italian opera that emerges in the letter is connected with the practice of soliloquy, as mentioned in the section on Shaftesbury above. For the third Earl underlines how music is especially suited to those portions of the opera devoted to reflection, 'such as soliloquys and the real parts of the Chorus (who should be *one*, and is *one* in the action, tho' representing *many*). These if reserv'd for the great art of the musician, and attended by the symphonys, would have their due effect upon the audience [...].'[63] We have already seen how in the philosophical soliloquy one is summoned to set up a sort of internal theatre, that Shaftesbury calls a *sounding mirror*; the letter adds that, if the sounding mirror is sung and its action is staged with the corroboration of the music, its action will be all the more powerful. Here, the philosopher par excellence of speculative orientation, whose idea of music was that most closely tied to the ancient tradition of cosmic harmony, reveals himself in this rapid *aperçu* as the only cultivated supporter of Italian opera.

Addison and Steele: critique and practice of music

Addison expounds his critique of opera along two main lines: the first concerns the use of stage effects, the second the language.[64] In no. 31 of the *Spectator*, he resorts to an expedient to express in a satirical way his own attitude towards the aforementioned aspects of operatic production, and imagines the proposal by a gentleman for a new model of opera. The gentleman is preoccupied with the welfare of London ladies and deplores the fact that they have to take long journeys through the town in order to attend the several entertainments necessary for their education: monkeys, puppets, opera and lions are scattered at the four corners of the city, poor things! The only way out of this difficulty is to create a new kind of opera that would comprise the most important forms of show. The subject proposed is the 'Expedition of Alexander the Great', in which Alexander will ride a dromedary called Bucephalus and will encounter King Porus, whose steed will be an elephant. Having met, the sovereigns will go to a puppet show and all the

---

⁶³   In T. McGeary, 'Shaftesbury on Opera, Spectacle and Liberty', p. 540 et seq.

⁶⁴   On Addison's critique of opera, see Franz Montgomery, 'Early Criticism of Italian Opera in England', *Musical Quarterly*, 15 (1929), pp. 415-425; Sigmund A. E. Betz, 'The Operatic Criticism of the *Tatler* and the *Spectator*', *Musical Quarterly*, 31 (1945), pp. 318-330, and H. Knif, *Gentlemen and Spectators*.

most wonderful stage machines will be employed to entertain the two royal guests. The opera will, of course, be sung in Greek:[65]

> which was a tongue he was sure would wonderfully please the ladies, especially when it was a little raised and rounded by the Ionic dialect; and could not but be acceptable to the whole audience, because there are fewer of them who understand Greek than Italian.

If Addison censures opera for the use of machines and live animals on the stage as a discrepancy, owing to an improper mixture of appearance and reality, his criticisms of its language are even sterner: it risks total incomprehension. This may occur for several reasons. Addison identifies three moments in the history of Italian opera in England and shows how in each of them the language is a stumbling block.[66] At first, the texts were translated into English, but the versions left something to be desired; second, the text was sung in the singer's mother tongue – with a jumble of Italian and English in one and the same performance – and this, as we shall see, involved problems of a 'political' nature in allotting the roles between Italian and English singers; and, in the third and last stage, the opera was sung entirely in Italian, with the result that nobody understood the plot any more.

The production of operas in English 'after the Italian manner' took place between 1705 and 1709 and the greatest success was *Camilla*.[67] In the *Spectator* no. 18, Addison dwells on the quality of the translation of the text and explains how the translator went about 'to make the numbers of the English verse answer to those of the Italian, that both of them might go to the same tune',[68] paying no attention whatever to the sense of the words. And the situations thus produced were of the following type:[69]

---

[65]   J. Addison, *The Works*, vol. II, p. 293 (*The Spectator*, 31).

[66]   *The Spectator*, 18. Note that this article quotes Horace's distich 'iam migravit ab aure voluptas / Omnis ad incertos oculos et gaudia vana […]'.

[67]   A reworking of *Il trionfo di Camilla* (first performed at Naples in 1696) with libretto by Silvio Stampiglia and music by Giovanni Bononcini. For the fate of this opera in early eighteenth-century London, see Lowell Lindgren, '*Camilla* and *The Beggar's Opera*', *Philological Quarterly*, 59 (1980), pp. 44-61. The operas of Italian kind written in that period also included the sole attempt by Addison himself, who wrote the libretto of *Rosamond* to music by Thomas Clayton (first performed 4 March 1707), which was a resounding flop. In this connection, see H. Knif, *Gentlemen and Spectators*, pp. 174-179.

[68]   J. Addison, *The Works*, vol. II, p. 269 (*The Spectator*, 18).

[69]   Ibid. Lindgren explains how the revival of *Camilla* in 1717 involved thoroughgoing revision of the translation and improvement of the passages criticized in the *Spectator* (L. Lindgren, '*Camilla* and *The Beggar's Opera*', p. 53).

Thus the famous song in Camilla,

> 'Barbara t'intendo'

Which expresses the resentments of an angry lover, was translated into that English lamentation,

> 'Frail are a lover's hopes', &c.

And it was pleasant enough to see the most refined persons of the British nation dying away and languishing to notes that were filled with a spirit of rage and indignation.

Led on by the sense – or nonsense, as Addison frequently underlines – of the sung text, the spectators whom our author is ridiculing interpret a music that should express indignation as a lover's lament! The article reviews other instances of translation of the text that take no account of the music that accompanies it with disgraceful results. For example, Addison amuses himself by quoting hosts of articles and prepositions that have become instances of musical florilegia and preciosities.[70] But perhaps even an excellent translation could not produce really worthy results: a second criticism levelled by Addison is 'the making use of Italian *recitativo* with English words'.[71] Thus, as every language has its own accents and its own way of expressing the passions, so the music of every country, too, has its particular way of doing this:[72]

> Thus the notes of interrogation, or admiration, in the Italian music, (if one may so call them,) which resemble their accents in discourse on such occasions, are not unlike the ordinary tones of an English voice when we are angry […] both nations do not always express the same passions by the same sounds.

This is why English composers should not be too wedded to Italian recitative. Not that Addison intends to close the door to an influence of Italian music on English. His wish is that England may see the birth of a 'Signor Baptist Lully'[73] who will employ anything good that may come from Italy to forge a style that will

---

[70]   'I have known the word *and* pursued through the whole gamut, have been entertained with many a melodious *the*, and have heard the most beautiful graces, quavers, and divisions bestowed upon *then*, *for*, and *from*; to the eternal honour of our English particles' (J. Addison, *The Works*, vol. II, p. 270 (*The Spectator*, 18)).

[71]   J. Addison, *The Works*, vol. II, p. 288 (*The Spectator*, 29).

[72]   Ibid., p. 289.

[73]   Ibid., p. 290.

be English. All this will not be possible if we seek only for rules within the art itself, without taking taste into account:[74]

> music, architecture, and painting, as well as poetry and oratory, are to deduce their laws and rules from the general sense and taste of mankind, and not from the principles of those arts themselves; or, in other words, *the taste is not to conform to the art, but the art to the taste.* Music is not designed to please only chromatic ears, but all that are capable of distinguishing harsh from disagreeable notes. A man of an ordinary ear is a judge whether a passion is expressed in proper sounds, and whether the melody of those sounds be more or less pleasing.

In Addison's view, art must not be a law unto itself and, above all, must never lose sight of the common man. Music is not a matter for the sophisticated ear alone; anyone capable of comfortably distinguishing the pleasantness of its sounds must be enabled to appreciate it. Since every people has its own particular mode of expressing feelings and thoughts, any music that aspires to communicate will have to take account of the language spoken by the public to whom it is addressed. To utilize Italian-style music with an English text indicates, according to Addison, a lack of taste and of attention to the listeners. Art cannot merely go its own way, as if the person who consumes it were not a historically determined individual.

The second stage of the Italian opera in London Addison deals with is even more pernicious than the first: the case of bad translations is ultimately used to ridicule a supposed audience of 'connoisseurs' who are not even aware of the discrepancy in expression between music and text; and if an English text is set to Italian-style music no fit communication with the audience will be possible. The second stage, instead, where Italian and English singers tread the boards simultaneously, results in a political kind of embarrassment. For Addison underlines how in this type of opera the Italian singers always end by taking the leading roles, while the English are demoted to their slaves:[75] it is not hard to see why the political message conveyed by this situation was not exactly gratifying to the English.

The last stage of the Italian opera in London described in the *Spectator* sees the complete abandonment of the English language. As Addison narrates with his characteristic irony, the audience, tired of understanding only half of what was sung:[76]

---

[74]　Ibid., p. 291 (my italics).

[75]　Lindgren, too, emphasizes how the Italian singers assumed the serious roles, while the English performers were allotted the comic ones: 'so far as is known, all the Italian singers who appeared in early eighteenth-century London performed only heroic serious roles, and comic ones were therefore excluded from the opera house together with the English language in 1710. In Italianate operas of 1705-1710, such parts had always been played by English actor-singers [...]' (L. Lindgren, '*Camilla* and *The Beggar's Opera*', p. 55).

[76]　J. Addison, *The Works*, vol. II, p. 269 (*The Spectator*, 18).

> to ease themselves entirely of the fatigue of thinking, have so ordered it at present, that the whole opera is performed in an unknown tongue […]. I cannot forbear thinking how naturally an historian who writes two or three hundred years hence, and does not know the taste of his wise forefathers, will make the following reflection, 'In the beginning of the eighteenth century the Italian tongue was so well understood in England, that operas were acted on the public stage in that language'.

As well as being exposed to a non-English musical idiom, if the audience must also deal with a foreign tongue, this may result in what Dennis found so reprehensible in opera – namely, that it appeals exclusively to the senses, leaving reason aside. And if, according to Addison, the aim of every cultural production must always be the improvement of human nature, a music that speaks an unknown language cannot partake of this higher purpose:[77]

> Music is certainly a very agreeable entertainment, but if it would take the entire possession of our ears, if it would make us incapable of hearing sense, if it would exclude arts that have a much greater tendency to the refinement of human nature, I must confess I would allow it no better quarter than Plato has done, who banishes it out of his commonwealth.

Here we find the same impeachment that Dennis made of opera, though couched in finer, more moderate style, in the tone proper to the *Spectator*. Though Addison dwells on the problems of language and communication, the last passage quoted reveals how that foreign music that resounds in the London theatres is able to 'take possession' of our hearing and, by so doing, to render the audience incapable of listening to things endowed with more sense. Dennis would write that the facile contentment brought by hearing opera inculcates a bad habit in us and makes us unwilling to partake of more solid enjoyments.

We can get a fairly precise idea of what sort of spectacle represented a valid example for Addison from a periodical published between 1715 and 1716, *Town-Talk in a Letter to a Lady in the Country*, by Richard Steele, co-author of the *Spectator*. From some numbers of this periodical and some epistolary evidence, we learn of an attempt by Steele to organize poetical-musical evenings intended as an alternative to opera.[78] The project was pursued over several years but seems to have come to fruition on only one occasion, the birthday of George I, 28 May 1715. A letter of 1713 from George Berkeley to John Percival[79] informs us that Steele's

---

[77]   Ibid., p. 271.

[78]   See John Loftis, 'Richard Steele's Censorium', *The Huntington Library Quarterly*, 14 (1950), pp. 43-66.

[79]   John Percival, first Earl of Egmont (1683-1748), friend of George Berkeley and profound lover of music, especially of Handel's operas (see W. H. Grattan-Flood, 'Handel and the Earl of Egmont', *The Musical Times*, 65 (1924), pp. 1016-1017).

project was already at an advanced stage, with York Buildings, the venue for the event, already decorated for the purpose and only the two pictures representing Virtue and Eloquence still awaiting completion:[80]

> he [Steele] is proposing a noble entertainment for persons of refined taste. It is chiefly to consist of the finest pieces of eloquence translated from the Greek and Latin authors. They will be accompanied with the best music suited to raise those passions that are proper to the occasion.

In the fourth number of *Town-Talk* we find the first description penned by Steele of his project. His intention is to present a selected London public of around two hundred persons of both sexes with a spectacle lasting two and a half hours, less expensive than opera and in which the leading arts – in particular, music, eloquence and poetry – join forces in the aim to direct the taste of the audience 'in politeness, wit and learning'.[81] Steele says he has taken care of every detail of the hall: the seats are arranged in a semi-circle, there are paintings of human figures and architectural features, lights, ornaments – everything is organized so that the scene may be as beautiful as possible – this because the projector aims to promote virtue by means of pleasure. If, as we saw in Dennis and Addison, pleasure is so powerful a device to influence humankind, instead of leaving it up to shows of doubtful morality – like the opera – it will be best to try and exploit it and give it a form oriented in the desired direction:[82]

> An improvement of the publick taste in pleasures, which is rather corrupted thro' the insolence of fortune, arising from sensual gratifications [...] is industriously to be laboured. [...]. Philosophy in vain attempts contempt of pleasure, which is the gift only of the most sublime and exalted spirits; but it may, with much more ease, give law and bounds to pleasure, and make us all its followers.

Prohibition only makes desire the sharper. To direct it without repressing it is the best solution. Steele chose to call this institution of his by the curious name of *Censorium*.[83] This choice, he explains, was not dictated by any intention to indicate contents to be accepted or rejected, but because he wished the name to refer to the organ of sense, to its specific place. Note here that the term 'sensorium' at the beginning of the eighteenth century is clearly connected with the name of

---

[80]   Letter of 7 March 1712/13, in *The Works of George Berkeley Bishop of Cloyne*, ed. A. A. Luce and T. E. Jessop (London, 1964² (1956)), vol. VIII 'Letters', p. 62.

[81]   Richard Steele, *Town-Talk in a Letter to a Lady in the Country*, 4 (6 January 1715-16), in *Richard Steele's Periodical Journalism 1714-1716*, ed. Rae Blanchard (Oxford, 1959), p. 209.

[82]   Ibid., p. 209 et seq.

[83]   In some articles this is spelt *Sensorium*, but sound and sense remain the same.

Sir Isaac Newton, who had described infinite space as the sensorium of God, where He[84]

> sees the things themselves intimately, and throughly perceives them, and comprehends them wholly by their immediate presence to himself: Of which things the images only carried through the organs of sense into our little sensoriums, are there seen and beheld by that which in us perceives and thinks.

The sensorium, then, is the place of perception and in Newton, as in Steele, it is connected with the idea of knowledge. In Newton, God, in the infinite sensorium, perceives everything intimately, knows it; man, instead, is endowed with a 'small sensorium', but it is there that he reflects on what he perceives. In the same way the *Censorium* created by Steele is intended to be a place for the exaltation of virtue, which by means of particular sensory stimulations will generate 'knowledge by diversion'.[85]

After explaining the purpose of the *Censorium*, then, in the sixth number of the periodical (20 January 1716) Steele gives a detailed description of the performance that took place there. The men and women were seated on opposite sides of the hall and there was a throne upon which sat a person representing George I apparelled with the insignia of Liberty. The spectacle began with a recited prologue, composition of which has been ascribed to Steele himself:[86]

Prologue
Spoken at the Sensorium *on His* Majesty's *Birthday*

For bright assemblies, and for tastes refin'd,
This little theater was first design'd,
In which the well-pleas'd founder hopes to treat
An audience rather elegant than great;
[…]
To please you here shall different ages strive,
New arts shall flourish, and the old revive.
To the raw tribe of Templars shall be shown
The *Grecian* gesture and the *Roman* tone:
Virgil shall be the talk of every beau,
And ladies lisp the charms of *Cicero*.
The land shall grow polite from you, who sit
In chosen ranks, *the cabinet of wit*;
To you shall bards their virgin-works reveal,
And hoarse contending orators appeal;

---

84   Sir Isaac Newton, *Opticks* (London, 1704; New York, 1952), p. 370 (*Query* 28).
85   R. Steele, *Town-Talk*, 4.
86   Ibid., p. 239 (*Town-Talk*, 7).

> For your applause the rival arts shall sue,
> And Musick take its melody from you.
>
> [...]

Steele addresses the audience to explain the aim and contents of the event; the public consists of the 'beau monde', eminent persons who should set an example to society with their good taste and whose education is therefore all the more important. The purpose is to fill the head of the 'beau' – dissected by Addison in the *Spectator* no. 275 and found appallingly empty! – with verses from Virgil, to make the ladies sigh at the sound of Ciceronian *concinnitas* and, ultimately, to draw a new melody from such a harmonious disposition of minds. The Prologue was followed by an ode in honour of the king, and Steele describes its setting to music as follows:[87]

> the language of it approaches that simplicity and purity of expression, which has made the natural and easy thoughts of the antients, on subjects of meer mirth and gaiety, and writ as if only for the diversion of the present hour, descend to our times [...] Men of taste will extreamly applaud the art of making the ear tingle with pleasure, at the same time that the heart exults with triumph, as in this ode. [...] The audience feel a noble delight, at once enjoying the benefit, and expressing their sense of it on the united power of musick and poetry.

From these remarks, from Steele's overall conception of his project and from the attempt by Addison himself to write an opera libretto, we may deduce how deeply interested in music these two critics were. As against that, we should not forget that their interest is inseparably linked with the aim they attribute to music and to the other arts: education to good taste, promotion of knowledge, improvement of humanity.[88] What the authors of the *Spectator* demand from artists and composers is an assumption of responsibility: they cannot remain exclusively preoccupied with their own art and its development; for, since their activity is performed in public places, it must take account of the effect their creations may have on the audience. On the one hand, then, they must avoid speaking exclusively to an audience of specialists and connoisseurs and, on the other, they must exploit

---

[87]   Ibid., p. 228 (*Town-Talk*, 6).

[88]   In a letter to James Harris, dated 24 November 1739, the fourth Earl of Shaftesbury gives an account of a domestic evening similar to the kind of entertainment aimed to in the *Censorium*, and refers to it as a *rational entertainment*: 'I never spent an evening more to my satisfaction than I did the last – Jemmy Noel read through the whole poem of Sampson Agonistes and whenever he rested to take breath Mr Handel (who was highly pleas'd with the peice) played I really think better than ever, & his harmony was perfectly adapted to the sublimity of the poem. This surely, to use Cibber's phrase upon a former occasion, may be call'd *a rational entertainment*' (cited in D. Burrows and R. Dunhill (eds), *Music & Theatre in Handel's World. The Family Papers of James Harris (1732-1780)* (Oxford, 2002), p. 80.

the potential that art offers them to perform a useful public service, with the aim of improving society.

Conclusions

From the foregoing, I think we may get a clearer idea of what was said at the beginning of the chapter in regard to the relation between music, pleasure and education in the context we are dealing with. Criticism and philosophy pit themselves in the same field and may arrive at the same conclusions, albeit by different paths. We have seen, for example, the attention devoted to the subject of listening by Addison and Shaftesbury. Both of them demonstrate its importance, each in the sphere of life that most interests him. For Addison, listening is a social virtue that regulates the behaviour and the talk of the man of good taste; in Shaftesbury, listening is entirely inner-directed, oriented first and foremost to the understanding of 'self'. Among the authors we have reviewed there appears to be only one instance of flat rejection of music. This was John Dennis, but we must not forget that his criticism is addressed solely to operas 'after the Italian manner'. In all the other cases we find a keen desire that music be directed towards the improvement of humanity. Addison uncovers certain defects of opera that would seem to impair the exercise of the noble end of education attributed to music; Steele's project of the *Censorium* shows the way for a right use of music as, in the main, consistent in accompanying a poetry that will express socially shared values.

In the cases reported, the necessity (or not) for music to combine with a verbal text appears in direct relation with a conception – more or less elaborated from a theoretical point of view – of how music acts upon man. Where it is recognized that music influences the senses alone, its connection with words appears necessary: once more, John Dennis's position seems the most radical; in Milton's words '… eloquence the soul, song charms the sense'.[89] Music involves only the senses and therefore, without the support of words to direct the meaning, it is confined to lulling the ear of the listener, thereby inducing a state of perilous abandon to sensual seduction. The case of Addison is more complex but, as with Dennis, he too seems to see music as acting mainly on the senses and for this reason his discussion turns on its vocal version. However, among the articles cited there is one – dealing with sacred music, in the *Spectator* no. 405[90] – where Addison appears to indicate a different action of musical sound. In this case, he underlines a particular function of music: when combined with words, not only does it make the text more enjoyable, it also has a precise function of emphasizing the meaning, thus enabling the latter to leave a solid and lasting impression in the mind. But

---

[89]   John Milton, *Paradise Lost*, II, 556.

[90]   See above, p. 29.

Addison does not specify 'how' this may come about and which are the faculties brought into play.

To conclude: among the examples cited here that of Shaftesbury is perhaps the richest; he appears almost to succeed in restoring to eighteenth-century man Boethius' trinitarian vision of music. Opera, *music instrumentalis*, has the task of leading art back to the simplicity of the Ancients and of reawakening in man that critical knowledge that alone makes him free; the soliloquy, the sounding mirror, *musica humana*, brings man into contact with himself, enables him to perceive the internal harmony. Lastly, only when man can recognize the harmony within himself will he be able to lift his gaze to the macrocosm, to that *musica mundana* that gives a meaning to existence.

Chapter 2
Anthropologies and psychologies
of listening

In the first chapter we examined the remarks on music of some critics and philosophers between the end of the seventeenth century and the early eighteenth century, and showed how the discussion went on against a background of moral interest. We now take a step forward in time and – taking our cue from a writer closely linked with the authors just dealt with – proceed towards the midpoint of the century, defined by Reinhart Koselleck as a *Sattelzeit*, literally 'saddle-period', or – as one could say – watershed.[1] This period saw the birth of at least three philosophical disciplines: the philosophy of history, philosophical anthropology and philosophical aesthetics. According to Odo Marquard,[2] these dealt with the redefinition of man and, above all, played a part in counterbalancing the loss of a vital human world (*Lebenswelt*) that resulted from *inter alia* the crisis of the theodicies and the doubt about mankind's being responsible for the existence of evil in the world.[3] In reflecting on the meaning and function of contemporary aesthetic experience, Marquard underlines how art provides a fund of experience in an epoch in which man is increasingly distant from experience of the world; and we may note how in the eighteenth century art not only enables us to 'undergo' experiences, as is the case in any period, but also how aesthetic experience itself is used as a 'laboratory'. Aesthetic experience is a human cultural characteristic and can be employed in the same way as a 'scientific experiment', supplying data and indications for understanding humankind itself. While we 'undergo' experience we also observe and study, in this way attempting to deduce the causes of the effects produced on us by art. And these causes are identified not so much in the qualities of the individual objects that have conveyed the experience as in the inner workings of the mind – only aroused by the object – that have produced those effects.[4]

---

[1]   Reinhart Koselleck, *Futures Past*.

[2]   See in particular Odo Marquard, *Der angeklagte und der entlastete Mensch in der Philosophie des 18. Jahrhunderts*, in *Abschied vom Prinzipiellen* (Stuttgart, 1981), pp. 39-66; English trans. R. Wallace, *Farewell to Matters of Principle* (Oxford, 1989).

[3]   This process of accusing man vis-à-vis himself is defined by Marquard as Übertribunalisierung, hyperimputation of human vital reality.

[4]   For example, evidence of how aesthetic experience can simultaneously be an object of study and a device for theorization can be found in the following passage from Archibald Alison: 'I speak upon an art [music] of which I have no theoretical knowledge, and of

As we shall see, the considerations of music that follow combine both psychological elements – or, rather, 'philosophy of mind' – and anthropological ones: on the one hand, the study of human nature, and especially of the mechanisms of perception, emerges as fundamental for the approach to questions of an 'aesthetic' nature, and particularly for justification of the effects of music on the human mind; while, on the other, it is acknowledged that if nature shapes us as equal, culture and education make us different. And the debates on the differences of taste among nations, but also among individuals, are underpinned by these reflections of a more anthropological kind.

All this can already be found in an author like Francis Hutcheson, who occupied the chair of moral philosophy at the University of Glasgow as from 1729 and wrote important treatises on the passions.[5] The text of greatest interest here is the *Inquiry into the Original of our Ideas of Beauty and Virtue* (1725), which shares that concern with *eudaimonia* that we found in the authors dealt with previously. In the preface to the work, Hutcheson begins by recognizing that a correct knowledge of human nature is an essential part of philosophy, but we are not told what purpose it serves. The aim Hutcheson ascribes to conscious development of thought is happiness. This may be achieved if man has a clear notion of which is 'the greatest and more lasting Pleasure', and hitherto no philosopher has ever taught distinctly 'how it is that knowledge or truth is pleasant to us'.[6] He fears, moreover, that 'we have made philosophy […] by our foolish management of it, so austere and ungainly a form, that a gentleman cannot easily bring himself to like it […]. So much is it changed from what was once the delight of the finest gentleman among the antients […].'[7] By drawing on the knowledge of human nature, the task of philosophy, then, will be to show man the path towards happiness and to teach him to cultivate lasting pleasures. As we shall see, music, conceived both as harmony and as art, has an important role to play in this project.

According to Hutcheson, philosophers do not offer an adequate discussion of the pleasure that derives from the senses and neglect an important aspect of it: for they seem to dwell only upon the 'mere ideas of sensation' – that is, on

---

which I can judge only from the effect that it produces on myself' (*Essays on the Nature and Principles of Taste* [1790] (Hildesheim, 1968), p. 178). The very fact of not identifying the causes of the effects in the objects in themselves but, rather, in the inner workings of the mind also enables persons not claiming to be expert in one specific art to theorize the functioning of aesthetic experience in that specific art of which they possess no theoretical knowledge.

[5]   On Hutcheson's role in the history of aesthetics, see Peter Kivy, *The Seventh Sense. Francis Hutcheson and Eighteenth-Century British Aesthetics* (New York, 1976).

[6]   Francis Hutcheson, *An Inquiry into the Original ...*, p. iv. On the topic of aesthetic pleasure and perception see Emily Michael, 'Francis Hutcheson on Aesthetic Perception and Aesthetic Pleasure', *British Journal of Aesthetics*, 24 (1984), pp. 241-55; and Mark Strasser, 'Hutcheson on Aesthetic Perception', *Philosophia*, 21 (1991/92), pp. 107-118.

[7]   Ibid. p. viii.

the individual sound, colour and so on – 'but there are vastly greater pleasures in those complex ideas of objects, which obtain the names of beautiful, regular, harmonious'.[8] The peculiar nature of these ideas is that they are not perceived through the five external senses but, rather, through a specific *inner sense*. The internal sense of harmony enables pleasant ideas to arise in our mind 'from the composition of sounds', while we call 'a good ear [...] a power of perceiving this pleasure'[9]. As we see, the inner sense remains that faculty already pointed out by Shaftesbury, a sort of instinct – in a word, a power existing in any person of any epoch. But while Shaftesbury's inner sense belonged within a Neoplatonic context, Hutcheson treats it in a Lockeian phenomenology of mind.

In examining the position taken by Addison in the numbers of the *Pleasures of the Imagination* with regard to music's place in the 'modern system of the arts' – to use the expression coined by Paul O. Kristeller[10] – we noted how his emphasis on the sense of sight and the mimetic principle made it hard to place the art of sounds among the arts grouped around the 'secondary pleasures of the imagination'. For the latter are based on the work of comparison that the mind sets in motion when it finds itself faced with artistic objects that recall others of these, already present in our mind and normally belonging to the realm of nature; and for this reason music encounters difficulty in the 'representation of visible objects'.

Likewise, in the system propounded by Hutcheson, we find a distinction that appears to hark back to that of Addison between primary and secondary pleasures – the separation between *original or absolute beauty* and *comparative or relative beauty*.[11] Pride of place in Hutcheson is awarded, no longer to pleasure and imagination, but to the beautiful and the inner sense. Not that pleasure disappears, but it is indissolubly linked with beauty, the perception of which is the necessary outcome.

The distinction between the two kinds of beauty is based, indeed, on whether or not the mimetic principle obtains. In the case of absolute beauty 'we [...] understand only that beauty which we perceive in objects without comparison to any thing external, of which the object is suppos'd an imitation, or picture',[12] whereas in the case of relative beauty the opposite principle holds. Hutcheson specifies that one and the same object may partake of both kinds of beauty, but it is important to distinguish them, since the pleasure that derives from them stems from two different sources. The source of pleasure conveyed by absolute beauty is the principle of *uniformity in variety*. Examples of absolute beauty are geometrical

---

[8]   Ibid. p. 6.

[9]   Ibid. p. 7.

[10]   P. O. Kristeller, 'The Modern System of the Arts*'*.

[11]   On the relationship between Addison's and Hutcheson's thought, see Clarence DeWitt Thorpe, 'Addison and Hutcheson on the Imagination', *English Literary History*, 2/3 (1935), pp. 215-234; and R. L. Montgomery, 'Addison and Hutcheson', in Charles Fox (ed.), *Psychology and Literature in the Eighteenth Century* (New York, 1987), pp. 149-166.

[12]   Hutcheson, *An Inquiry into the Original ...*, p. 14.

figures, the works of nature, mathematical theorems and *harmony*, where by 'harmony' Hutcheson intends the art of composing. In 'good compositions', he opines, the unity is assured by a[13]

> general unity of key, an uniformity among the parts in bars, risings, fallings, closes. The necessity of this will appear, by observing the dissonance which would arise from tacking parts of different tunes together as one, altho both were separately agreeable. A greater uniformity is also observable among the bases, tenors, trebles of the same tune.

Whereas variety is guaranteed by dissonance:[14]

> There is indeed observable, in the best Compositions, a mysterious Effect of Discords: They often give as great Pleasure as continu'd Harmony; whether by refreshing the ear with Variety, or by awakening the Attention, and enlivening the Relish for the succeeding Harmony of Concords, as Shades enliven and beautify Pictures.

In Hutcheson's system, then, music assumes a special place. While the other arts are discussed in the light of the principle under whose heading comparative beauty belongs, music belongs to the kind of beauty whose pleasantness is connected with the principle of uniformity in variety. But Hutcheson shows himself not entirely satisfied with this analysis of music and admits to being aware that other factors may lie behind the particular pleasure it is capable of arousing. Thus in another paragraph of the *Inquiry* – in the section of the work devoted to demonstrating the universality of the sense of beauty in man – he returns to dealing with music:[15]

> There is also another charm in musick to various persons, which is distinct from the harmony, and is occasion'd by its raising agreeable passions. The human voice is obviously vary'd by all the stronger passions; now when our ear discerns any resemblance between the air of a tune, whether sung or play'd upon an instrument, either in its time or key, or any other circumstance, to the sound of the human voice in any passion, we shall be touch'd by it in a very sensible manner, and have melancholy, joy, gravity, thoughtfulness excited in us by a sort of sympathy or contagion. The same connection is observable between the very air of a tune, and the words expressing any passion which we have heard it

---

[13]   Ibid., p. 26.

[14]   See the edition edited by Wolfgang Leidhold (Indianapolis, 2004), p. 43. Only at this point, the reader is referred to a different edition of the *Inquiry*, since the text included in the complete works by Olms reprints only the first edition (1725), whereas the passage cited above appears in the three subsequent editions (1726, 1729, 1738) but is absent from the first.

[15]   Ibid., 1st treatise, section VI, p. 77 et seq.

fitted to, so that they shall both recur to us together, tho but one of them affects our senses.

Here Hutcheson makes mention, though only briefly, of a principle that will recur in British thought: *sympathy*. As with the term *harmony*, its extraordinary semantic range includes a special musical significance, linked with the phenomenon of sympathetic vibration. In this perspective it must be emphasized that it was possible for sympathy to be understood as a principle operating in a physical way on man, whose nerves were likened to the strings of a musical instrument.[16] Although Hutcheson says nothing specific about his idea at this point, the fact that he used the term 'contagion' as well as 'sympathy' to describe the action of music would seem to project us into a field of terminology that rubs shoulders with medicine. Whatever the case, this ulterior source of pleasure that can be found in music has some analogy with comparative beauty. For Hutcheson speaks of a 'resemblance' that our ear detects between a melody and the particular tone assumed by the human voice when stirred by the passions. It is also interesting to note that these statements suggest, in Hutcheson's view, how the pathetic effect of an instrumental composition resides in the analogy with the accents of the human voice. In fact, he seems to conceive of instrumental music as an imitation of the states of mind expressed by the voice. I must emphasize how in Hutcheson there is no hierarchy between absolute and comparative beauty. They are two distinct kinds of beauty, and comparative beauty is not compelled to imitate objects endowed with absolute beauty in order for it to be pleasing.

Note that according to Hutcheson – as Diderot, too, would argue under the heading of 'beauty' in the *Encyclopédie*[17] – it is not necessary for the partaker to perceive distinctly what constitutes the uniformity or the variety of the beautiful object in order to experience pleasure. For the perception of beauty is immediate and necessary, and cannot be modified in accordance with purely rational considerations. A friend of ours may spend hours explaining why an object that has struck him is beautiful, but if that object has not aroused the idea of beauty in us, the feeling of pleasure connected with it cannot be awakened in others by his rationally argued discourse. For the author of the *Inquiry*, while beauty is unquestionably a subjective idea, it possesses an objective component. In other words, beauty is subjective inasmuch as it is that idea that is aroused in us by a particular object. But, whatever the case, the idea can be aroused only when an object displays determinate characteristics: when it is endowed with uniformity in variety, or when it imitates another object. While the *inner sense* is that faculty that allows us to feel pleasure before objects that present determinate qualities, the obvious diversity of human tastes depends, instead, on habit, education,

---

[16]   In the current of thought under study, this conception can be found in David Hartley's *Observations Upon Man, his Frame, his Duty and his Expectations* (London, 1749).

[17]   A goodly part of Diderot's article is devoted to discussing Hutcheson's theory.

expectations and associations. For, Hutcheson says, expectation may alter our perception:[18]

> thus bad musick pleases rusticks who never heard any better, and the finest ear is not offended with tuning of instruments if it be not too tedious, where no harmony is expected, and yet much smaller dissonancy shall offend amidst the performance, where harmony is expected.

If habit, education, expectations and associations play a fundamental role in our perception of beauty, clearly the educators – parents, teachers, and so on – will have a very important task. For instance, Hutcheson stresses how fear of the dark derives from an association of ideas originating in faulty upbringing, and before him Locke had already enjoined nurses not to tell their infant charges ghost stories that would engender an association between the idea of the dark and the existence of supernatural beings.

To sum up, we can say that Hutcheson seems to have found in his predecessors the necessary encouragement to develop a complex aesthetic theory. The inner sense of Shaftesburian origin prepares the Lockeian mind to accept the idea of beauty and the pleasures theorized by Addison become the two different sources of beauty. And in all this the central objective of discussion is never lost sight of: man. For the reflection on the arts finds scope within a debate regarding the possibility of happiness.

Music and 'natural sympathy'

With no claim to being exhaustive, let us now analyze in detail certain theories that seek to explain the action of music upon man, calling into play the psychology of the mind. We start from sympathy, a concept we already encountered in Hutcheson and that represents one of the ways in which music is held to operate on man, influencing his state of mind. In many cases, with no further attempts at definition, sympathy remains a hidden cause that in mysterious ways produces effects that can be experienced by any person.[19] Sympathy, however, can be understood in a mechanical sense, as a phenomenon of resonance that enables the air that is made to vibrate by a sounding body to cause the sympathetic vibration of our 'internal strings', the nerves.

---

[18]   Hutcheson, *An Inquiry into the Original ...*, p. 66.

[19]   Roger North, for example, objected to this mode of intending sympathy in his *Cursory Notes of Musicke*, in a section devoted to the physical phenomenon of sympathy, beginning a paragraph with the statement 'I intend not this [the sympathy of sounds] in the sence of unmechanicall people, as many adorers of musick are, who fancy a sort of magick in sound' (Roger North, *Cursory Notes of Musicke (c. 1698-c. 1703)*, ed. M. Chan and J. C. Kassler (Kensington, 1986), p. 127).

James Harris's work *A discourse on Music, Painting, and Poetry* is the second of his *Three Treatises* (1744).[20] These treatises consist of a general discourse on Art (*A dialogue concerning Art*), a detailed discussion of the means and subject appropriate to three specific arts, leading to a statement of the aim of human life in the third treatise, *Concerning Happiness*. Before dealing with the discourse on music, painting and poetry, it will be as well to consider the first dialogue of the work, which will also allow us to contextualize what Harris has to say.

Two sources lie behind the *Dialogue concerning Art*: its literary genre bears the imprint of Shaftesbury, who was Harris's uncle on his mother's side,[21] while some of the main ideas in the dialogue, as well as the sequence of the argument, come from Aristotle. Together with the *Poetics*, the main texts of reference are the *Nicomachean Ethics* – providing the concepts of 'work' and 'energy' that Harris employs to divide the arts into two large groups – and the *Physics*, which supplies the scheme to organize the dialogue. He propounds a series of definitions of 'art', articulated according to the four forms of causality (material, formal, efficient and final) distinguished by Aristotle in Book II of the *Physics*, which serve to explain the generation not only of the entities of the natural world but also those produced by the human arts. The concept of art Harris uses is still that of the ancient τὲχναι, among which he cites music, painting, medicine, poetry and agriculture. What clearly emerges from this dialogue is a view of the arts as not merely ornamental to the life of the individual, but a kind of production intimately connected with the human constitution itself. Music, painting and poetry are defined by Harris 'as inseparable from our being, as perspiring, or circulation',[22] in virtue of the argument by which human nature cannot bear the absence of joy and pleasures and all that it claims to be its own good. In pursuing pleasure through the arts, man only continues his eternal quest for that 'complex being called good',[23] but he does this in a particular way that compels him to self-improvement, since the kind of good he seeks through the arts exceeds his faculties in the natural state. Art, then, responds to a natural need of man and drives him to perfect his own nature. The

---

[20] For a complete and documented biography of Harris, see Clive Probyn, *The Sociable Humanist: the Life and Works of James Harris 1709-80. Provincial and Metropolitan Culture in Eighteenth-Century England* (Oxford, 1991). On the contemporary reception of Harris's treatise on the arts see also the letters from the fourth Earl of Shaftesbury (15 [?] April 1737) and from Robert Warner (20 November 1738), in Burrows and Dunhill (eds), *Music & Theatre in Handel's World*, p. 24 and p. 64; and the private conversations with King George III and Queen Charlotte noted in Harris's conversation diary on 29 November 1772 and 26 January 1774 (ibid., p. 695 and p. 758).

[21] James Harris's mother was Elisabeth Ashley Cooper, sister of the third Earl of Shaftesbury. His father, also James, had in 1704 married Catherine Cocks, who died the following year while giving birth to a daughter. In 1707 Harris senior married Elisabeth Ashley Cooper, by whom he had three sons, James being the eldest.

[22] James Harris, *The Works of James Harris* (Bristol, 2003), vol. I, p. 19.

[23] Ibid.

efficient cause of art is man himself, his power of becoming cause of determinate effects; Harris gives very pregnant expression to this idea: not only is art a cause, but man himself becomes a cause.[24]

If man is the origin of art, Harris wonders what may be its end, its fulfilment, and finds this in the individual works, whose characteristic it is to be units made up of parts according to an order. These parts may coexist or follow one another: on the basis of this distinction Harris classifies them as 'work', or 'movement' or 'energy'.[25] The distinction comes from the *Nicomachean Ethics* – not from the small section dealing with the arts (VI, 4, 1140a) but from the preliminary discussion regarding the definition of human happiness in Book I. Aristotle's two concepts of 'work' and 'energy' do not actually refer to the products of art; it is Harris who transfers them from a moral context to an artistic one. In Aristotle, ἐνέργεια is the act that leads the work (ἔργον) to fulfillment, and in the *Nicomachean Ethics* the term is repeatedly employed where Aristotle tries to establish what is the good of man, ultimately finding it in 'an activity (ἐνέργεια) of the spirit according to its virtue' (I, 7, 1098a, 16-17).

In the category of 'energy' Harris places life itself, the activities performed in time, such as speech, and two of the arts: music and dancing. The arts like painting and sculpture are, instead, placed under the heading of 'work', and Harris also shows how in their 'energetic' phase – that is, in the *becoming* of the work – they are not perfect and hence are not to be taken into consideration. In the one case, then, the perfection of the art stems from the process itself; in the other, from the outcome of the creative process.

The second source of this dialogue, as we said, is the third Earl of Shaftesbury. Firstly, the very choice of literary genre and the pastoral setting are redolent of *The Moralists* and, secondly, as in that work, the peroration is analogous to the ecstatic praise of Nature sung by Theocles in Shaftesbury's text. In Harris, after the main character of the dialogue has systematically expounded his own definition of art, he reveals that he has already himself written a few lines on the subject and offers to recite his composition to the friend who has been his patient listener up to now. This is the cue for a long digression in praise of Art, in poetic language and emphatic style. The first topic dealt with in the elogium is the relationship between art and nature, and here Harris declares at once that the merit of art is not confined to *imitation* of Nature, 'but (what is more) even to adorn her with graces of thy

---

24   Ibid., p. 12: 'Let us then say […], not only art is a cause, but that it is man becoming a cause'. This definition is in line with what Aristotle argues in the *Nicomachean Ethics*, VI, 4, 1140a: 'All Art deals with bringing something into existence; and to pursue an art means to study how to bring into existence a thing which may either exist or not, and the efficient cause of which lies in the maker and not in the thing made' (trans. H. Rackham (London and Cambridge, MA, 1962), p. 335).

25   J. Harris, *The Works*, vol. I, p. 23.

own'.[26] Art is thus summoned to a dual and important task: on the one hand, it improves Nature in the widest sense of the term, decorating it with fresh beauties while, on the other, in the narrower domain of human nature – as we saw above – it compels man to perfect himself, since the need from which it sprang cannot be satisfied by use of man's faculties in the natural state alone, but requires that these faculties be refined. The elogium continues with a list of the powers of the arts over the four natural elements and, in the part dealing with air, Harris states that thanks to art even air may minister to our pleasure, for 'at thy command it giveth birth to sounds, which charm the soul with all the powers of harmony'.[27]

From these passages we can already see not only how Harris removes music from the category of the imitative arts, but also how – unlike many others of the authors who doubt the possibility of music to imitate – this in no way implies a negative assessment of the art of sounds, and actually places it in the class of arts that improve nature itself. For, in the case of music, the art exploits a natural element (air), modifying it so as to enchant the spirit by means of harmony. The elogium closes shortly afterwards with an important, conclusive definition of art not as 'ornament' of the mind, but as 'mind' itself, mind that becomes 'form': 'shall I call thee ornament of mind; or art thou more truly mind itself? It is mind thou art, most perfect mind; not rude, untaught, but fair and polished; in such thou dwellest, of such thou art the form.'[28]

The theses discussed in the dialogue are of use for fully understanding the *Discourse on Music, Painting, and Poetry* that followed in 1744. This treatise starts out from a definition of what links the arts; the principle identified *in primis* by Harris as common immediately reveals his main interest: 'all arts have this in common, that they respect human life'.[29] Right from the start, then, it is evident that what concerns Harris is not so much the means common to the arts as their end, and this end is man himself. In line with what he averred in the previous dialogue, Harris insists on the fact that also music, painting and poetry can be considered as 'necessary' arts on a par with medicine or agriculture. Since man is concerned with more than simply living, his hallmark is not mere subsistence, like other animals, but, as with the Ancients, the desire to 'live well'. Harris's intention in this short essay is to discuss the resemblances and differences between the three arts in order to decide which is the best.[30]

The discussion begins by identifying the senses involved in the perception of artistic objects, namely sight and hearing. Through them ,'these arts exhibit to the mind imitations, and imitate either parts or affections of this natural world,

---

[26]   Ibid., p. 26. The second person singular in the passage cited refers, of course, to Art, apostrophized at the start of the dialogue.

[27]   Ibid., p. 27.

[28]   Ibid., p. 28.

[29]   Ibid., p. 33.

[30]   About the topic of the comparison of the arts in Britain, see James Malek, *The Arts Compared: An Aspect of Eighteenth Century British Aesthetics* (Detroit, 1974).

or else the passions, energies, and other affections of minds'.[31] By means of sight and hearing, then, art affords the mind imitations of the natural world, but also that congeries of processes that make up the activity of the mind. Harris firstly identifies the means employed by the arts: music, which makes use of the ear, can imitate thanks to *sound* and *movement*; painting thanks to *colours* and *figures*; poetry, like music, uses hearing and therefore, as regards imitation, can utilize only the selfsame means as music. But Harris immediately adds that poetry, thanks to language, has the faculty of rendering the sounds of complex meanings and thus to employ them as vehicles of ideas.[32] This distinguishes it from the other two arts, since it enables it to make use of an *artificial means*. The three arts, then, have their 'modality' in common, imitation, and differ by their 'means'.

Having established the means of the arts, Harris explains how – in order to decide to which of music, painting and poetry the primacy belongs – we should deal with the subjects that each one may imitate. For their dignity will depend on the subject for imitation. As we might have expected in a discussion of this sort, music is at a disadvantage. Harris acknowledges its power to imitate certain realities of the natural world (for example, winds, waters, birdsong), as well as certain sounds peculiar to man and, in particular, those that express pain and anguish. But these last are merely imitations of 'imperfect' type for, according to him, musical sound and natural sound are fundamentally different, and their differences consists in the fact that musical sounds are the product of equal vibrations, whereas natural sounds stem from unequal vibrations.[33]

His conclusion is that musical imitation can, at most, attain the sphere of 'resemblance' but can never be identical, and thus 'is greatly below that of painting, and that at best it is but an imperfect thing'. But immediately afterwards he adds: 'as to the efficacy therefore of music, it must be derived from another source, which must be left for the present, to be considered of hereafter'.[34] In order not to interrupt his discourse on imitation Harris intends to proceed with the comparison between painting and poetry, but he decides to inform the reader in advance that his judgement on music has not yet been proclaimed. Without troubling ourselves

---

[31]   J. Harris, *The Works*, vol. I, p. 34.

[32]   James Harris also wrote an important essay on language (*Hermes, or a Philosophical Inquiry concerning Universal Grammar*, London, 1751) and had occasion to discuss language and philosophical method in letters exchanged with James Burnett (Lord Monboddo), author of the well-known *Of the origin and progress of Language* (Edinburgh, 1773-1792).

[33]   Harris is not very precise in adducing the theory of vibrations. Although his reference is very briefly made, he obviously has in mind the theory of consonance as coincidence of the vibrations. In the case of consonance, the pleasure derives from the fact that the vibrations of the two sounds come to coincide; but where dissonance is concerned, the *ictus* of the two sounds fall at different moments and therefore do not meet.

[34]   J. Harris, *The Works*, vol. I, p. 41.

to follow his rigorous train of argument, we go on to the section of greatest interest for our purposes: the sixth and last chapter of the essay, entirely devoted to music.

The chapter focuses on music's power to arouse the affects, connected with the *natural sympathy* that enables our mind to establish links between affects and ideas. Harris explains how, for example, the idea of a funeral generates a feeling of melancholy within us; and how, conversely, when we feel affected by melancholy our thoughts may turn to ideas like that of a funeral. The affect, however, has such power on the mind that it is able to alter the effect of one and the same idea on the same individual at different moments. Thus, if a person were to find himself in a cheerful state of mind, the idea of a funeral would not exert the same effect on him as when he is sad. The effect of greatest impact on the mind is attained, therefore, when affect is united with idea. This argument underpins Harris's assertion that an 'irresistible force' may derive from the union of poetry and music.[35] For poetry is supremely capable of conveying ideas to the human mind, but is often unable to achieve the desired effect on its audience because the latter is not in the appropriate state of mind to receive those ideas: if the feeling of the public is not in tune with the idea conveyed by the text the sympathetic vibration will not occur. Moreover, if poetry should be initially concerned with arousing feelings, and subsequently with conveying the ideas, it would dissipate its own forces. This, therefore, in Harris's view, is the most important task of music:[36]

> For here a double force is made co-operate to one end. A poet, thus assisted, finds not an audience in a temper, averse to the genius of his poem, or perhaps at best under a cool indifference; but by the preludes, the symphonies, and concurrent operation of the music in all its parts, roused into those very affections, which he would most desire. An audience, so disposed, not only embrace with pleasure the ideas of the poet, when exhibited; but, in a manner, even anticipate them in their several imaginations.

In line with the foregoing, Harris also spends a few words in favour of opera and oratorio, asserting that only a person devoid of sensitivity to music can remain unmoved by the joint effect of music and poetry, with the justification that this sort of expression is not 'probable'. For anyone will be willing to surrender a little verisimilitude in favour of a superior power of impact on the feelings that will involve him in the action 'with double energy and enjoyment'[37]. Here, as we see, Harris does not postulate the need for simultaneous presence of word and music; instrumental music, too, has a place in his discourse. Not only does it set the mind of the listener in tune with a particular feeling, it also activates his imagination, stimulating it to *anticipate* the ideas that will follow. Listening as postulated by Harris, then, is an active phenomenon, well in line with the characterization of

---

[35]   Ibid., p. 58.

[36]   Ibid., p. 57 et seq.

[37]   Ibid., p. 59.

music as 'energy'. If, however, it is desired to attain a 'well-rounded' effect, music must be accompanied by a poetic text: otherwise, the risk is that the ideas aroused in the imagination of the individual listener will vanish when the sound ceases, without leaving any deep impression on the individual's mind.[38]

Certain parts of Harris's argument display a remarkable kinship with a key text in the eighteenth-century's reflections on the arts: namely, the *Réflexions critiques sur la poésie et sur la peinture* by Jean-Baptiste Du Bos, the complete edition of which in three volumes, containing an ample discussion of opera, appeared in 1733 in Paris, eleven years prior to Harris's text. The first English edition of Du Bos's writing was published in 1748, but it is not altogether unlikely that Harris had occasion to consult the French original. Although the two works diverge in their decision of which art should be held to predominate over the others – Du Bos gives the palm to painting, Harris to poetry – the choice of arts, the distinction between the use of natural and artificial signs, and several of the arguments regarding the subject of painting are identical, as is the idea that the pleasures conveyed by art respond to a 'need' in man and are therefore necessary. Note, in particular, how close are Harris's view, as given above, of the limits of poetry considered by itself and certain ideas expressed by Du Bos in chapters XL and XLV of the first part of his work. In chapter XL, where painting is accorded pride of place, Du Bos writes:[39]

> The most tender verses can affect us only by degrees, and by setting the several springs of our machine successively to work. Words must first excite those ideas, whereof they are only arbitrary signs. These ideas must be ranged afterwards in the imagination, and form such pictures as move and engage us. All these operations, 'tis true, are soon done; but it is an uncontestable principle in mechanics, that the multiplicity of springs always debilitates the movement, by reason that one spring never communicates to another all the motion it has received.

The idea, exactly as it was to be in Harris, is that, if poetry, as well as awakening ideas, should contrive to activate the imagination to 'strike us', then part of its force would be lost. Du Bos holds that, in this connection, the sense of sight is much more powerful than that of hearing. He admits, however, that human ingenuity has succeeded in giving fresh vigour to verses by availing itself of three further means that increase the pleasure of poetry: recitation, declamation and *singing*. Music in

---

[38]   Note that, as we saw in Hutcheson, the discussion on the arts often centres not only on the idea of pleasure but, more specifically, on which are the 'lasting' pleasures, in which man could profitably invest.

[39]   Jean-Baptiste Du Bos, *Critical Reflections on Poetry, Painting and Music, with an Inquiry into the Rise and Progress of the Theatrical Entertainments of the Ancients*, trans. Thomas Nugent (London, 1748), pp. 322-323.

Du Bos becomes that which transforms 'pleasure of the ear into pleasure of the heart'. He describes the relation between music and poetry as follows:[40]

> The natural signs of the passions, which music collects and employs with art, in order to increase the Energy of the words she sets, ought to render them more capable of moving us, because these natural signs have a surprizing power over us.

And he goes on to claim 'some truth in the recitatives of opera', and to explain how instrumental music, too, can be held to be imitative. Although Harris prefers not to attribute the effects of music to imitation, to assign them to the connection between feelings and ideas through 'natural sympathy', the similarity between the two arguments appears evident, and it remains significant even without supposing him to have borrowed anything from Du Bos. On the basis of their common reflections on the means employed by poetry, painting and music, both authors identify a lack of expression in poetry that desiderates music as an art able to constitute a 'powerful ally'[41] for the first of these.

The second essay that concerns us here is the above-cited *Essay on the arts commonly called imitative* (1772) by Sir William Jones, a teacher of orientalia. It commences with an immediate critical reference to those who – adducing the authority of Aristotle without any detailed knowledge of him – claim that poetry and music are 'imitative' arts. Jones proposes a comparison between music and poetry and starts his analysis from the origin of the two arts. According to his reconstruction, poetry, in its various genres, is the child of four sentiments: ecstatic-religious feeling before the beauty of nature, love, aversion to vice and hatred. The commencement of the passages devoted to the origin of music comes not from history but from physics. Jones desires to say something, without going into detail, on the nature of sound, and the phenomenon that most interests him is that of harmonics. In order to explain the distinction between a 'common sound' and a 'musical sound', he adduces an image of geometrical type: common sound, he states, is like a point and is isolated; musical sound, instead, is like a circle, whose figure consists of a multitude of points located at the same distance from the centre. The points that form the circumference of the musical sound are the harmonics, upon which the modern system of harmony is based.[42] After this brief specification, Jones defines the poetical texts expressed in song as 'music of the origins' – these songs 'would then be pure and original musick; not merely soothing to the ear, but affecting the heart; not an imitation of nature, but the voice of nature

---

[40]   Ibid., p. 362.

[41]   Harris, *The Works*, vol. I, p. 54.

[42]   Sir William Jones, *Essay on the arts commonly called imitative* (Oxford, 1772), in *The Collected Works of Sir William Jones*, ed. Garland Cannon (London, 1993), vol. X, p. 367.

herself'.[43] Poetry and music are therefore linked by their both representing a genre of natural and spontaneous expression of humankind. At which point, after a brief digression to illustrate the Greek musical system and its principal differences from the modern system,[44] Jones reiterates what 'real' music is and expresses a decided antipathy towards modern music, which[45]

> paints nothing, expresses nothing, says nothing to the heart, and consequently can only give more or less pleasure to one of our senses; and no reasonable man will seriously prefer a transitory pleasure, which must soon end in satiety, or even in disgust, to a delight of the soul, arising from *sympathy*, and founded on the natural passions, always lively, always interesting, always transporting.

Sympathy, then, is the real principle common to music and poetry, and in this context – though it will not always be so – Jones uses the term only to denote the capacity of the two arts to express feelings: sympathy represents music's way of action and, as in Harris, is based on the idea that there exists a natural relation between sounds and feelings.[46] Along with sympathy, Jones identifies a second mode of action of the arts, which he calls *substitution*[47] and considers of lesser importance. He employs this term to indicate what many other authors call 'imitation': for 'substitution' identifies those descriptive representations whose aim is to arouse within us feelings analogous to those we experience before the respective natural objects described (for example, a landscape). At which point we understand even more clearly the reason why the author insists on distinguishing the phenomenon of imitation – and of substitution – from that of sympathy: while imitation expresses a resemblance between what it imitates and what is imitated, music and poetry do not 'imitate' emotions, nor do they copy them, but 'are' themselves emotion. The artist's task is therefore not so much to imitate nature as

---

[43]   Ibid., p. 368. Note this continual return – as we also found in Du Bos – of the opposition of between what strikes the ear alone and what speaks to the heart. This was to be one of the main objections to instrumental music.

[44]   Jones here shows a good knowledge of music, explaining the concept of 'tonic' and the difference between major and minor modes, and characterizing certain tonalities: e.g. F minor 'pathetick and mournful to the highest degree, for which reason it was chosen by the excellent Pergolesi in his *Stabat Mater*' (ibid., p. 370 et seq.). Recall that Jones, who lived for a long time in India, was the author of an essay on the *Musical modes of the Hindus*.

[45]   Ibid., p. 371 et seq. (my italics).

[46]   But while in the 1740s it was normal for this relation to be acknowledged without question, in the period when Jones was writing – as we shall see later on – the need to distinguish the nature of sound from that of the emotions was taken as established; so Jones's stance is scarcely up with the times.

[47]   Jones is the only one of my sources where I have found this term used.

to exploit her very power 'causing the same effect upon the imagination, which her charms produce to the senses'[48].

In a later work, whose first version belongs to 1784, and which was subsequently enlarged, Sir William Jones returns to the subject he dealt with more than ten years earlier. The object of the essay is to illustrate the Indian system of modes, of which he had first-hand acquaintance. Having travelled to India in 1783 he had taken up residence in Calcutta where, in the year following, he had founded the Asiatic Society of Bengal for the promotion of oriental studies. Before describing Indian music, however, he offers some remarks on western music. Here, he divides music into two parts: *music* considered *as science*, which comes under the head of natural philosophy and seeks to explain the causes and properties of sounds, and *music* considered *as art*, which combines those sounds considered by philosophy in isolation and whose function is to delight the hearing. To this bipartite view of music – already classic in the 1780s – he adds *music* considered as a *fine art*, whose task is 'to captivate the fancy while it pleases the sense, and, speaking, as it were, the language of beautiful nature, to raise correspondent ideas and emotions in the mind of the hearer'[49].

The main difference between this essay and the one devoted to the question of imitation is that Jones now deals at greater length with the physical causes of the action of sound on the human body. This also leads him to provide a less general explanation of the principle of sympathy he had previously stated, specifying that, if a person 'had merely described the human frame as the noblest and sweetest of musical instruments, endued with a natural disposition to resonance and sympathy, alternately affecting and affected by the soul, which pervades it, his description might, perhaps, have been physically just'.[50] In this case, then, the mysterious connection between music and emotions is explained through a 'sympathy' of natural-physical kind, based on a precise view of the human constitution: if musical sound produces on the nerves the same sympathetic effect experienced on the strings of an instrument, the impact of music upon man can be explained according to a mechanical model. In this case, sympathy is no longer, as in Harris, an alternative form of 'association' where there exists a correspondence between emotions and ideas, but can be adduced to explain a cause-effect nexus on a mechanical basis.

Sympathetic emotions: vocal and instrumental music according to Lord Kames

In his reflection on music James Harris addresses some important and delicate questions: what kind of influence may musical sound have on human nature? Is

---

[48]   Ibid., p. 378.

[49]   Sir William Jones, *On the Musical modes of the Hindus: written in 1784, and since much enlarged*, in *The collected Works*, vol. II, p. 166.

[50]   Ibid., p. 169.

there any difference between the effects produced by musical sound accompanied by words and those produced by purely instrumental music? Harris does not spend much time on this distinction, but his theory leaves us in no doubt that the sound of music, whether vocal or instrumental, arouses emotions in us in virtue of 'natural sympathy'. What poetry adds are ideas; the words of music, then, assist in specifying the object of the emotion that the music awakens. A similar problem is addressed in a celebrated work published in 1762 in Edinburgh: the *Elements of Criticism* by Henry Home, Lord Kames.[51] The author's aim in this essay is to create a 'science of criticism' that will enable man to refine his taste. Study of the fine arts – poetry, painting, sculpture, music, gardening and architecture, according to Kames – is of particular importance, since he claims a special virtue for them: they refine the sympathetic sentiments that underpin the cohesion of society.

Unlike other arts, music is not granted special sections of its own in the *Elements of Criticism*, and only in one instance does Kames devote a paragraph to it as such (II.1.2). Nonetheless, a fairly complex picture of Kames's view of music emerges from the essay. As we shall shortly see, Kames, too, discusses the relation between sound and feeling and offers some reflections on the difference between vocal and instrumental music, according full legitimacy to the latter.[52] But for a full understanding of his ideas on music we must concentrate on certain theories expounded in the first two chapters of the work regarding the working of the human mind and the distinction between passions and emotions.

The first chapter of the *Elements of Criticism* is titled 'Perceptions and ideas in a train', where the author identifies the main element responsible for the concatenation of ideas in our mind – that is, the principle of *association*.[53] Kames's description recalls that of Hume, who writes in the *Treatise on Human Nature* (1739) that there is[54]

---

[51]   Notwithstanding the relevance of this work, in the second half of the century the *Elements of Criticism* have been seriously neglected. A recent explanation of the causes of this neglect, and a study of the work can be found in Beth Innocenti Manolescu, 'Traditions of Rhetoric, Criticism, and Argument in Kames's "Elements of Criticism"', *Rhetoric Review*, 22/3 (2003), pp. 225-242.

[52]   This is infrequent in the period; nor, as far as I can see, has it been noted in the secondary literature, which has preferred to dwell on Adam Smith's consideration of music in his later reflections (see, for example, Wilhelm Seidel, 'La musica va annoverata tra le arti mimetiche? L'estetica dell'imitazione riveduta da Adam Smith', *Il Saggiatore Musicale*, 3 (1996), pp. 259-272; Nikolaus De Palézieux, *Die Lehre vom Ausdruck in der englischen Musikæsthetik des 18. Jahrhunderts* (Hamburg, 1981).

[53]   On the use of the principle of association in contemporary critical theories, see Martin Kallich, *The Association of Ideas and Critical Theory in Eighteenth-Century England* (The Hague, 1970).

[54]   David Hume, *A Treatise of Human Nature*, I, ed. T. H. Green and T. H. Grose (Aalen, 1964; reprint of the London 1886 edition), p. 321 (I, ɪ, § 4).

> a kind of attraction which in the mental world will be found to have as
> extraordinary effects as in the natural, and to shew itself in as many and as
> various forms. Its effects are every where conspicuous; but as to its causes, they
> are mostly unknown, and must be resolv'd into *original* qualities of human
> nature [...].

Kames, like Hume, argues that the concatenation of ideas (*train of thoughts*)
resides in the constitution itself of human nature, and underlines how associations
have an internal order:[55]

> Every man who attends to his own ideas, will discover order as well as
> connection in their succession. There is implanted in the breast of every man
> a principle of order, which governs the arrangement of his perceptions, of his
> ideas, of his actions.

The pleasure, then, that man experiences from regularity stems from an inner
natural constitution. All this is of consequence in considering the arts. For Kames
acknowledges that the relation between the objects has the power to impact
considerably on the production of emotions and passions, yet, in his view, not all
relations are equally effective. We must therefore examine which kinds of relation
exert most influence on the mind. At this point, Kames notes how the name of
'passion' or 'emotion' – thereafter to be distinguished from one another – is accorded
only to the feelings aroused in us through the media of sight or hearing, the senses
that underlie all the Fine Arts. Hence the study of these becomes the fundamental
object of the treatise, since the principles of the Arts 'appear [...] to open a direct
avenue to the heart of man'.[56] Thus, as the observation of the train of ideas in thought
is utilized to understand how the principle of association works, so the functioning of
the Fine Arts must be observed in order to comprehend how passions and emotions
may be aroused in the best way for conveying pleasure to man.

Kames, as we said, separates the feelings into passions and emotions, and
his reflection on these differences is important for the considerations on music.
According to him, the main difference between *emotion* and *passion* resides in
desire: for passion is a motion of the mind joined with a desire; it incites us to act
upon an object in order to satisfy the desire aroused and appease it. Emotion has
none of this. Its nature is more contemplative and, I should say, 'gratuitous'. Music,
says Kames, is unable to excite passions but, rather, emotions and further kinds of
feeling which he can only call *sympathetic emotion*,[57] whose essence consists in
the fact that it undoubtedly excites desire but without object. The classic instance
of 'sympathetic emotion' he finds in the emotion aroused by virtuous actions. If

---

[55]   Henry Home, Lord Kames, *Elements of Criticism*, in *Collected Works of Henry
Home, Lord Kames*, ed. J. V. Price (London, 1993), vol. I, p. 22.

[56]   Ibid., p. 33.

[57]   Ibid., chap. I, § 4.

we go to witness a spectacle and are impressed by a particular act of gratitude, not only will we esteem the author of the act (in which case we would experience a simple emotion), we will also feel a desire to perform a similar act. There exists, then, a type of emotion that appears to incite the mind to action, which, even in absence of a particular object on which to act, creates tension in our mind. Now, according to Kames, sympathetic emotion is precisely that type of emotion that can be aroused by purely instrumental music:[58]

> The emotions raised by music, independent of words, must be all of this nature: courage roused by martial music performed upon instruments without a voice, cannot be directed to any object; nor can grief or pity raised by melancholy music of the same kind have an object.

Unfortunately, Kames does not pursue his own thought. Nevertheless, in the literature we are examining this simple statement is absolutely novel and denotes a profound spirit of reflection. The writings of the period often attribute a generic indeterminacy to music. It is not credited, for example, with the power to excite particular passions, only general ones (like joy or sadness). The novelty in Kames lies in the kind of indeterminacy he ascribes to instrumental music: the typical assertion regarding the lack of 'object' in music without words takes on a different nuance in his writing. We have no longer to do with a limitation, but with a specific type of emotion that is manifested precisely in the want of an object to act upon.

One of the criticisms often made of instrumental music by various authors, including Harris, and deriving from the fact that it does not enable us to fix our attention on the object, was that it left only transitory impressions. But this criticism, too, is surmounted by Kames's theory of how the mind functions and by his reflection on the nature of the emotions. As we have seen, Kames finds a continuous flux of emotions in the mind, and hence every thought, emotion or passion of ours cannot be lasting. This state springs from a wise consideration on the part of nature, which knows well that[59]

> were it the nature of an emotion to continue, like color and figure [...] the condition of man would be deplorable: it is ordered wisely, that emotions should more resemble another attribute of manner, namely motion, which requires the constant exertion of an operating cause, and ceases when the cause is withdrawn.

Music and emotions, then, exhibit precise 'structural' analogies. Both, as Harris would say, are 'energy', movement. Both exist only in their unfolding, for as long as there is an operative cause. And in this Kames detects not only nothing negative, but indeed a project of Nature herself. The perception of a close analogy between the functioning of sounds and emotions can be seen in another remark of

---

[58]   Ibid., p. 63.

[59]   Ibid., p. 115.

his, on the fourth page of the *Elements*, where he sets out to explain how emotions and passions coexist and which effects they produce when they are united; to illustrate the combination of the two kinds of feeling Kames makes reference to the combinatorics of sounds that engender consonances and dissonances. According to his (albeit somewhat imprecise) reconstruction, two sounds are consonant when they 'unite' before reaching the ear. Instead, when they strike the ear 'separate' they are discordant and their effect is unpleasing even though their sound considered separately be pleasing. The conjunction of emotions works in the same way, therefore 'two emotions are said to be similar, when they tend, each of them, to produce the same tone of mind'.[60] As we see, not only do the emotions behave like sounds that produce consonances and dissonances, but the mind itself is musical in Kames's view, since the combinatorics of the emotions endow it with a 'tonality' of its own. The internal effects generated by the combinatorics of the emotions may be of two kinds 'of which, the one may be represented by addition in numbers, the other by harmony in sounds'[61]. Where there coexists a series of emotions of the same type, like those that may derive from the different components of a passage, in the combined vision of a tree, a stream and hills, their pleasure is summed together and the combinatorics answer to the model of an arithmetical sum. In the opposite case, where emotions of different type coexist – if, for example, we add to the afore-mentioned landscape the twittering of the birds or the scent of a flower and thus several senses cooperate to attain the same effect – the pleasure will be the greatest possible and this combinatoric will respond to the musical model that can be resumed in the adage *Harmonia est discordia concors* ('Harmony is discordant concord'):[62]

> As that pleasure resembles greatly the pleasure of concordant sounds, it may be termed the *harmony of emotions*. This harmony is felt in the different emotions occasioned by the objects of different senses; as where the emotions of the eye are combined with those of the ear.

Music, then, is used by Kames also as a model to explain, by analogy, the action of the emotions. The use of the analogy, however, suggests merely a structural correspondence. In reality, Kames specifies how there is no resemblance between sound and movement, or sound and feeling, as he notes in a chapter (XVIII) of the *Elements* devoted to the 'beauties of language', where he discusses the imitative power of words with respect both to mere sound and to the relation between sound and meaning. And here Kames also has something to say on the question of imitation in the arts. He understands the term 'imitation' in the strictest sense,

---

[60]   Ibid., p. 126.

[61]   Ibid., p. 128.

[62]   Ibid., p. 129.

as a simple 'copy of nature', restricting the imitative arts solely to painting and sculpture:[63]

> An ornamented field is not a copy or imitation of nature, but nature itself embellished. Architecture is productive of originals, and copies not from nature. Sound and motion may, in some measure, be imitated by music; but for the most part music, like architecture, is productive of originals.

Kames admits, as does Harris, that music can imitate sound or motion, but he ascribes no great importance to musical imitation. He stresses how imitation, in order to be such, must be based on resemblance. At the same time he denies the possibility of resemblance between objects of different senses; in particular, sound 'resembles not in any degree taste, smell, or motion: and as little can it resemble any internal sentiment, feeling or emotion. But must we then admit, that nothing but sound can be imitated by sound?'[64] The answer lies in the principle already identified: as regards imitation, music has very limited means at its disposal, but in order to communicate it may rely on the principle of sympathy, which harks back not to the concept of 'resemblance', as in the case of imitation, but to that of 'consonance'. Determinate sounds, says Kames, 'accord' with their own significance, in the chain of associations that make up the human mind determinate musics summon up likewise determinate emotions. Opposite to the principle of imitation, then, which operates within very narrow confines, stands the idea of 'sympathy' and 'consonance'. The sole resemblance between sound and emotion resides in their effects, and we can only say that 'emotions raised by sound and signification may have a resemblance; but sound itself cannot have a resemblance to any thing but sound'.[65]

Hitherto we have seen how Kames's reflection on music always revolved around the concept of 'emotion'. But there is a passage in the *Elements of Criticism* upon which we must focus, for it contains something quite surprising. Shortly after establishing the analogy between the combinatorics of emotions and sounds – in the second chapter, dealing with emotions and passions – Kames dwells on the pleasantness of vocal and instrumental music. His position regarding vocal music is substantially very like Harris's (for which music must accord with the feeling expressed in the text), but in relation to the previous discussion it takes on a new significance. We saw how the emotions gain in intensity when they are summed together and when they derive from different means and how they need to be 'in tune' in order for their effect not to be annulled and turn into dissonance. Indeed, they must meet 'before reaching the ear'. In this context, then, the need for word and music to agree receives a further justification and must be situated within the play that Kames calls *'harmony of the emotions'*. But the real novelty lies in his consideration of instrumental music – though here again, alas, it is only made in

---

[63]   Ibid., vol. II, p. 3.

[64]   Ibid., p. 86.

[65]   Ibid., p. 88.

passing. Kames writes that this music, 'having no connection with words, may be agreeable without relation to any sentiment: harmony, properly so called, though delightful when in perfection, has no relation to sentiment'.[66] Music can therefore please even in virtue of acoustic harmony alone, without any consideration for meaning. By sheer paradox, the pleasant nature of sound becomes for Kames the justification of Opera. For, after laying down a series of precepts on how music and word must agree, he states that 'it is true, that not the least regard is paid to these rules, either in the French or Italian Opera'[67]: and according to Kames the success of opera with the public lies precisely in the music itself, considered as pure sound![68]

> In these compositions the passions are so imperfectly expressed, as to leave the mind free for relishing music of any sort indifferently; and it cannot be disguised, that the pleasure of an opera is derived, chiefly, from the music, and scarcely at all from the sentiments.

Summarizing these complex reflections of Kames, we can see how his perspective has become richer than Harris's. Music in the *Elements* appears in two guises: the first is its 'substantial' or sound aspect, which is expressed in the remarks on vocal and instrumental music; the second is its 'formal' aspect, expressed in the analogies made between the formation of consonances and dissonances – however fleetingly conveyed from an acoustic point of view – and the combinatorics of the emotions. Moreover, these two aspects overlap in the explanation of the pathetic action of vocal music, which finds its justification in the theory of the harmony of the emotions. Instrumental music, lastly, is considered from two angles: in the first place it may excite a particular kind of emotion, sympathetic emotion, devoid of object. But it can also do entirely without specific emotions, since its sound may be pleasant even without appeal to anything but itself. We have seen how the whole period in which Kames is writing is pervaded by the idea that pleasure is a fundamental element of the life of man, and one towards which he tends. And, in line with this, Kames has no troubling in acknowledging that a music that conveys pleasure, even without appealing to anything else, can be fully enrolled among the Fine Arts that shed lustre to humanity.

A 'mechanical' musical sympathy: Daniel Webb

The authors dealt with up to now, who made use of the concept of 'sympathy' in their attempt to find a way round the obstacle placed before music by the cardinal

---

[66]   Ibid., vol. I, p. 138. Kames's use here of 'may' reminds us that instrumental music, as we saw, can *also* be related to an emotion of sympathetic type.

[67]   Ibid., p. 141.

[68]   Ibid.

principle in the comparison among the arts – namely, imitation – employ the term in a mostly general sense. If we except the work of Sir William Jones on Indian music, where we find a precise reference to the physical phenomenon of sympathy, Harris, Jones in his essay on the imitative arts and Lord Kames do not go into detail in their account of 'how' that phenomenon comes about. As is already clear from Kames's limpid writing, they argue that we cannot assert that there is a resemblance between sound and emotions, even though each of us may have intimate experience of how the effects of music resemble those produced by the emotions. As with these authors, we may choose this consideration as a starting point for reflection, without penetrating beyond the principles that underpin the resemblance of the effects. But we can go a little further and base the resemblance on physiological foundations. This was what Daniel Webb did in three essays on the arts. In 1761 he published a dialogue devoted to painting, a second dialogue[69] on poetry appeared in the year following, succeeded in 1769 by an essay titled *Observations on the Correspondence between Poetry and Music*.[70]

The last-named writing starts out from the problem just mentioned: wherein does the relation between sound and feeling consist? Webb is not satisfied with the solution provided by the principle of association,[71] according to which we associate our emotional state with a piece of music that we have just heard. Association, education and habit are not sufficient to account for a mechanism that seems to be embedded in the very constitution of human nature. Webb loses no time in giving the solution, and proposes a theory based on the principle of vibration that, although he does not quote, smacks of the theories of David Hartley (1705-1757), philosopher and physician, author of *Observations Upon Man, his Frame, his Duty and his Expectations* (1749). In that work, Hartley orients the Newtonian natural philosophy from the exterior to the interior of man and attempts to develop the speculative hypotheses on the properties of matter of which Newton had sketched a theory at the end of the *Opticks* (1704). The concept of *vibration*, in particular, is of central importance in Hartley's theory. We recall how the analogy advanced by Newton between the musical octave and the spectrum of colours was based on the fact that the properties of sounds and colours depended on the specific frequency of their vibrations, leading him to propose a quantitative analysis not only of sound

---

[69]   Namely, *An Inquiry into the Beauties of Painting and into the Merits of the most celebrated Painters Ancient and Modern* (1761) and *Remarks on the Beauties of Poetry* (1762), both published in London.

[70]   On this essay, see James Malek, *The Arts Compared*; and Jerome D. Wilbert, 'Poetry and music as observed by Daniel Webb', *Studies on Voltaire and the Eighteenth-Century*, 193 (1980), pp. 1730-35.

[71]   The principle of association is of crucial importance in the thought we are dealing with, and was exploited to its highest potential by Archibald Alison in his *Essays on the Nature and Principles of Taste* (1790). In this connection see the recent contribution by Steven A. Jauss, 'Associationism and Taste Theory in Archibald Alison's *Essays*', *The Journal of Aesthetics and Arts Criticism*, 64 (2006), pp. 415-428.

– which was supported by a long tradition – but also of colour. As evidenced by Richard Allen, author of a monograph on Hartley, 'Newton's analogy of spectrum and octave held out the promise of a science that could discover the fundamental "harmonic" principles that structured all physical reality, including the brains and nervous systems of living organisms'.[72]

Hartley's view of man is founded on the idea that the human mind is a mechanism whose impulse to act stems from the vibration of the nerves, which generates sensations of pleasure and unpleasure. For the study of vibration Hartley availed himself largely of experiments in acoustics and analogies with sounds; in addition, the *Observations* contains some paragraphs devoted to music. The most interesting point for understanding Webb's thought on music comes in the section of the treatise on man dealing with the sense of hearing, where Hartley specifies that musical sounds, whether vocal or instrumental, are pleasing in virtue of their physical, quantifiable properties. The theory of vibration thus enables musical sound to be considered without the mimetic paradigm; and this theory sets itself to explain music's impact on man, adducing the 'mechanism of the human mind' that is based on the mechanical principle of vibration, as well as the principle of association of ideas.

Along with Hartley's theories, the writings of medical character in which music is discussed in order to illustrate its thaumaturgic properties may have influenced the development of Daniel Webb's thought on music. Richard Browne's *Medicina Musica* (1729) and the *Reflections on Antient and Modern Musick* by Richard Brocklesby (1749) belong within this eighteenth-century current of thought. In the case of Browne, it is interesting to note that to the benefit that may accrue to man from listening to music he adds a second benefit from the practice of singing. While the pleasure of listening stems immediately from the 'agreeable percussion of the vibrating air upon the auditory nerves',[73] singing, which activates a reciprocal pressure 'of the diaphragm and abdominal muscles',[74] influences the animal spirits that regulate the circulation of the blood. This model, then, resolves the influence of sound on man into a mechanical communication of impulses.[75]

The mechanical theory of the action of sound upon man comes to the aid of Webb in explaining the analogy between sound and emotions. As we have already seen in the writings cited above, it is mainly based on the fact that both phenomena can be reduced to the concept of *movement*. The passions sway and agitate the

---

[72]   Richard C. Allen, *David Hartley on Human Nature* (Albany, 1999), p. 102.

[73]   Richard Browne, *Medicina Musica: or, a Mechanical Essay on the Effects of Singing, Musick, and Dancing, on the Human Bodies* (London, 1729), p. 35.

[74]   Ibid., p. 9.

[75]   And in 1784 Thomas Robertson was to write: 'We are to look upon the human body, consisting of bones and nerves, as a kind of musical instrument mounted with strings. Musical Sound, playing upon it, may sometimes prove more powerful than any medicines that are known. These are explications, at least, which we can listen to; and the marvellous disappears' (Thomas Robertson, *An Inquiry into the Fine Arts* (London, 1784), vol. I, p. 34).

mind in the same way as sounds sway and agitate the air, which impresses itself in our body through the organ of hearing. To this simple scheme Webb adds a further element, the nerves. Passions and sound do not act in a general way on the human 'mind' – rather, they stimulate it to activate the specific parts of the body:[76]

> We are then to take it for granted, that the mind, under particular affections, excites certain vibrations in the nerves, and impresses certain movements on the animal spirits. I shall suppose, that it is in the nature of music to excite similar vibrations, to communicate similar movements to the nerves and spirits. For, if music owes its being to motion, and, if passion cannot well be conceived to exist without it, we have a right to conclude, that the agreement of music with the passion can have no other origin than a coincidence of movements.

As the passions initiate a process whereby the mind communicates an impulse, a movement, to the nerves and the spirits, so also music succeeds in exerting on the body an effect similar to that of the mind. Note that in Webb's analogy it is not music and passions that are 'on a par', since it is not the passions that directly move the nerves, but music and mind. At this point Webb defines four classifications of movement that refer to a similar number of emotional spheres; for he is at pains to specify how mere movement is not sufficient to identify a determinate passion, but how it refers to genuine 'areas' containing several passions of similar type. For example, an impetuous musical movement consisting of rapid transitions will correspond to those passions that lead to a violent agitation of the nerves – anger, courage or indignation. Other movements refer to the emotional areas of love and benevolence, pride and glory, pain and melancholy.

The only musical examples adduced by Webb in this connection come from the instrumental repertoire (Jommelli and Geminiani): just when the link between passions and music is explained by a principle of mechanical sympathy, the gap between instrumental and vocal music narrows.[77] For both of them, as regards sound, make use of the same means: vibration. Verbal meaning, then, no longer becomes the sole device to connote a piece, since one of the faculties of inarticulate sound is to awaken determinate classes of emotions. Nonetheless, the eventual

---

[76]   Daniel Webb, *Observations on the Correspondence between Poetry and Music* (London, 1969), anastatic reprint in *Ästhetische Schriften*, ed. I. Kerkhoff (Munich, 1974) p. 6 et seq.

[77]   No reference is given to specific works by either Jommelli or Geminiani, the author just indicates two genres cultivated by the two composers in hearing which 'we are, in turn, transported, exalted, delighted': the overture and the concerto. The variety which these genres entail falls well within Webb's discussion of the types of agogic movement (sudden transitions, placid succession of lengthened notes, climax in sounds) which generate the different classes of passions.

addition of a text to the music may enable further specification of the kind of feeling evoked, so that we move from a class of emotions to a specific passion:[78]

> Let eloquence co-operate with music, and specify the motive of each particular impression, while we feel an agreement in the sound and motion with the sentiment, song takes the possession of the soul, and general impressions become specific indications of the manners and the passions.

In the connection between sound and word, however, Webb, unlike authors such as Harris and Kames, does not insist on the role played by meaning, by semantic content. All the remainder of the essay aims to demonstrate with examples drawn from literature – Milton above all – how the principle of movement governs also the effectiveness of the poetic text through the rhythmic function performed by the verse, which Webb defines as 'the music of language'.[79] Rhythm and metre are two fundamental constituents of music and poetry, and these parameters underpin the 'correspondence' between the arts to which the title of the essay refers. Movement, then, is promoted to the principal cause of the pleasure conveyed by music and poetry. And here again we get an unmistakable glimpse of the Aristotelian thought in the background, though adapted to the conceptions of modern physiology. In dealing with Harris we saw how the good is defined in the *Nicomachean Ethics* as an *activity* of the soul, and how activity and movement were central to Aristotle's thought, and to this we can add the passage in the *Rhetoric* where pleasure is defined: Aristotle dubs it 'a certain *movement* of the soul' (κίνησίν τινα τῆς ψυχῆς).[80] In the eighteenth century the 'movement of the soul' changes into a kinesis of the complicated organs that make up the human machine, as Webb himself often refers to it, and the nerves function as its transmitters: the means change but the principle remains the same.

We have seen how the difference between vocal and instrumental music in Webb is based on a greater or lesser degree of definiteness of the feeling aroused. In addition to which, he does not consider indeterminacy in itself to be a negative factor. Whereas in Kames we read that the imperfect expression of the passions in opera left 'the mind free for relishing music of any sort',[81] Webb appears to adduce new arguments. For he underlines how, in dealing with the passions, one cannot go beyond a definite degree of precision; in particular, it is not possible '[to] fix an unalienable sign on each particular feeling'.[82] This, far from being a defect of the species, is its good fortune. For, if man possessed a complete knowledge of the passions and the operations of the mind:[83]

---

[78] D. Webb, *Observations*, p. 11 et seq.

[79] Ibid., p. 14.

[80] Aristotle, *Rhetoric*, I, 11, 1370b.

[81] See above, p. 77.

[82] D. Webb, *Observations*, p. 35.

[83] Ibid., p. 36.

> every proposition would be reduced to a simple affirmation, the operations of the
> understanding would cease, and the beauties of the imagination could have no
> existence. Providence has judged better for us, and by limiting our powers has
> multiplied our enjoyments.

Indeterminacy, then, is a factor of stimulus for both intellect and imagination. Instrumental music, more indeterminate than its vocal counterpart, will hence not be penalized but, rather, as it activates our imagination it will bring us new pleasures. In Webb's system, the arts also become an epistemological tool, counterposed to philosophical argument, as well as – especially in the case of music – a means of promoting morality. Webb claims that he can dispense with philosophy, because what interests him are the 'signs' of the passions and it is the arts themselves that bring these signs to our attention in the most evident way. Music is viewed as a guide in everything that regards the identification of the passions on the basis of internal movements; painting will be best able to indicate the external signs of the passions; and poetry – as in Harris, the most complete of the arts – will lead us to discover both, since 'her imitations embrace at once the movement and the effect'.[84]

The special connection between music and morality derives, instead, from the kind of passions music may excite: at which point we come face to face with the classical idea by which music has the power to regulate the passions. But here, too, there is some divergence from the ancient tradition. While Greek thought on music's power over the passions could also generate unruly reactions and hence its use was scrupulously regulated, in the eighteenth century it is frequently asserted that music deals solely with the passions which are somehow the vehicle of pleasure and promote the social virtues. Kames, in the *Elements of Criticism*, argues that music 'must be pleasant, or it is not music',[85] and Webb maintains that it cannot arouse excessively painful passions, for the 'measure' itself is its hallmark. Hence:[86]

> the movements of music being in a continued opposition to all those impression
> which tend either to disorder or disgrace our nature, may we not reasonably
> presume, that they were destined to act in aid of the moral sense, to regulate
> the measures and proportions of our affections; and, by counter-acting the
> passions in their extremes, to render them the instruments of virtue, and the
> embellishments of character?

Webb's reflection is thus focused entirely on the pathetic function of rhythm, metre and movement, and provides an alternative explanation of the effects of music to the associative one. The new medical science, the studies on the nerves

---

[84]   Ibid., p. 39.

[85]   Lord Kames, *Collected Works*, vol. I, p. 139.

[86]   D. Webb, *Observations*, p. 37.

and on the phenomenon of vibration added further elements to explain the mechanism of the human body, and these were also of use in studying the Fine Arts. Faced with the challenge of going beyond the Cartesian mind-body dualism, British writers of the eighteenth century would often assert the need to study man in his entirety and thence to derive basic principles that would jointly account for the working of body and mind. The theory of vibration as activating man's mind and nerves, and thus giving rise to the passions, succeeded partly in recomposing this unity – and music, too, as we have seen, was co-opted into the enterprise.

Musical expression

The theories examined up to now have always found the application of the imitative principle to music highly problematic. The difficulty that emerges, in particular, is to imagine what music may be a 'copy' of. To be sure, all the authors agree in acknowledging that imitation of the sounds of the natural world does not suffice to explain the pleasure that comes from listening to music; indeed, close musical imitation may be seen as a form of pedantry.[87] The works reviewed in the previous chapter highlight how music enjoys a particular relation with the emotive sphere, and deny that this relation can be of an imitative nature since it is difficult to give reasons why sound should be able to 'imitate' a passion. Thus we encountered theories aiming to demonstrate 'how' music can *produce* emotions instead of confining itself to copying them or *re*producing them. This emphasis on a poetical capacity of sound with regard to the emotions gives rise to another important principle in the British debate in the eighteenth century: expression. The leading contribution to the elaboration of the concept of 'musical expression' was made by Charles Avison who, in 1751, published an important and much read work titled *An Essay on Musical Expression*. Here I will make only brief references to this work, since it will be more amply discussed in the next chapter, where I shall also show how much it owes to the writings that preceded it, especially the essay by Harris.[88] But it will be important to understand from the outset what Avison means by 'expression' and what his definition implies. He defines expression as a combination of the two components of music – that is, melody and harmony – and as 'no other than a strong and proper application of them to the intended subjects'.[89] Unlike imitation, which according to Avison stimulates the intellect because it

---

[87]   This subject is dealt with in the eighth of the *Thirty Letters on Various Subjects*, published by William Jackson in 1783, where the author complains of the fact that 'the most common mistake of composers is to express words and not ideas' (W. Jackson, *On musical Expression*, in *Thirty Letters on Various Subjects* (London, 1783), p. 49).

[88]   See below, pp. 121-129.

[89]   Charles Avison, *An Essay on Musical Expression* (London, 1752), anastatic reprint of the edition of 1753 (New York, 2004), p. 57.

suggests a comparison between objects, expression must arouse emotions of the soul.[90]

Avison's definition of expression seems to have a very important consequence: the principle of expression, that assumes a correct use of harmony and melody, far from finding its centre in music itself depends, rather, on the 'intended subject'. If to the previous definition we add an indication Avison gives to composers intent on producing 'true musical expression', we will have a clearer idea of where this argument leads. For Avison advises composers 'to blend such an happy mixture of air and harmony, as will affect us most strongly with the passions or affections which the poet intends to raise'.[91] And here is the point: Avison develops and emphasizes a particular aspect of Harris's theory which recognized music as the best ally of poetry – a formula Avison often cites. As we shall shortly see, in the next writing to be dealt with, James Beattie's *Essay on Poetry and Music, as they affect the Mind* (1762), in the discussion on music the adoption of the expressive in place of the sympathetic principle implies a closer link between sound and word, leading to a theoretical predomination of vocal music over instrumental.[92] This is not a matter for arguing over individual 'preferences'. We know that Avison composed mainly instrumental music and there is no reason to suppose that he did not hold it in great esteem. As a rule, however, while the theories based on the sympathetic effect of sound on man tend to deal with sound *tout court*; and are therefore based on a principle valid for every sort of music, a theory founded on the principle of expression sends us back, as in the case of imitation, to the age-old question of 'what' is expressed by music. Avison replies that music expresses the feeling that the poet wishes to arouse, and the expressive principle is evidently better suited to explaining the effects of vocal than of instrumental music.

As we said, the dynamic just described can be well represented by Beattie's *Essay* devoted to poetry and music, where the author wavers between one position and another according to the principle to which he appeals. For, when he refers to the theory of associations between sounds and emotions and to the effect of

---

[90]   A similar theory of music, clearly influenced by Avison and Harris, was worked out by John Gregory in *A Comparative View of the State and Faculties of Man with those of the Animal World* (London, 1765). This writing is examined in Maria Semi, 'Musica e perfezionamento dell'uomo: John Gregory e l'Inghilterra del Settecento', *Intersezioni. Rivista di Storia delle Idee*, 28/2 (2008), pp. 209-234; see also Penelope Gouk, 'Music's Pathological and Therapeutic Effects on the Body Politic: Doctor John Gregory's Views', in P. Gouk and H. Hills (eds), *Representing Emotions: New Connections in the Histories of Art, Music and Medicine* (Aldershot, 2005), pp. 191-207.

[91]   Charles Avison, *An Essay ...*, p. 69.

[92]   On Beattie's general aesthetic theory, see Karen Kloth, *James Beatties ästhetische Theorien. Ihre Zusammenhänge mit der Aberdeener Schulphilosophie* (Munich, 1974); on his ethics of music and its relation to musical life in eighteenth-century Aberdeen, see Catherine Jones, 'James Beattie and the Ethics of Music', *British Journal for Eighteenth-Century Studies*, 30 (2007), pp. 55-71.

vibrations on the human body, he places instrumental and vocal music on the same plane, whereas when he argues for the importance of expression, voice and word become the paradigm.

From the start of the essay, Beattie states that he does not consider music to be an imitative art unless to a very small extent, but he adds that this does not demote music from its position among the Fine Arts. It has great influence on the human mind and, he says,[93]

> I grant, that, by its power of raising a variety of agreeable emotions in the hearer,
> it proves its relations to poetry, and that it never appears to the best advantage
> but with poetry for its interpreter.

Here, then, is the basic position he maintains up to the end of the essay – namely, that the poetic text must interpret the emotions expressed by the music, otherwise the music will risk never becoming a 'rational entertainment'.[94] Music, in Beattie, is compared with the sort of pictorial art whose subject can only be understood through the bubbles coming out of the characters' mouths. For this reason he will not define it as an 'imitative art': if we were not told explicitly that there is an imitation to be noted or if there were no text, we could not understand what the music is imitating.

The second consideration by which Beattie excludes music from the category of imitative arts is that imitation plays no part in the pleasure conveyed by music. In painting, if we fail to understand what is represented in a picture and if, therefore, the imitation is imperfect, we can derive no pleasure from it; whereas in music it is otherwise: 'an air may be pastoral, and in the highest degree pleasing, which imitates neither sound nor motion, nor anything else'.[95]

At which point, Beattie addresses the problem that recurs incessantly in the writings we have examined: what kind of analogy or resemblance can there be between musical sounds and emotions. Here, rather from habit, he adopts the associative explanation. For example, it leads us to associate certain instruments with certain contexts: the organ with a church, and hence with solemnity and congregation, the drum with warfare, and hence with bravery, and so on. At the same time Beattie argues that sound vibrations probably have a mechanical effect on the human body – suffice it to think how in church the echoes of certain notes of the organ lead us to perceive the vibration of some parts of the building itself. And, in this context of association and sympathy, Beattie focuses on instrumental music and asserts 'be that however as it will, it admits of no doubt, that the mind may be agreeably affected by mere sound, in which there is neither meaning nor

---

[93]   James Beattie, *An Essay on Poetry and Music, as they affect the Mind* (Edinburgh, 1776), in *The Philosophical and Critical Works of James Beattie*, ed. B. Fabian (Hildesheim and New York, 1975), vol. I ('Essays'), p. 441.

[94]   Ibid., p. 469.

[95]   Ibid., p. 452.

modulation'.[96] Note, moreover, that he speaks not merely of 'arousal of the sense', but refers to the stimulation of the mind by the sound of the music alone, with no other support. With instrumental music, he adds, composer and player must pay attention to the sweetness, fullness and variety of the sound; by these means they can convey the idea of greatness and vastness and thus 'they excite a pleasing admiration, and seem to accord with the lofty genius of that soul whose chief desire is for truth, virtue, and immortality, and the object of whose most delightful meditation is the greatest and best of Beings'.[97]

Up to this point instrumental music, too, appears to be fully endowed with those powers unanimously accorded to music in general. But in a few sentences the atmosphere changes. What happens? In the non-linear development of the argument on the causes of music's effect on man, Beattie introduces the principle of expression:[98]

> but pathos, or *expression, is the chief excellence of music.* Without this, it may amuse the ear, it may give a little exercise to the mind of the hearer, it may for a moment withdraw the attention from the anxieties of life, it may show the performer's dexterity, the skill of the composer, or the merit of the instruments; and in all or any of this ways, it may afford a slight pleasure: but, without engaging the affections, it can never yield that permanent, useful, and heart-felt gratification, which legislators, civil, military, and ecclesiastical, have expected from it. [...] Music would not have recommended itself so effectually to general esteem, if it had always been *merely instrumental.* For, if I mistake not, the expression of music without poetry is vague and ambiguous.

Thus, a little at a time, Beattie goes one by one through the positive aspects previously listed of instrumental music, always using the formulas 'it is indeed true that' and 'it cannot be denied', but his conclusion is inexorable and leads him to assert that it is only thanks to the connection with words that music can transform a simple affection of the mind into a genuine emotion. Instrumental music is relegated within a narrow margin of feeling, similar to that of an audience hearing an oration, fervent as it may be but declaimed in a foreign language whose accents are audible but whose content remains obscure. In this way, the appearance of the principle of expression – which he takes from Avison – leads Beattie away from his previous assertions. Almost nothing remains of the musical sound that succeeds in shaking the massive walls of churches and causing them to vibrate, and the instrumental sound becomes alien, external and remote.

In the 1760s and '70s another important philosopher links music with expression: Thomas Reid, member of the Aberdeen Philosophical Society – along with Beattie, Gregory and Gerard, among the authors cited by us – and later

---

[96]   Ibid., p. 457.
[97]   Ibid.
[98]   Ibid., pp. 461 et seq. (my italics).

successor to Adam Smith in the prestigious chair of Moral Philosophy at Glasgow.[99] Reid's perspective differs from the others we have mentioned also because his model of the relation between mind and perception does not correspond to the one encountered hitherto: against Hume's theory – which envisages a gap between objects and perceptions, since the mind can detect only the latter – Reid posits the distinction between *sensation* and *perception*. While sensation has itself as object and lives in the mind alone, perception always has an object and this object is a *quality* of what is perceived. Common speech employs the same term and does not facilitate the distinction, but Reid discriminates, for example, between the scent of a rose as a sensation of the mind and the scent as a perceived quality *belonging* to the rose. According to Reid, sensation is to perception as the sign is to the signifier. Sensations are therefore of fundamental importance because they are the *sign* of something other, of which we can perceive a quality.

In the *Inquiry into the Human Mind* (1764) Reid focuses on the nature of the sensations conveyed by the five external senses, hearing among them. He is especially interested in the use of sound as vehicle of language. In this connection he distinguishes between a language consisting of artificial signs and a second one consisting of natural signs. The languages of individual peoples are the fruit of a human invention, founded on a mutual agreement of convenience, and are therefore artificial signs of thought. But in order for such artificial signs to be created, there had to be a pre-existing natural language that would make communication possible: 'The elements of this natural language of mankind, or the signs that are naturally expressive of our thoughts, may, I think, be reduced to these three kinds: modulations of the voice, gestures and features'.[100] Song is thus one of the original languages of mankind and was a vehicle of *expression*. Reid adds that to these very signs may be attributed the force and energy of language: the inflections of the voice, the accents, rather than the words in themselves, are what make a discourse effective. But what remains of these natural signs in our modern epoch? According to Reid they are bit by bit supplanted by the artificial signs, so that:[101]

---

[99]   On the topic of music's perception in Reid's writings, see Leslie Ellen Brown, 'Thomas Reid and the Perception of Music: Sense vs. Reason', *International Review of the Aesthetics and Sociology of Music*, 20/2 (1989), pp. 121-140. Her article provides a useful reading, although I do not agree with her statement that Reid's comments concerning the perception of music 'appeared at a time when most writings on music in Britain dealt almost exclusively with the aesthetic sense point of view and either ignored or downplayed the rationalist approach. Reid's discussions on music function as components of broader analyses on the activities or processes of the human mind.' As I hope my book demonstrates, Reid's discussion of music in this respect follows a well-established British tradition.

[100]   Thomas Reid, *An Inquiry into the Human Mind on the Principles of Common Sense*, ed. Derek R. Brookes (Edinburgh, 1997), II, pp. 51-52.

[101]   Ibid., p. 33.

> It were easy to show, that the fine art of the musician, the painter, the actor, and the orator, so far as they are expressive – although the knowledge of them require in us a delicate taste, a nice judgment, and much study and practice – yet they are nothing else but the language of nature, which we brought into the world with us, but have unlearned by disuse, and so find the greatest difficulty in recovering it.

Music, in Reid, is expressive inasmuch as it is a natural sign, for artificial signs 'mean but do not express'. What 'thing', then, does music express? The answer can be sought in two writings not published in Reid's lifetime: the *Lectures on the Fine Arts*, not printed until 1973 when Peter Kivy transcribed them from an original manuscript,[102] and from some papers published in 2005 in volume V of the works of Reid (Mss. 2131/8/I/16). In the *Lectures* (written in 1774) Reid asserts roundly that music is a material representation of the emotions of the mind,[103] and that this representation acts in an immediate way and is not a result of experience. One music may provoke sadness, another joy: according to Reid our recognition of musical expression is founded in the constitution of human nature, which provides for the production within us of determinate feelings by determinate sounds. In the above-cited manuscripts Reid states that the very fact that we describe sounds as sweet, hard, weak[104]

> shows that they are expressive of something beyond themselves, which is agreeable or disagreeable [...]. Nature has established a connexion between the disposition of the Mind and the Sound of the Voice. And Nature teaches each Men to discern the one in some degree by perceiving the other. Now everything which is signified or expressed by sound may be expressed by Music. This expression is the capital thing in all compositions of Music, and this evidently depends upon this connections between Sounds and thought, between things sensible and things intellectual.

While, then, in Avison expression was the aim of music, or in Beattie its means, with Reid it becomes the very essence. Music is expression inasmuch as it is a natural and sensible sign of states of mind.[105] But at this point we cannot fail to see how misleading the use of categories like 'expression' may be; for the authors dealt with above evidently did not employ the term in the same meaning, and that in Reid the expression is much more akin to sympathetic association than

---

[102]   The manuscript consists of lectures notes and it is not in Reid's hand; see J. Charles Robertson, review of *Thomas Reid's Lectures on the Fine Arts*, *Canadian Philosophical Review*, 14 (1975), pp. 710-714.

[103]   See Peter Kivy, *Thomas Reid's Lectures on the Fine Arts* (The Hague, 1973), p. 30.

[104]   Thomas Reid, *On Logic, Rhetoric and the Fine Arts*, ed. Alexander Brodie (Edinburgh, 2005), pp. 287-88.

[105]   Leslie Ellen Brown, 'Thomas Reid and the Perception of Music: Sense vs. Reason'.

to the meaningful support for sound performed by the word, as asserted by Avison and Beattie.

Mimesis and imitation in music: Aristotle and the Moderns in the comparison of Thomas Twining

The problem of terminology posed above becomes of great importance in a work of 1789 by Thomas Twining,[106] which appeared in the context of a new English translation of Aristotle's *Poetics*. Aristotle's text was amply commented by Twining, who also provided the edition with two essays devoted to the concept of 'imitation' in its application to poetry and music.[107] The title of Twining's dissertation – *On the different Senses of the Word, Imitative, as applied to the Music by the Antients, and by the Moderns* – already marks a departure from the previous contributors: instead of asking himself whether music is an imitative art, he speculates on the actual meaning ascribed to the term 'imitation' in relation to music.

From the outset, Twining evinces the need to instil system into the discussion of music and, in the first twenty lines, succeeds in giving a consistent organization to all the aspects we have sought to describe up to now. He begins by distinguishing three different 'objects' on which music exerts its particular effects: the ear, the passions and the imagination. The effect on the ear is immediately set aside since it has nothing to do with imitation, refers to nothing and imparts a 'simple and original' pleasure, like that aroused by the scent of a rose. In the other two cases – passion and imagination – the effect is not on the sense but on the human mind. Music, says Twining, may awaken ideas in two ways: through an association of immediate type (acting by means of sound and movement), or through an association that works through the medium of the emotions. Here Twining quotes the essay by Harris, to which he makes frequent reference, and the conception developed therein[108] – namely, that ideas and emotions are connected in the mind by means of association. Twining loses no time in stating that all the effects just cited will not be the subject of his essay, since they have no relation with the principle, imitation, he seeks to clarify. Immediately excluded from the discussion, then, are physical stimulation and association, the two principles by which, as a rule, vocal and instrumental music are ensured an equal consideration.

The author recalls how the previous literature on the subject has unanimously stated that musical imitation acting through the sole medium of *sound* – for

---

[106]   Thomas Twining conducted an important correspondence with Charles Burney – with whom we shall deal in Chapter 4 – and was of great assistance to the latter in compiling his *General History of Music*.

[107]   On these essays, see James Malek, 'Thomas Twining's Analysis of Poetry and Music as Imitative Arts', *Modern Philology*, 68/3 (1971), pp. 260-268.

[108]   See above, pp. 62-71.

instance, the imitation of birdsong – lends very little prestige to the art; and how all the authors (Hutcheson, Harris, Beattie, Kames and Avison are the most quoted) have sited music's greatest worth in the fact of its arousal of emotions: 'but this is so far from being regarded by them as imitation, that it is expressly opposed to it. The ideas, and the language, of the antients, on this subject, were different'.[109] Twining's underlying thesis, based on analysis of the texts of Aristotle and the Moderns, is that the latter give the name 'expression' to what the former called *mimesis*: this quarrelling over the counterposition of expression and imitation is thus, in his view, merely the result of a wholesale misunderstanding and of a problem wrongly posed. Twining proceeds to a conscientious review of the passages in Aristotle that may help us to comprehend what must be meant by *mimesis* with reference to music, and it will be of use to follow him in his review.

He deals with three texts of Aristotle: *Poetics*, *Politics* and *Problems* (in particular nos. 27 and 29 of section XIX, devoted to harmony). Twining evidences how in dealing with music Aristotle uses the terms μίμησις (imitation) and ὁμοίωμα (resemblance) and also specifies what he means is imitated or resembled by music: it resembles customs, dispositions (τοις ἤθεσι) and, precisely, the irascible or mild state of mind, redolent of strength (ἀνδρεία) and temperance (σωφροσύνη). Aristotle adds that the devices by which music achieves resemblance are rhythm and melody. Twining compares these passages of Aristotle, in which music is considered according to its function of arousing emotions, with the passages in Harris and Beattie where they deal with the same subject, and he notes how the last two use the term 'expression' in the same circumstances in which Aristotle uses 'imitation' or 'resemblance'. Whence Twining continues with some remarks on the differences between vocal and instrumental music. At first glance his discussion appears to be the standard one:[110]

> The expressions of music considered in itself, and without words, are, (within certain limits,) vague, general, and equivocal. [...] The effect of words, is, to strengthen the expression of music, by confining it – by giving it a precise direction, supplying it with ideas, circumstances and an object [...].

We might almost be reading Beattie. Moreover, Twining adds that ancient music was seldom heard without a text and therefore it may be supposed that for the listeners it retained a 'vocal style' even when played by instruments alone, perhaps in virtue of the analogy between musical rhythm and the rhythm of language. But, he warns, it is useless to seek to interpret the literature of the Ancients on music by

---

109   Thomas Twining, 'On the different Senses of the Word, Imitative, as applied to the Music by the Antients, and by the Moderns', in *Aristotle's Treatise on Poetry, translated: with notes on the translation, and the original; and two dissertations, on poetical, and musical, imitation* (London, 1789), pp. 44-61: 46.

110   Ibid., p. 48.

reading their texts and thinking of our own music. The instrumental music of the Moderns seems to have no kinship with that of the Ancients.

On the basis of the passage cited above, Twining would appear to side with the multitude of authors who assert the supremacy of vocal over instrumental music, owing to vocal music's greater 'precision' in expressing emotions or determinate ideas. But, as we shall soon see, Twining maintains a balanced position, which approaches rather the positions of Kames and Webb, who accord a positive value even to the indeterminacy of instrumental music. Here, Twining achieves a wonderful synthesis of ancient and modern and, starting from some remarks on the two Aristotelian *Problems* of section XIX, arrives at an encomium of instrumental music based on a faculty of particular importance for the eighteenth century: imagination.

The two *Problems* to which Twining refers are numbers 27 and 29, whose texts are very similar:[111]

27. Why is what is heard the only object of perception which possesses moral character? For every tune, even if it has no words, has nevertheless character; but neither colour, smell or flavour have it. Is it because sound alone has movement, though not of course the movement which it produces in us? For movement of this kind exists in other senses too, since colour moves our sight; but we are conscious of the movement which follows such and such a sound. This movement has a resemblance [ἔχει ὁμοιότητα] of moral character both by the time and by the arrangement of the higher and lower sounds, but not in their mixture. Consonance has no moral character. This character does not exist in the other perceptible. But the movements with which we are dealing are connected with action, and actions are symptoms [σημασία ἐστίν] of moral character.

29. Why do rhythm and tune, which are only an emission of the voice, resemble moral character, while flavours, colours and scents do not? Is it because, like actions, they are movements? Now, action is a moral fact and implies a moral character, but flavours and colours do not act in the same way.

As we read, and as Twining himself emphasizes, the text evidentiates how the resemblance between melody and mental disposition is not connected with the use of the word – a position Aristotle also maintains in Book VIII of the *Politics*,[112] where he also specifies wherein the difference consists between auditory sensations and others: 'the other objects of sensation contain no representation of

---

[111] Aristotle, *Problems*, ed. W. S. Hett (London and Cambridge, MA, 1961), pp. 395, 397 (I have inserted the Greek terms or locutions in brackets in the most important passages).

[112] See Aristotle, *Politics*, VIII, 1340a: 'everybody when listening to imitations is thrown into a corresponding state of feeling, even apart from the rhythms and tunes themselves', ed. H. Rackham (London and Cambridge, MA, 1959), p. 657.

character, for example the objects of touch and taste (though the objects of sight do so slightly) [...]. Also visual works of art are not representations (ὁμοίωματα) of character, but rather the forms and colours produced are mere indications (σημεῖα) of character [...].'[113] Twining wonders what Aristotle could have meant by the term 'sign', and interprets the passage from the *Politics* in the light of *Problem* 27. In short, while disclaiming anything more than an attempt at exegesis of some rather obscure passages, he tries to interpret Aristotle according to the theories of his (Twining's) own time. He imagines that Aristotle, like the writers we have dealt with above and whom Twining has in mind, could not have meant that there could be any real and direct resemblance between music and the emotions. This resemblance is only possible in mediated form, and the mediation comes from the concepts of movement and action. In substance, music would be in relation to movement as action to *ethos*. But in this case which movement and which action? Twining quotes the Ancient Aristoxenus and the Moderns Hutcheson and Rousseau (in particular the *Dictionnaire de Musique* of 1767) in support of his hypothesis: namely, that the analogy is to be understood as between the melody and rhythm of music and word. Hence the word, in the case of vocal music, or the analogy with its rhythmic and melodic impact, in the case of instrumental music, would be the cause of music's power to arouse emotions. Already at this point the relation between vocal and instrumental music no longer appears so unequal. But there is a further reflection in a long footnote where the author adds another reason for consideration of instrumental music:[114]

> in the best instrumental music, expressively performed, the very indecision itself of the expression, leaving the hearer to the free operation of this emotion upon his fancy, and, as it were, to the free choice of such ideas as are, to him, most adapted to react upon and heighten the emotion which occasioned them, produces a pleasure, which nobody, I believe, who is able to feel it, will deny to be one of the most delicious that music is capable of affording. But far the greater part even of those who have an ear for music, have only an ear; and to them this pleasure is unknown. The complaint, so common, of the separation of poetry and music, was never, I believe, the complaint of a man of true musical feeling [...].

Twining here provides evidence for more than one new and important aspect. First and foremost, to have an 'ear' for music is not sufficient in all cases; appreciation of instrumental music requires a 'true musical feeling'. Here it is the feeling that makes the difference. And not only. The essential element in favour of instrumental music in Twining is that its indeterminacy enables a greater freedom of thought in the listener: the latter, while hearing music without text, is

---

[113]   Ibid., pp. 657-659.

[114]   Thomas Twining, *Aristotle's Treatise on Poetry*, p. 49.

more active, and the faculty adduced is the *imagination*.[115] Twining finds a dual motive for the pleasure conveyed by instrumental music. On the one hand, sound without word activates the imagination, which is pleasant in itself (suffice it to recall Addison's *Pleasures of the Imagination*); on the other hand, imagination is a faculty that allows man individuality of feeling, and thus each may act in the sphere of liberty that instrumental music permits, 'freely' electing to focus on those ideas that are best fitted to excite and enhance personal emotion.

The beauty of the 'system': the new musical listening of Adam Smith

The imagination, as we shall shortly see, plays an essential role also in Adam Smith's reflections on the arts and on music. This section will deal in particular with his well-known essay *Of the Nature of that Imitation which takes place in what are called the Imitative Arts*, published posthumously in 1795. Its date of composition is not clear, but it must certainly have been subjected to a good deal of reworking. We know that in the early 1760s, before his journey in France (1764-66), Smith gave two lectures in Glasgow on the imitative arts,[116] and that during his stay at Kirkaldy in 1777 he was busy with 'another work concerning the imitative arts'.[117] The relation between the lectures and this work is, however, obscure; and at least a couple of passages in the essay on the imitative arts in relation to music suggest a late reworking of the text that has come down to us. The editors of the essay noted that Smith cites the division of Greek music into diastaltic, systaltic and medium, that he could have read in the first volume of Charles Burney's *General History of Music*, published in 1776. A second element, however, much more evident than the former, seems to have escaped the general attention – namely, the at times really surprising resemblance between certain passages of Smith's work and the essay by James Beattie (written in 1762 but not published till 1776), with which we dealt in the section on 'musical expression' above. Our analysis will focus on one passage in particular, which will be set against Beattie's version.

Smith ordered the executors of his will to destroy his unpublished writings, with a few exceptions, among which this essay on the arts and a youthful work, *The Principles which lead and direct Philosophical Enquiries; illustrated by the History of Astronomy*. And, as we shall soon have occasion to see, reference to

---

[115]   In this case Twining employs the term 'fancy', but imagination and fancy are synonymous in many authors of the period.

[116]   For all references to the problem of the draft of the work see the introduction by W. P. D. Wightman to *Of the Nature of that Imitation which takes place in what are called the Imitative Arts*, in Adam Smith, *Essays on Philosophical Subjects*, ed. W. P. D. Wightman and J. C. Bryce (Indianapolis, 1982; reprint of the Oxford University Press edition of 1980), pp. 171-175: 172-3.

[117]   Ibid., p. 171.

this latter will help us to understand certain passages in the work on music and, in particular, Smith's discussion of instrumental music.[118]

Of the Nature of that Imitation which takes place in what are called the Imitative Arts is divided into three parts. In the first, Smith sets out his own interpretation of the concept of 'imitation' – in particular, with examples drawn from painting and sculpture; the second is almost entirely involved with music, and the very brief third part deals specifically with dance. But what is 'imitation' for Adam Smith? He distinguishes two types: the first is the 'copy'. This, especially in the arts, does not confer beauty, it is actually a matter for blame. The second type of imitation that lends value to the arts rests on the *disparity* between the object imitated and the product of the imitation:[119]

> Though a production of art seldom derives any merit from its resemblance to another object of the same kind, it frequently derives a great deal from its resemblance to an object of a different kind.

Sculpture, for instance, closely resembles what it imitates, since it involves a solid that imitates another solid; whereas painting manages in two dimensions to represent three. The greater identity between the object imitated and the imitator causes the merit of the sculpture to be closely linked with the virtue of the object used as model, while in the case of painting even objects of scant interest in nature may bring pleasure to the senses. For, in this case, what excites the interest of the gazer is not the object in itself; rather, his attention and his pleasure are stimulated by wonder:[120]

> that pleasure is founded altogether upon our *wonder* at seeing an object of one kind represent so well an object of a very different kind, and upon our *admiration* of the art which surmounts so happily that disparity which nature had established between them.

Unlike the works of Nature which conceal her process, the products of art add to the pleasing wonder that stems from ignorance the even greater pleasure that derives from knowledge. Works of art, says Smith, seem to incorporate their own explanation. For we can explain 'how' they achieve a determinate effect, the

---

[118]   Among the scholars who have studied Adam Smith's theory of music see, in particular: Nikolaus De Palézieux, *Die Lehre vom Ausdruck*; Wilhelm Seidel, 'La musica va annoverata tra le arti mimetiche?', and, by the same author, 'Der *Essay* von Adam Smith über die Musik [Einführung und Text]', *Musiktheorie*, 15 (2000), pp. 195-204. See also the 'Postface' by M. Noiray in A. Smith, *Essais esthétiques. L'imitation dans les arts et autres textes* (Paris, 1997).

[119]   A. Smith, *Essays* ..., p. 178.

[120]   Ibid., p. 185 (my italics).

process of their creation and the means employed can be known to a far greater extent than is possible with the works of Nature.

Before examining what Smith has to say on music, it will be useful to focus on some suggestions that arise from this general theory of imitation based on the separation between the object that imitates and the object to which it refers. In the passage just cited, note the use of the terms 'wonder' and 'admiration' to explain the pleasure we derive from imitation; and Smith does not employ them in a general sense. Their importance and significance become clear from *The Principles which lead and direct Philosophical Enquiries; illustrated by the History of Astronomy*, mentioned above. In that work, before embarking on the history of astronomy, from Eudoxus to Newton, Smith summarizes, in line with the title, the principles that underpin philosophical study. The first of these harks back to a Platonic and Aristotelian context: *wonder*. Set alongside this we find surprise *and* admiration. Wonder is felt in the face of that which is uncommon, surprise before things we do not expect, while we admire beauty and greatness. When we experience these conjoint feelings in respect of one and the same object, their effect on the mind is enhanced. The section in which 'wonder' is defined opens with words that strike us by their familiarity: 'it is evident that the mind takes pleasure in observing the resemblances that are discoverable betwixt different objects'.[121] We see, then, how the importance assumed by the 'separation' in the case of imitation is but the reverse side of what, in general, underlies wonder: to say that the resemblance between two objects of different nature conveys pleasure, and to say that imitation conveys pleasure in relation to the diversity between the imitating object and what it imitates, is to say much the same thing.

Smith describes the process that wonder generates in our mind as follows. The mind tends to refer the individual objects it perceives to determinate classes, and when it is presented with a new object, the memory is unable to connect it with anything known and thus, along with the imagination, begins to be activated. Wonder corresponds to that movement. But the essay also contains a second description of wonder that directs us even more clearly to the source of these reflections. Smith explains how objects, albeit dissimilar, that normally follow one upon another are perceived by the imagination as connected, since 'the idea of the one seems, of its own accord, to call up and introduce that of the other'.[122] Thus the principle of association of ideas enables the imagination to anticipate the sequence of events according to their habitual presentation, without effort or impediment. The object that excites wonder interrupts this chain and 'surprises' the imagination, whose predictions turn out to be wrong. In this way, it signals the necessity to overcome the hiatus that has occurred in the process, and it tries to create a connecting bridge by which the problematic object will be inserted within a new sequence. Once this process is completed, the wonder vanishes: 'who wonders at the machinery of the opera-house who has once been admitted

---

[121]   Ibid., p. 37.
[122]   Ibid., p. 40.

behind the scenes? In the wonders of Nature, however, it rarely happens that we can discover so clearly this connecting chain'.[123] Here we have the same thesis – previously examined – that Smith would maintain when he speaks of the beauty of artistic imitation that 'bears within itself its own explanation', as in the case of theatrical machinery, counterposing it to the objects of nature which conceal it. This want of explanation that man finds in Nature gives birth to philosophy, whose aim is to represent the invisible chains that connect the principles of nature and, therefore, curb the movement of the imagination when faced with what amazes it. For Smith views philosophy as an art that addresses the imagination.[124] We may legitimately suppose that these reflections were somehow suggested to Smith from his reading of the *Treatise* of Hume and, in particular, from the analysis of the idea of cause (I, iii). For Hume did indeed speculate on the nature of what we call the cause–effect relation, reducing it to those chains of events we are accustomed to experience in succession and that lead the imagination to pass from one event to another:[125]

> when the mind [...] passes from the idea or impression of one object to the idea or belief of another, it is not determin'd by reason, but by certain principles, which associate together the ideas of these objects, and unite them in the imagination.

As in the process described by Smith, in examining his treatment of the principle of imitation in relation to the arts, we, too, experience 'wonder'. For, accustomed as we are to the *standard* reflections on the importance of resemblance in imitation, our imagination has found an obstacle in the way of the concept of 'difference'. It has therefore tried to remove the obstacle and re-establish a chain of reflections along which to travel without difficulty. This new chain starts from Hume's thoughts on the concept of cause, where he shows how the mind continually sets up relations between separate objects and how these relations are conducted by the imagination. Smith takes up this formulation and develops it, with particular attention to how the imagination responds when faced with what appears to cast doubt on the relations it has hypothesized and which surprise it. Philosophical knowledge is interpreted in the work on the history of astronomy in the light of this dynamic: its theories respond to the needs of imagination disturbed in its normal course.[126] In the case of the imitative arts, conversely, wonder does

---

[123]   Ibid., p. 42.

[124]   Ibid., p. 46.

[125]   D. Hume, *A Treatise*, I, p. 393 (I, iii, § 6).

[126]   With regard to the connection between surprise, admiration and philosophical knowledge, recall Hume's assertion that 'any thing propos'd to us, which causes surprize and admiration, gives such a satisfaction to the mind, that it indulges itself in those agreeable emotions, and will never be persuaded that its pleasure is entirely without foundation. From these dispositions in philosophers and their disciples arises that mutual complaisance betwixt them [...]' (ibid., p. 334 (I, ii, § 1)).

not need to be 'extinguished' by a philosophical theory. The peculiarity of artistic objects, as we saw, is that they carry their own explanation within themselves. Once the making of a work is revealed, once its coming into being is understood, the wonder ceases.

Let us now look at musical imitation, to which Smith devotes the second part of his work on the arts. Unlike painting and sculpture, which are discussed without any inner distinction, music is divided into three genres: vocal music, instrumental music connected with opera (for example, overtures) and instrumental music by itself.

Vocal music can be said to be 'imitative' in at least three cases: the music 'imitates' the discourse in songs; it imitates the passions through tone and movement; there is, lastly, the gesture with which the singer accompanies himself. Here Smith is clearly not concerned with identifying an imitation of the 'sound' in itself but, rather, of specific musical contexts. Hence, in the case of songs, thanks to the text there are 'rhythmus and melody, shaped and fashioned into the form either of a good moral counsel, or of an amusing and interesting story';[127] then there is the song that imitates something different, say, a discourse. In this connection, Smith mentions the well-known critique directed at operatic arias: what could be more unnatural than that a person should sing to express his own distress? But the appreciation of difference allows us to acknowledge a virtue in that genre of music in its very lack of 'naturalness', since the separation between the object imitated (a discourse resulting from a painful situation) and its imitation (the song) is of the greatest. The second case of imitation regards the relation between music and passions:[128]

> The tone and movements of music, though naturally very different from those of conversation and passion, may, however, be so managed as to seem to resemble them. On account of the great disparity between the imitating and the imitated object, the mind [...] cannot only be contended, but delighted, and even charmed and transported, with such an imperfect resemblance as can be had.

Here Smith refers to the theory – already expounded by several authors before him – that musical sound could express 'classes' of passions but not specific passions, for which latter poetry would come to the rescue. To this theory, however, Smith adds a new corollary regarding the reason why vocal music is so suited to the expression of passions, and wherein they resemble one another, despite their great diversity. And the resemblance is found in the principle of repetition. The passions render the individual a prey to madness, he is obsessed by a thought, by a recurrent idea that he can never shake off. Music, arias, can represent precisely this, with their repetitions, their incessant return of one and the same motif:[129]

---

[127] A. Smith, *Essays* ..., p. 190.

[128] Ibid., p. 191.

[129] Ibid.

> Neither prose nor poetry can venture to imitate those almost endless repetitions of passion. They may describe them as I do now, but they dare not imitate them; they would become most insufferably tiresome if they did. [...] It is by means of such repetitions only, that music can exert those peculiar powers of imitation which distinguish it, and in which it excels all the Imitative Arts.

Smith therefore introduces a new element upon which to establish a comparison between music and passions. Previous authors had often relied on the concept of movement, associating the velocity of sound with joy or its slowness with melancholy; Smith does indeed repropose these arguments, but he adds this special appeal to the cyclical movement, typical of passion, that music alone can reproduce without arousing boredom. The third type of imitation, like the first, is not to be attributed to sound but, rather, to the gestures of the singer: the latter, animated by the emotion excited by the music, acts with grace and naturalness in conformity with the feeling that governs him, thus enhancing its effect on his audience.

The brief passage quoted above also shows us how the second of the imitative modes of vocal music puts it in a position of privilege as compared with the other arts. Smith corroborates this assertion by illustrating a further difference between music and painting and sculpture: painting and sculpture add nothing to nature; although, according to the rules of the ancient *canon*, they can assemble parts that occur in different individuals and reunite them in a perfect exemplar, there is no detail in them that cannot be found in nature. Music, instead, thanks to its predominance over time, succeeds in bending nature to its own ends, and in 'clothing' nature, through melody and harmony, with a unique and peculiar beauty of its own. Though Smith does not mention it here, we can see how in this example, too, musical imitation is more agreeable in virtue of its distance from the object. Painting and sculpture, in Smith's analysis, assemble already existing parts of individuals, so that the separation with respect to the individuals in their own natural guise is not very important. The predominance over time, through rhythm and metre, that occurs in music marks, instead, a notable divergence from natural sound.

The passages in the essay that are devoted to instrumental music (composed for the stage) apparently start out with a realization that vocal music is superior to instrumental, and in these passages we find the similarities with Beattie's *Essay on Poetry and Music* already noted at the beginning of this section. Smith provides evidence for how instrumental music is hardly in line with the imitative principle and, to illustrate this, he takes an example already encountered in Beattie and discussed above.[130] Beattie wrote:[131]

---

[130]   See above, pp. 84-86.

[131]   J. Beattie, *An Essay on Poetry and Music*, p. 442.

> *Music is imitative, when it readily puts one in mind of the thing imitated.* If an explication be necessary, and if, after all, we find it difficult to recognize any exact similitude, I would not call such music an imitation of nature; but *consider it as upon a footing, in point of likeness, with those pictures, wherein the action cannot be known but by a label proceeding from the mouth of the agent* […]. *But between imitation in music and imitation in painting, there is one essential difference:* a bad picture is always a bad imitation of nature, and a good picture is necessarily a good imitation; but music may be exactly imitative, and yet intolerably bad; or not at all imitative, and yet perfectly good.

In Smith, the same thought is formulated thus:[132]

> In the imitative arts, though it is by no means necessary that the imitating should so exactly resemble the imitated object, that the one should sometimes be mistaken for the other, *it is*, however, *necessary that they should resemble at least so far, that the one should always readily suggest the other*. It would be a strange picture which required an *inscription* at the foot to tell us, not only what particular person it meant to represent, but whether it meant to represent anything. *The imitations of instrumental music may, in some respects, be said to resemble such pictures. There is, however, this very essential difference between them,* that the picture would not be much mended by the inscription; whereas, by what may be considered as very little more than such an inscription, instrumental music, though it cannot always even then, perhaps, be said properly to imitate, may, however, produce all the effects of the finest and most perfect imitation.

The similarity between the passages is striking and I have italicized the expressions that appear to replicate Beattie. Only in the conclusion does Smith show himself less 'Manichean', so to speak, than Beattie. He makes no rigid contrast between 'beauty' and 'badness', confines himself to saying that the inscription would not excuse a picture for the incomprehensibility of its imitation, whereas music – even where it is not precisely imitating – achieves the same effects as a perfect imitation. Even when it does not imitate, then, music pleases. And on that point Beattie and Smith return to agreement.

We have already mentioned how Smith, like his predecessors, deals with the intercurrent relation between movement of the sound and movement of the passions. The comparison is encouraged by the conception of the mind as an unceasing flow of ideas and thoughts. In the case of joy, for instance, Smith explains how the movement of the thoughts in the mind becomes livelier and swifter as the contrasts increase; music may do something similar thanks to a succession of sounds more or less rapid or grave. Like other previous authors, however, he specifies that there is no resemblance in the strict sense between sounds and passions. As we know, the relation between sounds and passions was

---

[132]   A. Smith, *Essays* ..., p. 196.

usually explained by the fact that, since their effects are the same, the mind tends naturally to link the two phenomena and occasionally to confuse them. But Smith denies that the relation is to be understood by imitation, or that it derives from sympathy, and prefers to ascribe human characteristics to music itself: This art[133]

> becomes itself a gay, a sedate, or a melancholy object; and the mind corresponds to the object which engages its attention. Whatever we feel from instrumental music is an original, and not a sympathetic feeling: it is our own gaiety, sedateness, or melancholy; not the reflected disposition of another person.

The better to illustrate his thought, Smith explains that what happens in music also happens in landscape. We commonly attribute emotive states to nature: a landscape shrouded in fog will be melancholy, another where the sun shines in a rural and verdant ambience will be joyful. In cases like these we do not say that the landscape 'imitates' melancholy or joy. The same is true of music, which does not imitate the passions but arouses them. Note that other writers in Smith's place, in a similar context, would have spoken of 'sympathy' to account for this strange form of music-feeling contagion, but in Smith's vocabulary sympathy – defined in the *Theory of Moral sentiments* (London, 1759) – is characterized by the feeling that occurs when one participates in the passions of another human being. Even if we cannot have direct experience of the feelings of our fellow humans, our imagination enables us to identify with the other person. The sentiments aroused by the impressions on our senses, if we should find ourselves in that person's situation, are awakened and we 'sympathize' with him. Smith, then, denies that music acts on man through sympathy, because – in line with the meaning he gives to the term – this would suggest a 'reflected disposition of another person'. Yet, in the very idea that music cannot imitate or 'be' melancholy in the same way as a landscape is, we can detect the nucleus of sympathetic activity: projection. For in all such cases I attribute to another (whether a person, a landscape, a music) feelings that are mine. But Smith fails to catch the resemblance.

Let us now look at Smith's last reflections on instrumental music, where I think we can find the most innovative aspect of his theory. As we have seen, he agrees with many of his compatriots that pure sound does not imitate, and that it expresses the passions in a less perfect way than vocal music – which touches the heart more. Yet the action of instrumental music – and here is the novelty – also has its effects, not on the sense but on the mind. By virtue of its pleasing nature, music awakens the *attention*, which begins to follow the train of sounds and the relations they conduct:[134]

> by means of this relation each foregoing sound seems to introduce, and as it were to prepare the mind for the following: by its rythmus, by its time and measure, it

---

[133]   Ibid., p. 198.
[134]   Ibid., p. 204.

disposes that succession of sounds into a certain arrangement, which renders the whole more easy to be comprehended and remembered. Time and measure are to instrumental music what order and method are to discourse.

The mind finds itself completely involved in this process; and, having already said something about the working of the mind in relation to Smith's writing on the history of astronomy, we may be able to understand why: Smith points out a substantial analogy between mental functioning, according to the Humeian model, and the musical construct. The mind consists of a continual flow of impressions and its essence springs from this uninterrupted succession; time and order represent fundamental needs, such that Hume specifies in the *Treatise* how 'the chief exercise of the memory is not to preserve the simple ideas, but their *order* and *position*'.[135] Note also that when, in the *Treatise*, Hume tries to explain the idea of time, he does this through a musical example and some of his remarks in this passage find a sort of echo in Smith. I quote the following passage:[136]

> Five notes play'd on a flute give us the impression and idea of time; tho' time be not a sixth impression [...]. These five sounds making their appearance in this particular manner, excite no emotion in the mind, nor produce any affection of any kind [...].

In the same way Smith emphasizes that what engages the mind in listening to music is the play set up between the memory and the imagination's capacities to anticipate, and that in this case music has no other significance beyond the combination itself of the sounds.[137] Music offers to the human mind that pleasure conveyed by complete and regular systems, for in listening 'the mind enjoys not only a very great sensual, but a very high intellectual, pleasure, not unlike that which it derives from the contemplation of a great system in any other science'.[138] The notion of 'system' had been defined by Smith in the *History of Astronomy*, and by this term he refers to the imaginary mechanisms that the fancy creates in order to connect different movements or effects encountered in reality.

---

[135] D. Hume, *A Treatise*, p. 318 (I, ı, § 3).

[136] Ibid., p. 343 (I, ıı, § 3).

[137] A similar interpretation can be found in *An Essay on Taste* (1759) by Alexander Gerard, where the author – with regard to the 'Taste of Harmony' – explains how 'Whenever our pleasure arises from a succession of sounds, it is a perception of a complicated nature; made up of a *sensation* of the present sound or note, and an *idea* or remembrance of the foregoing, which, by their mixture and concurrence, produce such a mysterious delight, as neither could have produced alone. [...] Sense, memory, and imagination, are thus conjunctively employed, in exhibiting to the interior organ a succession of sounds, which, properly disposed, especially in music, fill us with exquisite delight' (*An Essay on Taste*, ed. W. J. Hipple Jr. (New York, 1978; reprint of the 3rd edition, London 1780), pp. 58-59).

[138] A. Smith, *Essays* ..., p. 205.

Drawing together the threads of the discourse, we can say that Adam Smith's theory on the imitative arts and the interpretation of music are influenced in a determining way by his conception of the human mind. The faculties of memory and imagination, together with the triptych of surprise, wonder and admiration, constitute the foundations. For the emphasis on wonder enables Smith to centre his own idea of 'imitation' on the concept of 'difference': the human mind is stimulated in the face of objects that imitate other objects of different nature, because the surprise provoked by that perception urges the imagination to movement in order to explain the effect of this wonder, and generates pleasure.

In the case of instrumental music, the analogy with the unfolding of human thought leads Smith to consider music also beyond its pathetic dimension. The power of music is not confined to addressing the mind by awakening the passions. It can be the object of a purely intellectual pleasure, since it exhibits the characteristics of a system – that is to say, it develops in time according to a precise structure. Music thus becomes analogous to human thought, which continually unfolds, and in an orderly fashion, and its perception engages the imagination that experiences pleasure in performing and anticipating those movements that are so familiar to it.

Conclusions

The eighteenth-century British debate on the arts inherits certain fundamental questions from the past: which are the principles of the arts and by what are they linked? What is the relation between art and nature? How should we understand the imitation performed by music? How and what can a music without text communicate to man? What is the connection between music and passions?

Innumerable possible answers in detail can be given, as we saw, but the formulation of the problem remains the same. First of all, we can note how none of the authors dealt with, from Harris to Smith, understands the imitative dimension of music as mere mimesis of natural sounds. The pleasure of music has nothing to do with imitation of this kind. The problem most debated concerns the relation between music and passions. While the relation is unanimously acknowledged, there is disagreement over its interpretation: music can be said to 'imitate' the passions, or to 'express' them, or to arouse them by 'sympathy'. And each of these options implies consequences. The most obvious is the concept of 'expression' – imagined first by Charles Avison – as a possible response to the imitative principle. In actual fact, imitation and expression pose an identical problem that turns on the questions 'what?' and 'how?' The theories that emphasize the expressive dimension of music, as in Beattie, have a hard time explaining the pleasure produced in man by instrumental music; more effective results are achieved by authors who rely on the sympathetic principle, whether understood in a physical-mechanical sense (like Webb) or in the more general sense of 'natural resonance with something' as we find in Harris or Jones.

The theories that seem to answer best to the needs of music are those centred on the notions of *movement* and *time*, underlining the rhythmic and metrical dimension of music and relegating the semantic problem to second place. In these cases, the main references are to Aristotle and Hume. Aristotelian movement may find itself associated with the eighteenth century's discoveries in physiology and give rise to interpretations of a mechanical sort, like that of Daniel Webb, where the analogy between passions and music derives from the fact that both of these act on the mind in the same way and produce the same effects; or, as in Thomas Twining, it may take the form of a theory that employs the texts of Aristotle to interpret the relation between music and emotions, thence to exploit the modern concept of 'imagination' to complete a theory that seems to lack sufficient tools to account for the effects of instrumental music.

In this panorama the most complete and interesting arguments appear to be those of Lord Kames and Adam Smith. In some points, their ideas seem to repropound a new application of the classical concept of 'order': through their conception of a human mind ruffled by a continual passage of ideas and perceptions, they establish an analogy between the flow of human thought and the development in time of a piece of music.

It is of fundamental importance to understand how the aesthetic results of these authors' studies of music are conditioned by their choice of particular physiological or psychological theories. The thorniest questions of musical aesthetics in search of an answer included the nature of the relation between music and emotions and the meaning of music. The interface between a culture like that of eighteenth-century Britain, focused on the study of how the human mind works, and these problems of music turned out to be remarkably fruitful. Especially so was the encounter with Hume's psychology of the mind, where the concatenation of ideas in the mind of man is explained through categories of relation such as resemblance, identity, space, time and quantity, some of which lend themselves excellently to the description of how music unfolds, without any reference to the semantic dimension. The emphasis on the time dimension, on the incessant shifting of thought, and on the role of memory and imagination in the human mind found in music an ideal terrain for comparison, and this encounter supplied musical aesthetics with new possibilities of interpretation to account for the functioning and action of music. If the effects of music are always manifested in man, the study of man can be of enormous benefit for music.

PART II
An intellectual background for British musical theories and histories

In the first part of this work we aimed to show how music found its place in the arguments and reflections of men of letters and philosophers, and what part it played in their theories. This second part will be concerned with musical literature and how it received, integrated and utilized the aesthetic-philosophical concepts examined in the first part, in the aim of enriching its own art.

The first chapter of this section (Chapter 3) will deal, in particular, with the discussion of three works of musical theory: *A Treatise of Musick, Speculative, Practical and Historical* by Alexander Malcom (Edinburgh, 1721); *The art of Musick* by John Frederick Lampe (London, 1740) and the *Essay on Musical Expression* by Charles Avison (London, 1752). Chapter 4 will be concerned with a different kind of discourse on music, namely historical discourse. The celebrated writings of Sir John Hawkins and Charles Burney will be examined in the light of the eighteenth century's renewed interest in the historical past and framed within the process of formation of modern history-writing, along the lines developed, as from the 1950s, by Arnaldo Momigliano, who discerned in the dialogue between historians and erudites a salient opportunity for founding a new way of thinking about the past.[1] In our perspective, a discussion of these two well-known, seminal works seems necessary from several points of view. To be sure, a literature specifically centred on Hawkins and Burney does exist, but there have been few attempts to frame their works within a broad cultural context.[2] For a study that seeks to satisfy this need we have to go back to Warren Dwight Allen's *Philosophies of Music History* (1939, revised 1962);[3] in this work, however, the two histories of music with which we are concerned are dealt with almost as a genre in itself, detached from an argument that takes account of the concept of

---

[1] See, in particular, Arnaldo Momigliano, 'Ancient History and the Antiquarian'; and the same author's later *Le radici classiche della storiografia moderna*, (Florence, [1990] 1992), especially chap. III, 'L'origine della ricerca antiquaria', pp. 59-83.

[2] The principal study of Burney remains that of Kerry S. Grant, *Dr Burney as Critic and Historian of Music* (Ann Arbor, MI, 1983).

[3] Warren Dwight Allen, *Philosophies of Music History* (1939; republished in a slightly modified form, New York, 1962).

'historiography' in the eighteenth century in general. The French context includes an in-depth discussion of the history of music in the seventeenth and eighteenth centuries by Philippe Vendrix (1993), which attempts to explain the 'facteurs de l'interêt historique' in those centuries.[4] German writing on the subject features the important work done by Werner Friedrich Kümmel in the 1960s with his massive volume *Geschichte und Musikgeschichte*.[5]

A second, and permanent, factor of interest for a fresh study of the histories of Hawkins and Burney may also be found in the constant need of contemporary musicology to question itself on the nature of music history writing. The debate began in the late 1960s and continued until the 1980s with the studies by Dahlhaus, Wiora and Treitler,[6] and helped to define the problems and the concepts of a discipline whose outlines were rather vague. And yet, in addressing the eighteenth-century histories of music, even readers familiar with the afore-cited texts may find themselves wrong-footed. So, an attempt to understand how these histories were put together, and what currents of thought they drew on, may be useful for the contemporary musicologist in order to focus more attention on the historical nature of the categories employed, without ascribing an ontological dimension to them. Setting the concepts we use in a historical context may be a good way to avoid the Scylla and Charybdis of realism and nominalism, recognizing that terms like 'history' and 'music' do not always hark back to one and the same significance and are therefore not 'timeless' categories – without going to the opposite extreme and omitting to trace their general characteristics within precise historical and geographical contexts.[7]

In defining the task of music history, Guido Adler – acknowledged founder of the discipline of 'musicology' – writes:[8]

---

[4]   Philippe Vendrix, *Aux origines d'une discipline historique. La Musique et son Histoire en France aux XVIIe et XVIIIe siècles* (Geneva, 1993), especially chap. II, pp. 65-94.

[5]   Werner Friedrich Kümmel, *Geschichte und Musikgeschichte: die Musik der Neuzeit in Geschichtsschreibung und Geschichtsauffassung des deutschen Kulturbereichs von der Aufklärung bis zu J. G. Droysen und Jacob Burckhardt* (Marburg, 1967).

[6]   See W. Wiora, 'Musikgeschichte und Universalgeschichte', *Acta Musicologica*, 33 (1961), pp. 84-104; H. S. Powers (ed.), *Studies in Music History: Essays for Oliver Strunk* (Princeton, 1968); W. Wiora (ed.), *Die Ausbreitung des Historismus* über *die Musik* (Regensburg, 1968); B. S. Brook, E. O. D. Downes and S. V. Solkema (eds), *Perspectives in Musicology* (New York, 1972); C. Dahlhaus, *Grundlagen der Musikgeschichte* (Koln, 1977); G. Knepler, *Geschichte als Weg zum Musikverständnis: Beiträge zur Theorie, Methode und der Musikgeschichtsschreibung* (Leipzig, 1977); W. Wiora, *Ideen zur Geschichte der Musik* (Darmstadt, 1980); and L. Treitler, *Music and the Historical Imagination* (Harvard, 1989).

[7]   On how these two ways of relating to and understanding the categories in the area of historical musicology came to be articulated, see Leo Treitler, *Music and the Historical Imagination*, in particular chap. IV, 'On Historical Criticism', pp. 79-94.

[8]   Guido Adler, *Methode der Musikgeschichte* (Leipzig, 1919), p. 9.

Die Aufgabe der Musikgeschichte ist die Erforschung und Darlegung des Entwicklungsganges der tonsetzerischen Produkte; ihr Objekt sind die tonkünstlerischen Erzeugnisse und zwar ihre Entstehung und Ausbildung, ihre Zusammensetzung in Gruppen je nach der Zusammengehörigkeit und Unterscheidbarkeit, ferner die Abhängigkeit, Eigenentfaltung und die Einflußsphäre jeder tonkünstlerischen Persönlichkeit.

[The purpose of music history is the research and exposition of the way in which the musical products develop; its object are the composers' creations, and precisely their genesis and composition, their belonging to categories according to their similarities and differences, and furthermore the interdependence, individual evolution and the impact of every composer.]

At the centre of this model of music history, then, stands the musical product, the work. The history of music through the nineteenth and twentieth centuries is conceived firstly as a history of 'works of music'. As we shall see in the last chapter of this study, the eighteenth-century histories examined here start out from different assumptions.

Chapter 3
Musical knowledge and human knowledge

Examining the theories set out in the previous chapters, we may speculate on the diffusion of the categories hitherto encountered in artistic as well as philosophical and literary areas. As we know, the circulation of ideas in the cultured milieux in the eighteenth century was very effective, and the incredible increase in Britain of public opportunities to hear music can only have contributed to their spread. As recently recalled by William Weber, whose studies on the connection between society, politics and musical life are of primary importance for our research, 'basic to the modernity of English life in this period was the dynamism with which ideas and influences moved back and forth between closely adjoining areas of culture and society'.[1] What follows is aimed in this direction, analysing certain examples of writing on music in order to evidentiate how they partake of the cultural context described in the first two chapters.

Three texts of different nature have been chosen: an ample treatise, a short theoretical work, and an essay of musical-aesthetic type. Many other writers, not dealt with here,[2] would lend themselves well to our kind of analysis but – as with the first part of our study – the aim is not to ransack all the available material. We intend merely to highlight how in certain studies on music, belonging to different literary genres and written by authors of different background, one may come across theories and concepts stemming from philosophy that have contributed to enriching the discussion of music.

Alexander Malcolm: *A Treatise of Musick, Speculative, Practical and Historical* (Edinburgh, 1721)

Alexander Malcolm (1685-1763) is a little-known figure of the eighteenth century, to whom we owe a treatise on music published at Edinburgh in 1721. Theoretician and teacher, scholar of mathematics, Malcolm emigrated to America at some

---

[1]   William Weber, 'The *Beau Monde* in London, 1700-1870', in Susan Wollenberg and Simon McVeigh (eds), *Concert Life in Eighteenth-Century Britain* (Aldershot, 2004), p. 74.

[2]   Among which the *Cursory Notes of Musicke* and *The Musicall Grammarian* of Roger North or certain theoretical writings of William Jones – in which connection we note once again the brilliant studies by Jamie C. Kassler, especially *Inner Music. Hobbes, Hooke and North on Internal Character* (London, 1995) and 'The Systematic Writings on Music of William Jones (1726-1800)', *Journal of the American Musicological Society*, 26 (1973), pp. 92-107.

time before 1734 (when he emerges in New York) and continued in the teaching profession until 1759.[3] The *Treatise* not only betrays the author's clear interest in mathematics, it also reveals a knowledge of the Lockeian philosophy of mind and the philosophical debates of the time, and a particular concern with history. The work is dedicated to the Royal Academy of Music (1719-1728).[4]

The matter of the treatise is ordered as per the title. Chapters I-X are devoted to musical theory: they begin by defining the object and end of music, moving on to a discussion of the nature of 'musical sound'. Thereafter, the concepts of consonance, dissonance and harmony are defined and scales and chords are described. This is the section that takes up most space, accounting for half the work. The second part of the treatise (chapters XI-XIII) deals with the practice of composition. These pages, as the author explains in the introduction, are 'for want of sufficient practice' in musical art the work of the genius and the generosity of a 'friend',[5] whose name is not given. Chapter XIV, the last, is concerned with the historical aspect of music.

Malcolm's work is introduced by an *Ode on the Power of Musick, inscrib'd to Mr Malcom, as a Monument of Friendship, by Mr Mitchell*, which provides a typical example of the praise of music. The ode can, in all probability, be attributed to Joseph Mitchell (c. 1684-1738), Scottish poet and dramatist who, like Malcolm, attended the University of Edinburgh.[6] The last of the poem's thirteen stanzas closes with an encomium of Malcolm:[7]

> …the dear, deserving Man,
> Who taught in Nature's Laws,
> To spread his country's Glory can
> Practise the Beauties of the Art, and shew its
> Grounds and cause.

---

[3] The bibliography regarding Malcolm is very scanty. For biographical information we have relied on the entry 'Malcom, Alexander', in *The New Grove Dictionary of Music and Musicians*, ed. Stanley Sadie, 2nd edition (New York, 2001, vol. xv, p. 681 et seq.; there is also a doctoral thesis on Malcolm's treatise by Reppard Stone, 'An Evaluative Study of Alexander Malcom's *Treatise of Musick: Speculative, Practical and Historical*' (Catholic University of America, Washington D.C., 1974)).

[4] On the history of the academy, see Elisabeth Gibson, *The Royal Academy of Music: 1719-1728* (New York and London, 1989).

[5] Alexander Malcom, *A Treatise of Musick, Speculative, Practical and Historical* [Edinburgh, 1721], (New York, 1970), p. xxii.

[6] See Calhoun Winton, 'Mitchell Joseph', in *Oxford Dictionary of National Biography*, available on-line at http://www.oxforddnb.com/view/article/18846.

[7] A. Malcom, *A Treatise of Musick*, p. xii.

In the introduction Malcolm refers explicitly to Lord Shaftesbury and the topics dealt with by him in the *Soliloquy*,[8] especially regarding the relation between author and critic. As will be remembered, Shaftesbury had valorized the work of the critic and asserted that the progress of art could only stem from a fertile rapport between art and criticism. Hence Malcolm has no qualms about subjecting his own work to the judgement of the *criticks*, from whose negative remarks he will find matter for improvement. Nevertheless, there is a 'common place of criticism'[9] upon which he desires to focus and that will serve him to qualify his own work: namely, the discussion on what is a 'discovery', or novelty, in the sciences. Malcolm underlines the fact that the 'invention of new theorems is not the only thing of use for scientific knowledge, but also the proper relation and connection of the things already found, and the easy way of representing them to the understanding of others',[10] and thus he takes his place in the line of thinkers like Bacon, Descartes and Newton, who held the method and the classification of means to be as useful in the advancement of knowledge as the new discoveries themselves.

Malcolm's choice of the literary genre of 'treatise' – from time immemorial a device for systematizing knowledge – is thus consistent with the aims he sets himself: to organize the vast subject matter regarding the theoretical, practical and historical aspects of music by attempting to establish relations that will favour the understanding of it.

Musical sound in a Lockeian mind: Alexander Malcolm's speculative music

Of the 608 pages of the treatise, 323 are devoted to the speculative dimension of music. The starting-point is entirely Cartesian: 'music is a science of sound, whose end is pleasure'.[11] But times have changed and, unlike Descartes, Malcolm takes good care not to exclude the physical consideration of sound from his treatment. In the wake of the studies by Perrault and the discussion of the *Compendium* in the *Elucidationes Physicae* (1668) of Nicolas Poisson,[12] our author ventures into the thorny wood of the theories on the nature of acoustic production, though he tries not to be sidetracked and to keep on the straight path that must lead to the definition of what is 'that' sound that is the object of music.

---

[8]   See above, pp. 35-36.

[9]   A. Malcom, *A Treatise of Musick*, p. xx.

[10]   Ibid., p. xxi.

[11]   Ibid, p. 1. As we recall, the *Compendium Musicae* (1618) of Descartes began: 'Compendium musicae. Huius obiectum est sonus. Finis, ut delectet, variosque in nobis moveat affectus' (Descartes, *Abrégé de musique*, ed. F. De Buzon (Paris, 1987), p. 55).

[12]   On the role played by Poisson in disseminating the early work of Descartes, see the remarks by P. Gozza in P. Gozza and A. Serravezza, *Estetica* e *Musica. L'origine di un incontro* (Bologna, 2004), pp. 51-55.

Malcolm takes up Perrault's theorem according to which sound is caused by the mutual collision of particles, that communicates itself through the air until it reaches the air. The movement of the air impresses itself on the eardrum which, in turn, communicates that movement to the air within the ear, until it attains the auditory nerve where the sensory process ends and where the mind, by the laws of its union with the body, has that idea we call *sound*.[13] The Lockeian echo in this definition of 'sound' is unmistakable: Malcolm here takes over Locke's philosophy of mind and makes a clearcut demarcation between *sensations* and *ideas*.

What in his view differentiates an ordinary sound from a musical sound is that the latter 'being clear and evenly is agreeable to the ear'.[14] Pleasure, which is the end of music, is therefore the criterion on which to judge a 'musical' or non-musical sound. Now, in order for a sound to communicate an agreeable sensation and thus arouse the idea of pleasure, it must be 'clear and evenly' – that is, discernible. Clear identification of the sound is the necessary premise to performing the subsequent mental operation that enables the idea of 'pitch' to be conceived. Here again, Malcolm illustrates this process by means of Locke's theory of mind:[15]

> When two sounds are heard in immediate succession, the mind not only perceives two simple ideas, but by a proper activity of its own, comparing these ideas, forms another of their difference of tune, from which arise to us various degrees of pleasure or offence.

Here, in particular, Malcolm calls to his aid the pages devoted by Locke to the composition of ideas by means of simple ideas. In chapter XII of book II of the *Essay on Human Understanding* the latter writes that up to the stage of reception of simple ideas (in our case, the idea of sound) the mind is passive. Subsequently, however, it 'exerts several acts of its own, whereby out of its simple ideas, as the materials and foundations of the rest, the other are framed'; among the acts that the mind can perform with the materials supplied by simple ideas there is that of 'bringing two ideas […] together; and setting them by one another, so as to take a view of them at once, without uniting them into one; by which way it gets all its ideas of relations'.[16] Therefore, thanks to the mind's faculty of comparing the simple ideas of sounds without confusing them, we succeed in effecting a comparison between pitches, leading to the notion of *interval*.

Malcolm also uses Locke's theory of the mind in the attempt to supply a reasonable solution to one of the eternal questions of the philosophy of music: why are some sounds agreeable and others not? Combining mathematical proportions, vibratory movements and relations between ideas, he tries to give a personal

---

[13]   A. Malcolm, *A Treatise of Musick*, p. 4.

[14]   Ibid., p. 28.

[15]   Ibid., p. 66.

[16]   J. Locke, *An Essay concerning Human Understanding*, p. 276 (II, XII, 1).

answer to the question. He specifies that he is not interested in speculating on the 'first causes' of events – which rest in the mind of God – but he will focus on those laws or rules that can be deduced from the observation of phenomena constantly presented by Nature ('second' causes).[17] In Malcolm, the fact that an octave arouses a pleasant idea in the mind, whereas a second does not, has the same universal character (irrespective of epoch or culture) as gravitational phenomena and must therefore be referable to a law.

As was the case from the Renaissance onwards, Malcolm's starting point is the 'sounding number' or, as he writes, 'not […] numbers abstractly' but, rather, 'as expressing the very cause and difference of sound with respect to time, viz. the number of vibrations in the same time'.[18] The definition of 'consonance' that Malcolm takes from the studies of Mersenne and from the *Natural Grounds and Principles of Harmony* by William Holder (1694) is based on the frequency of the coincidence of the *ictus* transmitted by the vibration of the sounding body:[19]

> *Concord* is the result of a frequent union and coincidence of the vibrations of two sonorous bodies, and consequently of the ondulating motions of the air, which being caused by these vibrations, are like and proportional to them.

This theory of consonance was very common in late seventeenth-century England and can also be found in the *Curious Dissertation* of Robert Hooke (c. 1675-76) and in the *Philosophical Essay of Music* (1677) of Francis North.[20] The most delicate point of the theory – on which individual views diverged – lay precisely in the problem of explaining how a sequence of *ictus* was perceived as 'sound'. Locke's psychology, which sought to describe the process of formation of ideas and the relation between ideas and the sensations that generate them, must therefore have seemed an excellent tool for moving from the physical description of the nature of sound to its idea in the human mind.

---

[17]   The argument has an unmistakably Newtonian flavour and, indeed, Malcolm cites as example of this procedure the law of the fall of heavy bodies, where Newton's intention is not to explain 'why' they must fall, but to illustrate the phenomenon and evidence how it is a universal principle that follows determinate rules.

[18]   A. Malcom, *A Treatise of Musick*, p. 71 et seq. On the path that led to the development of the concept of the 'sounding number' and the transformation of the concepts of speculative music following the 'contact' between numbers and the idea of 'sounding body', see Guido Mambella, 'La risonanza nella scienza musicale del Cinquecento', *Intersezioni*, 25 (2005), pp. 209-235.

[19]   A. Malcolm, *A Treatise of Musick*, p. 84.

[20]   Essential reading for understanding the influence of studies and musical theories on the theories developed by authors such as Thomas Hobbes, Robert Hooke and Roger North is Jamie C. Kassler, *Inner Music. Hobbes, Hooke and North on Internal Character* (London, 1995). In this book Kassler highlights the use made by these authors of a musical symbology that leads to a physiological and ethical model of interpretation in a mechanical and computational key. See also Penelope Gouk, *Music, Science and Natural Magic in Seventeenth-Century England*.

Just as in the treatises of the sixteenth and seventeenth centuries, Malcolm proceeds from the discussion of the concept of 'consonance' to deal with one of the topoi of this kind of literature namely, the phenomenon of *sympathetic resonance* – citing the recurring list of experiments on strings, glasses, bells, and the phenomenon of beats. He then goes on to search for a foothold in Locke's theory that will supply a new argument in reply to the question of why consonances are pleasant; but here, as we shall see, he merely reiterates the ancient reply, not even very well disguised: consonances please in virtue of the simplicity of their numerical relations, since man is sensitive to harmony, order and proportion.

To pursue his reasoning, Malcolm relies on analogy, a procedure that was very much in fashion at the time. From the discussion on resonance he deduces that union and coincidence of movement are a necessary ingredient of consonance, and thus of the pleasure of hearing. After which, he bends Locke's theory a little in order to assert that, since every stimulus transmitted by each of the five senses is transformed into a *sensation* for the mind that receives it, the process is always the same in all cases.[21]

> [Thus] we have good reason to think, that it is not improper to compare one sense with another, as seeing and hearing; for tho' their objects are different, [...] yet they may be equally agreeable in their kind, and have some common principle in both cases necessary to the agreeableness.

Hearing and sight, in particular, become comparable because they have an element in common: movement. This is designated by Malcolm as the 'object' of sight, while in the case of hearing it is the 'cause' of the object of that sense (namely, sound). In the case of sight, he argues that visual pleasure evidently derives from the regularity of the movement and adduces the case of the pendulum: regularity and commensurability of the movements enable the human intellect to exert one of the important functions that Locke attributes to the mind – that of discerning and comparing, which underpin all the vast array of ideas comprised under the heading of 'relation'. Musical sounds, in virtue of the numerical relations that describe them, are subsumed into the category of 'regular and commensurable movements', and this is what enables the mind to make use of the 'bricks' (as Locke calls sensations) supplied by the acoustic experience in order to construct the lofty towers of human ingenuity: the operations of the mind (memory, composition, discernment, and so forth) allow the bricks to be put together in a new and elaborate shape, and this is what distinguishes men from animals.

Thus, as in previous authors, consonances are pleasing because they answer to a criterion of harmony and order and the proportions that express them are of the simplest: but with respect to ancient theory a small step forward has been taken, towards the interior of the human mind. The pleasure of hearing is, in this way, linked with the fact that the commensurability of musical sounds enables the

---

[21]   A. Malcolm, *A Treatise of Musick*, p. 92.

mind to act on them, to compose them – in a word, to discern the differences in unfolding their potentials, which alone generate knowledge.

Music and the human mind: a new goal for the music of the Moderns

We remarked earlier how the beginning of Malcolm's *Treatise* echoes, to the letter, the opening words of the *Compendium Musicae* of Descartes. It will have been noted, however, that in describing the 'end' of music, Malcolm takes up only the first part of the Cartesian definition: he claims that the goal of music is 'pleasure', but he makes no reference to its capacity to move the emotions. As we shall shortly see, the omission is intentional and finds its justification in the difference between ancient and modern music that Malcolm identifies in the historical section of his work.

This part consists of a chapter ('Of the Ancient Musick'), divided into six paragraphs. In form, modes and contents, it reiterates certain arguments that were standard in treatises on music: we begin with the definition of 'music' and proceed with its origins, then its praise, and something is said on the ancient writers who dealt with this art. A treatment of this kind could have been found in any relevant work of the sixteenth or seventeenth century and Malcolm says nothing new on the subject, but he does add a final section that deals with 'The ancient and modern Musick compared' and that belongs in the wide-ranging debate that arose from the *Querelle des Anciens et des Modernes*.

In these pages Malcolm not only opposes the harsh words addressed to the music of the moderns by Sir William Temple and Isaac Vossius, he also tries to clarify wherein the real and profound difference between the two musics consists. Malcolm's idea that ancient and modern music have different aims harks back to the position taken by William Wotton, Temple's adversary. Malcolm seems to reprise and corroborate the thesis expressed in *Ancient and Modern Music* (1694) where Wotton argues that the music of the Ancients and that of the Moderns cannot but display different characteristics, since they are addressed to different men. The crucial point in Wotton's reply to Temple rests on the idea that, although music is a physical-mathematical science founded on determinate and invariable rules, man is a historical being and subject to variation. This must be borne in mind when dealing with ancient and modern music. Wotton allows that ancient music could undoubtedly attain its goal – that of pleasing and arousing passions, in its own epoch. Modern music, however, has changed in order to respond to a need of modern man, that of being able to judge. While, of old, the merely sensory pleasure might suffice, modern man also requires that his intellect be stimulated. For ancient man[22]

---

[22]   W. Wotton, *Reflections upon Ancient and Modern Learning*, p. 287 et seq. (my italics).

> what is intricate, appears confused; and therefore he can make no *judgment* of
> the true excellency of those things, which seem fiddling to him only, for want of
> skill in musick. Whereas on the contrary, the skill or ignorance of the composer
> serve rather to entertain the understanding, than to gratifie the passions of a
> skilful master; whose passions are then the most thoroughly raised, when his
> understanding receives the greatest satisfaction.

What changes, according to Wotton, from ancient to modern times is the end itself
of musical art. In the age that witnessed the affirmation of the category of 'taste',
the ability to judge becomes a fundamental element.

Malcolm, in his comparison between the music of the Ancients and that of the
Moderns, considers two parameters: the principles of music and musical practice.
With regard to the former, the subject is soon dealt with: from the theoretical
point of view ancient music undoubtedly attains a level of excellence and the
writings that have come down to us bear witness to the richness of ancient theory.
This kind of knowledge, however, proceeds by 'accumulation', and hence the
Moderns enjoy an advantage inasmuch as they have been able to avail themselves
of the solid ancient foundations from which to progress in the investigation of the
principles of music.

More delicate is the argument relating to musical practice. Malcolm firstly
addresses one of the most debated questions on the music of the Ancients: did
the Ancients know polyphony?[23] No, says Malcolm. His negative is based partly
on interpretation of the ancient texts, partly on an argument regarding the *end* of
music that also involves a discussion of the *effects* of the music of the Ancients.
In his view, Ancients and Moderns differ, not so much in the 'capacity' to obtain
certain effects, as in the 'will' to obtain them: ancient use and modern use diverge.
The effects narrated of ancient music refer mainly to its power over the *emotions*.
Ancient music paid great attention to the bond between sound and word and, in
order to attain the intended effect, it was of paramount importance that the words
be fully understood. From this point of view, the goal attributed to music by the
Ancients would appear to exclude polyphony. The Moderns, however, know a
kind of music with which the Ancients were unfamiliar:[24]

> We have compositions fitted altogether for Instruments: the design whereof is
> not so much to move the passions, as to *entertain the mind* and *please the fancy*
> with a variety of Harmony and Rythmus; the principal effect of which is to raise
> delight and admiration.

---

[23]   A topic that had lost none of its relevance in the writings of Hawkins and Burney,
fifty years later.

[24]   A. Malcolm, *A Treatise of Musick*, p. 589 (my italics).

Here, then, is the main difference between ancients and moderns: their music is of different stamp because their aims are not the same. And while pleasure remains a term in common, heart and emotions yield place to mind and admiration.

The power to act on the mind Malcolm ascribes primarily to harmony and rhythm. At which point he links up once more with the argument developed in the theoretical section of his work. For, previously, we saw how the mind is facilitated in its action in the world of musical sounds in virtue of their commensurability. Harmony, the result of a continual integration and succession of consonances and dissonances, satisfies the mind and the imaginative capacity in the highest degree, generating what Malcolm calls 'an intellectual beauty'.[25]

In his view, the Moderns attribute less importance than the Ancients to the action of music on the passions because the latter have no need of it for them to be summoned to morality and virtue; which enables music to be directed to other goals. Moreover, Malcolm insists that to confine the power of music to dominion over the passions would relegate it to a position subordinate to the other arts:[26]

> If we look upon a noble building, or a curious painting, we are allowed to admire the design, and view all its proportions and relation of parts with pleasure to our understandings, without any respect to the passions. We must observe again, that there is scarce any piece of *melody* that has not the same general influence upon the heart; and by being more sprightly or heavy in its movements, will have different effects; tho' it is not designed to excite any particular passion, and can only be said in general to give pleasure, and recreate the mind.

This passage contains several remarks worthy of note in relation to instrumental music. Firstly, we find a topic already dealt with: instrumental music does not arouse determinate passions, yet it influences the mind – thanks, in particular, to a fast or slow movement. But Malcolm adds that, while other arts based on a harmony of proportions, like architecture, do not act on the passions, they are nonetheless considered noble owing to the way they satisfy our intellect. Therefore, even when an instrumental concert does not excite any definite passion in us, it may involve our intellect with pleasure. Malcolm does not deny that the pleasure conveyed by 'intellectual beauty' is less easily felt than the action of music upon the passions and necessitates 'experience'. Such difficulty, however, he thinks 'is no fault in the thing':[27]

> what, in musick and painting, would seem intricate and confused, and so give no satisfaction to the unskilled, will ravish with admiration and delight, one who is able to unravel all the parts, observe their relations and the united *concord* of the whole.

---

[25] Ibid., p. 598.

[26] Ibid., p. 599.

[27] Ibid.

Here again, Malcolm's argument finds itself perfectly at home within the genesis and development of Locke's analysis of the mind. Locke, it will be recalled, focused attention on the gradual way the human faculties are disclosed. Ontogenetic development follows the same sequence according to which the moment of experience always precedes that of reflection. In the construction of knowledge, the individual *first* perceives and feels sensations, and derives from these the ideas that he will use thereafter to compare them, compose them with one another, and so on. This occurs even in individual development, since in the very beginning – in infancy – more use is made of the powers of perception, which – it must be emphasized – are passive, and only later on in life does one become more able to reflect and concentrate on perceptions and utilize the mind in an active way.

In the description Malcolm gives of the two possible ways in which music acts upon man exactly the same process occurs. The music of the Ancients was first and foremost intended to excite the passions: Malcolm sees this as more immediate, it requires less experience and effort and is, indeed, a 'passive' pleasure. In this case the mind finds itself invaded and transported by the power of sound, without having to 'operate' on it. However, where music aiming at intellectual beauty is concerned –beauty represented by modern instrumental production – there is no stopping short at the level of passivity: the music derives its force from the fact that the ideas of the sounds can be combined and compared by the mind, thus restoring the idea of harmony as a dynamic unity rich in variety and contrasts. Which is why Malcolm cannot view the greater complexity of modern music as a defect but, rather, as a characteristic that melds perfectly with the combinatorial capacities of the mind, conducing the latter to an activity at one with its own purpose.

John Frederick Lampe: *The Art of Musick* (London, 1740)

John Frederick Lampe (1703-1751) was one of the numerous foreign musicians who arrived in England at a young age (in 1725 in the case of Lampe) and spent the rest of their lives there. Bassoonist and composer, he is known mainly to scholars of Handel and of the history of Italian opera in England; for, in 1732-33, he was involved in the attempt to establish a season of opera in English at the Little Haymarket, for which he wrote the opera seria *Amelia*.[28]

Here we shall say something about a short theoretical writing of his, *The art of Musick*, which gives a simple account of the reception and circulation of certain ideas on music in eighteenth-century England. Written after he had already been resident for fifteen years, from the outset his little work speaks the language of his

---

28   On the complex history of this season at the Little Haymarket, see Robert D. Hume and Judith Milhous, 'J. F. Lampe and English Opera at the Little Haymarket in 1732-33', *Music & Letters*, 78 (1997), pp. 502-531; on Lampe, see also Roy Johnston, 'The Pleasures and Penalties of Networking: John Frederick Lampe in the Summer of 1750', in Wollenberg and McVeigh (eds), *Concert Life in Eighteenth-Century Britain*, pp. 219-241.

new country – as witnessed by his quotation of a passage from Bacon's preface to the *Advancement of Learning*, where the Lord Chancellor marks the interpretation of Nature by man as the sole fount of knowledge. And this appeal to the search for the principles of music in Nature is one of the hallmarks of Lampe's text.

The short essay consists of sixty pages plus some plates with musical examples, and is not divided into chapters. Though the initial table of contents sets out the subjects dealt with, the text is continuous, broken only into paragraphs, but it can be subdivided into two parts. In the first twenty pages the author discusses music and its principles in the light of the main known theories: Pythagorean tradition, acoustic studies, Lockeian psychology. The remaining pages are devoted to the practice of composition. The link between the two parts is supplied by the illustration in the first plate, which shows the harmonic series of a sound: this furnishes the connecting link between scientific speculation and the theory of composition. For, on the one hand, the harmonics are a 'natural product' of the sound, to which our mind is accustomed by dint of the incessant repetition of one and the same sequence of sounds; on the other hand, that given succession of sounds reveals itself as particularly significant in compositional practice. All this, in Lampe's view, is 'a convincing argument, how much it is the business of a master to observe closely the dictates of nature, if they would ever reach the peculiar elegancy and beauties of musick'.[29]

Lampe's frequent exhortation to study Nature refers both to investigations in natural philosophy, and specifically to the study of human nature. With regard to the latter, Lampe argues that a knowledge of compositional technique in the absence of a knowledge of human nature will fail to obtain the effects desired of music:[30]

> To know only the right use of concords, the preparations and resolutions of discords, or to make subject upon subject, without knowing how *to touch the passions*, the work most probably will be dull, flat, and insipid.

This passage follows a quotation from Locke, where the latter focuses on the relation between sense and intellect, criticizing the idea that the imperfection of our knowledge would stem from an imperfection of the senses. Locke invites us to reflect on the fact that our cognitive difficulties are determined, rather, by a lack of attention and by not exercising our thought to concentrate on our perceptions.

In the citation from Lampe above it can be seen how the antithesis between the figure of 'talent' and the figure of 'genius' – which in the eighteenth century, especially in the second half, would often become a *locus classicus* – is here given a different interpretation: in order for compositional technique to produce the desired effects it must be underpinned, not by a form of 'natural instinct', but by a different kind of knowledge based on examination of the working of the mind.

---

[29]   John Frederick Lampe, *The Art of Musick* (London, 1740), p. 23.

[30]   Ibid., p. 5.

As we see, then, Lampe derives from Locke's philosophy the exhortation to urge the mind to reflection on its own sensations: for only by focusing attention on the perception of the sound will it be possible to identify the very existence of the harmonics.

Concerning the study of the nature of sound, Lampe, in line with the empirical spirit described above, rejects the mathematical-speculative current of thinking on music and denies that the principles sought may be derived from mathematical knowledge. Knowledge is attained through the senses, and only by paying more attention to the sense of hearing can one recognize the natural phenomenon that underlies the principles of music upon which Lampe holds that 'a true system of musick' can be founded.[31]

The existence of the upper harmonics was well known, and had been described for the first time in a systematic way by Marin Mersenne in the seventeenth century, but had not been satisfactorily explained. In England between the seventeenth and eighteenth centuries important steps had been taken towards understanding the phenomenon, particularly with the identification of the 'nodes' of the string,[32] as reported by John Wallis in 1677, and the formula for calculating the fundamental frequency of a vibrating string, published by Taylor Brook in the *Philosophical Transactions* (1713). It is, however, to a Frenchman, Joseph Sauveur, that we owe the fundamental connection between the existence of the nodes and the production of the harmonic sounds,[33] it would be Jean-Philippe Rameau's acquaintance with the studies of Sauveur – following the publication of the *Traité de l'harmonie* (1722) and thanks to the mediation of the Jesuit Louis-Bertrand Castel – that enabled Rameau to supply a natural-physical basis for the principle of *basse fondamentale*.[34]

The extent to which the new mode of viewing the mind, its processes and its faculties was by now common property can be gauged from the following passage, where Lampe explains wherein musical composition consists:[35]

---

[31]   Ibid., p. 21.

[32]   In other words, the points at which the string is in a state of repose.

[33]   The problem is set in the general framework of the harmonic theories of J. P. Rameau by Thomas Christensen, *Rameau and Musical Thought in the Enlightenment* (Cambridge, 1993), especially pp. 133-168, and in the same author's 'Eighteenth-Century Science and the "Corps Sonore": The Scientific Background to Rameau's "Principle of Harmony"', *Journal of Music Theory*, 31 (1987), pp. 23-50.

[34]   Lampe was undoubtedly acquainted with Rameau's studies, in particular the *Traité*, from which he quotes (in the original French) on p. 46, but it is not certain whether he knew the *Géneration harmonique ou traité de musique théorique et pratique* of 1737. Among the theorists cited we find Mattheson again and – in a highly polemical tone – Johann Christopher Pepusch (like Lampe, an English-naturalized German) and his *Treatise on Harmony* of 1731.

[35]   Lampe, *The Art of Musick*, p. 5 et seq.

by fixing our thoughts on the beforementioned principles, inspired by *fancy*, and *reason* assisting to keep due order and method, we shall discover infinite beauties, and vast variety of *expressions* in music, the more we know, the more we shall wish to know, as perceiving tho' knowledge be gained every day, yet the boundless prospect of fancy and invention lay open, reflection will branch out variety of beautiful images, which if disposed in a proper manner, must produce the desired effect, by a regular and nervous performance to instruct and please.

The Art of Musick is an interesting work because it highlights a central aspect of our study – the mutual and fruitful exchange between philosophical and musical reflection. In Malcolm's text this blend of interests might seem more to be expected, given the speculative nature of the treatise and the author's background. In the case of Lampe, with a text written by a musician and composer for practical purposes, the recourse to natural philosophy and psychology underlines once more how the contribution from these disciplines was seen as extremely useful for developing musical science.

Charles Avison: *An Essay on Musical Expression* (London, 1752)

The last example to illustrate how and to what extent theoreticians and practitioners of music made use of concepts elaborated in the philosophical area in order to enrich their thinking on their own art is the celebrated *Essay on Musical Expression* by Charles Avison (1709-1770), already mentioned in the first part of our work in regard to the concepts of 'imitation' and 'expression'.

Avison spent his life in Newcastle-upon-Tyne as organist and teacher of music. Founder and director of the Newcastle Music Society, he was an active promoter of concerts – together with John Garth he organized a regular concert series in Durham – as well as a composer.[36] And the writing of the *Essay* was undoubtedly stimulated by the intermesh of readings in philosophy and musical practice and teaching, combined with a particular attention to the problems of performance.

The essay is divided into three parts, preceded by a brief glossary of musical terms (melody, harmony, modulation, and so on), perhaps inspired by his reading of Pepusch's *Treatise on Harmony*, which adopts a similar device. As in the case of Lampe, it is the first part of the *Essay* that most evidences Avison's involvement in the mass of ideas with which we have become familiar in the course of our study: the search for the foundations of music in human nature, the idea of the presence of an internal sense enabling us to perceive beauty and harmony, the importance of the association of ideas. All these elements are used by Avison in the first section of the work, dealing with 'The Force and Effects of Music', followed by a comparison between music and painting. The second part of the *Essay* is devoted

---

[36]   For more details of Avison's biography, see the introduction to Pierre Dubois's edition of the *Essay on Musical Expression* (Aldershot, 2004).

to composition and especially to the relation of equilibrium between melody and harmony that is necessary for the success of a piece. Avison lastly turns to the concept of *musical expression* – in relation both to composition and performance – which takes up two-thirds of the work.

Avison's *Essay* was already hailed by his contemporaries as breaking new ground in the thinking on music. Charles Burney, in the *Essay on musical Criticism*, that opens the second volume of his history of music, would indicate Avison as the first author to devote a systematic treatment to 'musical criticism'.[37] As we shall see, several of the reflections of the Newcastle composer can be traced back to previous writers, especially James Harris. Nevertheless, the sense of novelty aroused by the publication of Avison's work must be taken into serious consideration: what was it exactly that enabled it to enjoy such success?

From a comparison with the literature examined hitherto, the most striking aspect is the excellent balance of Avison's writing between its readability,[38] its relevance and its precision of thought. Introducing his recent edition of the *Essay*, Pierre Dubois states that 'what is actually noteworthy in Avison's approach is the fact that he endeavoured to write for the general public', testified according to him by 'the very fact he should feel it necessary to define such technical terms as "melody", "harmony", "modulation", "cadence", at the beginning of the *Essay* [...]'.[39] In fact, the idea of supplying readers with a glossary was not new, and neither, in itself, was the attempt to address a general public extending beyond professional musicians. However, the writings preceding the *Essay* were often guilty of too much generality, lack of system or excessive difficulty. Avison's work, by contrast, would succeed in explaining the fundamental characteristics of music while maintaining a '*Spectator*-like' tone. Both Malcolm and Lampe had essentially attempted something similar, but the former had gone too far into the technical details of acoustics and composition to reach a large public, while Lampe managed to keep to a popular style only in the first part of his work, relinquishing it as soon as he came to deal with the rules of composition.

Avison would avoid these problems – on the one hand, by choosing the freer form of the essay, a literary genre more suited to popularization than the treatise, and, on the other hand, unlike the arduous texts we have dealt with hitherto, leaving aside all discussion of intervals, scales, consonances and suchlike. Since he is not

---

[37] C. Burney, *A General History of Music. From the Earliest Ages to the Present Period* [1776-1789] (New York, [1935] 1957), vol. II, p. 7. On Avison's influence on his contemporaries see also Roger B. Larson, 'Charles Avison's "Stiles in Musical Expression"', *Music & Letters*, 63/3-4 (1982), pp. 261-275.

[38] As William Weber put it: 'it reads as if it were the notes from a weekend of stimulating conversations' ('The Intellectual Origins of Musical Canon in Eighteenth-Century England', *Journal of the American Musicological Society*, 47/3 (1994), pp. 488-520: 511).

[39] C. Avison, *An Essay on Musical Expression* (London, 1752), anastatic reprint of the edition of 1753 (New York: Broude, 1967), p. xxii.

addressing future composers, he sees no point in furnishing this information. His aim is, rather, to train competent judges and performers attentive to the special properties of the art of music. His work is not an 'Essay on Music', nor does it claim to be an exhaustive study: Avison is concerned to focus attention on what, in his view, is the aspect of composition and performance most directly connected with the effectiveness of music, which he calls 'expression'.

Avison's ability consists in resuming a set of reflections that had already been made in the writings of some of his compatriots, clothing them in more attractive dress. While his predecessors still felt the need to explain and justify each single assertion, Avison was working on ground already tilled and could allow himself to take certain concepts for granted: imagination, internal sense, association of ideas were by now part of a shared and assimilated vocabulary.

The foundations of the art of music: the philosophical background of Charles Avison

In tune with the literature dealt with up to now, Avison starts his essay by reflecting on the cause of the effects music has on man. He credits music with the power to act on the imagination or the passions. Its effect on the imagination is attributed to the use of harmony and melody, while 'when to these is added the force of *Musical Expression*, the effect is greatly increased; for then they assume the power of exciting all the most agreeable passions of the soul'.[40] Although Avison is very synthetic in these remarks, the discussion on the distinction between action on the imagination and on the passions seems to hark back to Joseph Addison's reflection on the primary and secondary pleasures of the imagination, corroborated by reading Hutcheson and Harris.

Firstly, Avison sides with those who attribute the capacity to derive pleasure from beauty to an *internal sense* innate in man and, to denominate it, he employs exactly the same definition as Hutcheson, speaking of an 'internal sense of harmony'. We recall that Hutcheson, in the wake of Addison's remarks on the *Pleasures of the Imagination* published in the *Spectator*, had distinguished between absolute and relative beauty in a close analogy with the distinction between primary and secondary pleasures: in both cases the distinction rests upon the fact that relative beauty, like the secondary pleasures, is connected with a particular operation of the mind: comparison. Note also that both Addison and Hutcheson spoke specifically of music's capacity to excite passions in terms of 'associations' of ideas. As already mentioned in the section on Addison in Chapter 1, in the numbers devoted to the *Pleasures of the Imagination* music is accorded very little space, since Addison's reflection hinges on the sense of sight alone.

In discussing the secondary pleasures of the imagination, however, he does refer to music and argues that the ability of the masters of that art to 'set their

---

40   Ibid., p. 6.

hearers in the heat and hurry of a battle' and thus generate pleasure 'proceeds from that action of the mind, which compares the ideas arising from the original objects, with the ideas we receive from the statue, picture, description, or sound that represents them'.[41] According to Addison, then, the emotional capacity of music is in some way connected with the representation of an idea. Hutcheson, too, had acknowledged the need to explain the power of music to excite passions with a different principle from the internal sense of harmony, devoid of any idea of representation or content, and had suggested that the cause of that capacity lay in the resemblance between the sounds of the instruments and the inflections assumed by the human voice in different circumstances, which would enable the listener to move from one to another by association.

Avison's thought here is clearly indebted to these theories. Melody and harmony – categories that are in no way representative in themselves – are not credited with the capacity to excite emotions. This faculty is attributed instead to *expression*, by means of association and imitation. Avison points to the existence of 'certain sounds natural to joy, others to grief, [...] and by hearing these, we naturally sympathize with those who either enjoy or suffer'.[42] As in Hutcheson, then, musical sounds may enable us to experience 'melancholy, joy, gravity, thoughtfulness excited in us by a sort of *sympathy* or *contagion*'.[43] But the sounds may also be 'imitations':[44]

> Thus music, either by imitating these various sounds in due subordination to the laws of air and harmony, or by any other method of association, bringing the objects of our passions before us (especially when those objects are determined, and made as it were visibly, and intimately present to the imagination by the help of words) does naturally raise a variety of passions in the human breast, similar to the sounds which are expressed [...].

As we shall see, these remarks already suggest that 'expression' and 'imitation' are not opposite concepts in Avison's theory. Indeed, imitation turns out to be one of the possible means of expression.

Expression and imitation

Although the notion of 'musical expression' predates Avison's *Essay*, he can be credited with having highlighted it and investigated it in depth and described its possible applications. Where previous authors had mostly used phrases like 'capacity to excite the passions', 'pathetic action', etc., Avison subsumes the entire

---

[41]   J. Addison, *Spectator*, 416, in *The Works*, vol. III, p. 412.

[42]   C. Avison, *An Essay on Musical Expression*, p. 6.

[43]   F. Hutcheson, *Collected Works of Francis Hutcheson*, vol. I, p. 77 et seq.

[44]   C. Avison, *An Essay on Musical Expression*, p. 6.

sphere of effects that music may have on the human psyche in the concept of 'expression', and this will be further articulated according to whether it refers to composer, performer or individual instrument.

Avison takes his initial cue from the *Discourse on Music, Painting, and Poetry* (1744) by James Harris. In the first section of the *Essay* where Avison pinpoints the concept of *expression*, he pays open tribute to the work by Shaftesbury's nephew. It will be recalled that in the pages devoted to music Harris argued that the effectiveness of musical communication lies in a 'power, which consists not in imitations, and the raising ideas; but in the raising affections, to which ideas may correspond'.[45] Avison insists precisely on this separation between 'ideas', that come under the heading of rationality, and 'passions' that belong within the emotional sphere of man. If the principle of imitation is wrongly applied, the risk will be:[46]

> rather to fix the hearers [*sic*] attention on the similitude between the sounds and the things which they describe, and thereby to excite a reflex act of the understanding, than to affect the heart and raise the passions of the soul.

James Harris had insisted on the fact that poetry and music draw their maximum benefit from mutual support: for music may predispose the listener to receive the ideas conveyed by the poetic content by preparing the mind in advance and tuning it to the emotion most appropriate to the notes of that content. Avison shares this view and develops it. For him, poetry and music must cultivate the respective spheres of influence within a composition: if music is oriented towards a mere aping of the words, its very function is undermined. The composer must attend to the correct balancing of harmony and melody, generating expression from these alone, and must not introduce foreign bodies not consistent with the rest of the piece. This is the kind of imitation Avison rejects, forced imitation that distracts the listener and forgets that music 'obtains its end by raising correspondent affections in the soul with those which ought to result from the genius of the poem'.[47]

In the commentary to the modern edition of Avison's text, these criticisms of a certain conception of 'musical imitation' are seen as 'a decisive step towards granting music its autonomy as an art independent from poetry';[48] but this reading seems a little forced. In reality, the theory of Harris and Avison, rather than proceeding to an outright assertion of the autonomy of music with respect to poetry, confines itself to indicating how they act through different means and on different faculties of man. Music, in virtue of sound and movement, acts on the passions, involving the imagination but without reflection; whereas poetry, by means of its meaningful sound, addresses itself to the intellective faculties.

---

[45]   J. Harris, *The Works of James Harris*, vol. I, p. 58; see above, p. 67.

[46]   C. Avison, *An Essay on Musical Expression*, p. 24.

[47]   Ibid., p. 25.

[48]   Ibid., p. 62, n. 31.

Harris does not deny that music may arouse ideas, through imitation, or that poetry may employ meaningless sound (by onomatopeia, alliteration, and so on) to attain its ends, but he underlines how such cases produce a less effective result. Note how these remarks do not suggest a greater independence between the two arts; rather, they recommend a more discerning, more respectful application in both of them. As we saw in a passage from Harris quoted above, music and poetry are two 'allied' arts, and only in cooperation can they attain their end with maximum efficacy. Nothing could be further from the concept of 'independence' nor from the idea that one art can do without the other: in the theory of both Harris and Avison a dissociation between the two arts cannot but lead to an impoverishment of the aesthetic experience of the listener, who will no longer be enabled to feel that particular pleasure conveyed by the simultaneous arousal of imagination, emotions and rationality.

Avison's major contribution with respect to Harris's theorizing lies in his having added a series of practical indications 'by way of corollary to his theory',[49] that help us to understand better the use of the principles of imitation and expression. The first corollary of Avison, for example, immediately presents some practical spin-offs from the above-cited remarks on poetry and music. If the composition should feature sounds chosen as object of imitation, Avison advises that the imitation be entrusted to the instruments:[50]

> because it is probable, that the imitation will be too powerful in the voice which ought to be engaged in expression alone; or, in other words, in raising correspondent affections with the part. Indeed, in some cases, expression will coincide with imitation, and may then be admitted universally: as in such chromatic strains as are mimetic of the grief and anguish of the human voice.

Whereas if the composer relied on the voice for imitation of the sounds, it could no longer attend to the expression and so the effect of the poetic text would be nullified. As regards certain particular uses of the voice, however, Avison notes that imitation and expression may eventually coincide; which is the case when the sound imitates the object of the expression – that is, man's emotions.

In explaining the use of the artifices available to the composer, Avison establishes a parallel – which also belongs to the current of thought we have examined – between music and the art of oratory. A speech employs numerous rhetorical devices, but the audience must only experience the effects of these, without being aware of them. By the same token, in listening to a piece of music one must not be induced to consider the piece 'from outside' and thus recognize at which point the device of imitation occurs: the listener must be emotionally stimulated without being conscious of the compositional stratagems that make it possible. If the listener pauses to identify the imitation, that means that the

---

[49]   Ibid., p. 25.

[50]   Ibid.

composer has failed in his intent: 'a pompous display of art will destroy its own intentions'.[51]

These same observations also lead to the criticism of virtuosity, which is discussed in the section of the *Essay* devoted to the musical expression required of the performer:[52]

> as musical expression in the composer, is succeeding in the attempt to express some particular passion; so in the performer, it is to do a composition justice, by playing it in a taste and stile so exactly corresponding with the intention of the composer, as to preserve and illustrate all the beauties of his work.

Therefore, as the composer must respect the rules of harmony and the general sense of the text that he clothes in music, so the performer must take pains to bring out the beauty and construction of the piece, expressing not himself but the music. The virtuoso risks making the same mistake as the composer who exaggerates in the display of his own art and, by so doing, distracts the listener from the music to draw attention to his personal mastery. In Avison's view, those who 'strive, rather to surprize, than please the hearer',[53] whether composers or performers, are at fault.

Expression for Avison, then, is the goal at which every composition and performance aims, for the purpose of music remains that of arousing emotions in the human mind – as it was in the thought of his precursors. And in this the Newcastle composer sees no difference between vocal and instrumental music:[54]

> [for] though it is not the advantage of instrumental compositions to be heightened in their expression by the help of words, yet there is generally, or ought to be, some *idea of sense or passion*, besides that of mere sound, conveyed to the hearer: on that account he [the performer] should avoid all extravagant decorations, since every attempt of this kind must utterly destroy whatever passion the composer may have designed to express.

Many are the ways to attain perfect expression, and the author encourages composers to study diligently the works of their predecessors. As a general rule, however, in Avison's theory expression may be said to be linked by a dual connection to an ideal of *consistency*. Consistency in the balance between harmony and melody, in respect for the poetic text, where present, and on the part of the performer vis-à-vis the intentions of the composer:[55]

---

[51] Ibid., p. 28.
[52] Ibid., p. 41.
[53] Ibid., p. 15.
[54] Ibid., p. 51.
[55] Ibid., p. 55.

> how often does the fate of a concerto depend on the random execution of a set
> of performers who have never previously considered the work, examined the
> connection of its parts, or studied the intention of the whole?

In order to be expressive, then, music demands the concurrence of several elements
that must work together in a virtuous manner.

Musical perfection as the ideal combination of knowledge, deed and action

Avison's ideal of music is not confined to distinguishing aesthetic categories. His
reflection on *expression* abounds in implications drawn from areas traditionally
connected with the philosophy of music, moral and pedagogic in particular. The
attainment of perfection in music – that is, to allow full play to expression – entails
a profound mastery of theory and of know-how, but also of correct social action.

With regard to the last-named, Avison is at pains to emphasize the traditional
ethical value of the art of music. In line with the theories of Hutcheson and
Harris, he sees the arousal of emotions 'of the benevolent and social kind'[56] as
a characteristic peculiar to music, and it is important for him that this power be
perceived by and act upon the masters themselves of the art:[57]

> in truth, there is nothing enlarges the mind to every social and laudable purpose,
> so much as this delightful intercourse with harmony. They who feel not this
> divine effect, are strangers to its noblest influence: for whatever pretensions they
> may otherwise have to a relish or knowledge of its laws, without this criterion
> of the musical soul, all other pretended signatures of genius we may look upon
> as counterfeit.

This emphasis on the social dimension of music, along with his own practice
as music teacher, leads Avison to focus in an original way on certain aspects of the
study of composition by the performer. In compositions for several instruments,
the individual performers normally studied only their own parts from the sheet
music. But Avison urged the study of the piece as a whole, which led him to
demand that his *Concerti* be printed in full score. As we saw, expression requires a
knowledge of how the various parts interweave, and therefore an understanding of
the composition in its entirety: study of the individual parts alone impairs correct
instrumental playing, such that 'in all compositions for instruments in parts, which
are published in separate books, and seldom perused in score, most performers are
frequently at a loss, to know the composer's design'.[58]

---

56   Ibid., p. 6.
57   Ibid., p. 42.
58   Ibid., p. 53.

However, since the use of scores was costly and required more complicated printing, he devised a corrective for better use of the individual parts. This consisted in the insertion of a new musical sign – a sort of √ – called 'mostra', to be set above the first note of each musical subject, indicating the beginning of a phrase.[59]

The concerto is the musical genre with which Avison is most concerned and which he himself cultivated. It bears unmistakable witness to the need for a marriage between the spheres we have called 'knowledge', 'deed' and 'action'. From the composer's point of view, the concerto demands not only a careful balance between melody and harmony, but also full acquaintance with the expressive possibilities of each instrument, as well as a knowledge of the different styles of composition best suited to the eventual context of the music (especially regarding the distinction between *concerto da chiesa* and *concerto da camera*). The composer must therefore be the first to 'harmonize' the various components of musical composition in order to attain the desired end. The ideal of the composition's being consistent within itself has a spin-off for teaching: Avison instructs future instrumentalists that the study of the score is essential for a correct performance, and this conviction leads him to invent a specific symbol to guide the players in their understanding of the piece. In addition, the concerto supplies a virtuous example of a mode of social relation, basing itself on an integration and mutual valorization between *solo* and *ripieno*.

Avison's intention that the *Essay* should also reach the extensive area of amateur musicians is revealed in an interesting remark of his on the performance of ensemble music. After insisting that the aim of the kind of concerto described is 'to give a grand effect by uniting many', he pinpoints a particular type of pleasure that the performer may derive from having a limited role within the group of players:[60]

> nor let any lover of music be concerned if there is but little for him to execute, since he will thence have some leisure for the pleasure of hearing: for this reason, the under parts in good compositions are more ellgible to the performer, who would rather enjoy the whole than be distinguished alone.

This remark, together with the emphasis – in the concept of 'expression' – laid on cooperation between composer and performer, reflects the value attributed by Avison to music's social dimension as an art 'constructed together' and demanding understanding and respect for one's own role from all those involved.

---

[59]   An expedient similar to those adopted by composers of the Second Viennese School, like the 'H' (*Hauptstimme*) used to designate the principle phrase.

[60]   Ibid., p. 49.

Conclusions

Perhaps it may now have become clearer how the writings of musical theory were able to exploit the philosophical and aesthetic theories elaborated in the seventeenth and eighteenth centuries. The connection between musical knowledge and human nature described in these pages ranges from the use of the philosophy of mind to justify certain aspects of the perception of music to a theory of ensemble performance as a virtuous model of social relationship. In the case of Malcolm, moreover, it is of interest to note how he links the luxuriant production of instrumental music in his time with the characteristics of contemporary man. In this perspective, the widespread appreciation of instrumental music is intimately connected with the transformation of man through the centuries: in an epoch in which the operations of the mind and its activity were held in such high consideration, an art that succeeds in satisfying the mind and the imaginative capacity becomes the example of a form of beauty – 'intellectual beauty', exactly commensurate with the characteristics of modern man.

Chapter 4
Music and history

The generation in which there is no desire to know more or practice better than its predecessors, will probably neither know so much, nor practice so well.

ADAM FERGUSON, Principles of Moral and Political Science

As stated previously, the aim of this chapter is to focus on how the discipline of music history was conceived and organized in eighteenth-century England. In this perspective the *General History of the Science and Practice of Music* (1776) of Sir John Hawkins and Charles Burney's *General History of Music* (1776-89) provide two sources of especial interest: they are the first two modern histories of music in English,[1] and the task they set themselves is a gigantic one – namely, to summarize, document and organize more than two thousand years of musical history. Here our procedure cannot be to offer an analytical account of all the themes and contents of the two histories, but will confine itself to examining their conceptual bases.

Hawkins's and Burney's texts are entirely similar yet, at the same time, different. The material is the same, as is a great part of the sources on which they draw, but there is a fundamental difference that lies in divergent visions of the aim of the historiographic task, the nature of musical knowledge and the concept of progress.[2] Investigation into how these basic concepts influence the organization of the two works assists in "unveiling" the perspectives in which Hawkins and Burney start out. But that is not all. As we said, a procedure of this kind may also help towards critical reflection on the horizon from which we ourselves set out in formulating hypotheses on the nature of musical historiography. For, the

---

[1]   With the exception of the brief historical account given at the end of the *Treatise of Musick, Speculative, Practical and Historical* (1721) by Alexander Malcolm and the *Memoires of Musick* (1728) by Roger North, though both these works evidence different features from those of Hawkins and Burney and are much more limited attempts. An even earlier (c. 1576), and mostly unacknowledged, 'history of music' in English can be found in *The Autobiography of Thomas Whythorne*, ed. James M. Osborn (Oxford, 1961), pp. 222-248.

[2]   In this connection, I must say that I do not agree with William Weber's statement that: 'Hawkins and Burney [...] had a great deal in common in their sense of what music history should be about. They both attacked the tradition of studying the music of the antiquity; rejected the idea of imitation; and argued that music history, indeed musical learning, must be made independent of *belles letters* and scientific theory' (Weber, 'The Intellectual Origins of Musical Canon in Eighteenth-Century England', p. 514). As I hope will be clear from what follows, I firmly believe that the two historians of music had a very different idea of 'what music history should be about'.

application of a form of *Horizontabhebung* (differentiation of horizon)[3] in order to understand, at least in part, the different perspective of the two eighteenth-century historians also compels us to view contemporary historiography in a new framework. To discover that the 'history of music' was *thought* in a way very different from the one familiar to us also means that there may still be various ways of conceiving it in the future: comparison of the perspective from which it sets out today with those of the past can reveal many of the cultural concepts that underpin it and of which we are not always aware.

An important cue for reflection for what follows comes from the essays of Arnaldo Momigliano on the birth of modern history writing, and from studies by scholars who have pursued the argument.[4] One datum that emerges very clearly from reading the literature on eighteenth-century historiography and the musicological literature on Hawkins's and Burney's histories of music is the total absence of dialogue between the two literatures. Although current history of history writing has extended its focus to sources such as the British novel, and even to works on gardening,[5] one may search in vain there for citations, let alone discussion, of the work of Hawkins and Burney. Likewise, in the musicological literature on the two authors I have been unable to find anything that connects with the ongoing argument that raged among writers, historians and scholars in the serventeenth and eighteenth centuries in the attempt to work out a new historical method.[6]

This chapter aims to highlight the advantages of integrating the two literatures. In addressing their particular targets, historians of musical historiography should not sidestep the general historiographic context. In particular, the two texts here discussed display several of the characteristics described in Momigliano's study,

---

[3]   The concept of *Horizontabhebung* has been elaborated by Hans Robert Jauss in a critique of Hans Georg Gadamer's idea of *Horizontverschmelzung* (fusion of horizons). Together with the concepts of *Horizontwandel* (change of horizon) and *Erwartungshorizont* (horizon of expectation), it aims to escape from the state of passivity in the face of tradition as implied by Gadamer's method. (See H. R. Jauss, *Literaturgeschichte als Provokation der Litteraturwissenschaft* (Frankfurt am Main, 1967) and *Ästhetische Erfahrung und literarische Hermeneutik* (Frankfurt am Main, 1982).

[4]   For example, Momigliano's essay 'Ancient History and the Antiquarian', and Mark Salber Phillips, 'Reconsiderations on History and Antiquarianism: Arnaldo Momigliano and the Historiography of Eighteenth-Century Britain', *Journal of the History of Ideas*, 57/2 (1996), pp. 297-316. For an overview of the historical debate in eighteenth-century Scotland, see Murray G. H. Pittock, 'Historiography', in A. Broadie (ed.), *The Cambridge Companion to the Scottish Enlightenment* (Cambridge, 2003), pp. 258-279.

[5]   For example, the essay by Rebecca Bushnell, 'Experience, truth, and natural history in early English gardening books', in D. R. Kelly and D. H. Sacks (eds), *The Historical Imagination in Early Modern Britain. History, Rhetoric, and Fiction, 1500-1800* (Cambridge, 1997), pp. 179-209.

[6]   The most significant fruits of which included the *Allgemeine Geschichtswissenschaft* of J. M. Chladenius (1752) and the historical writings of Winckelmann and Gibbon.

and it will be interesting to reread them while bearing in mind the debates on eighteenth-century history writing.

Historians ascribe especial importance to the argument, that arose in the seventeenth century and continued in the eighteenth, between Pyrrhonists and anti-Pyrrhonists in working out a new historical method[7]. And it is in the light of this debate that Momigliano interprets the importance in that period of antiquarians, who 'by collecting much of their evidence outside the literary sources, helped to make the need for new histories apparent'.[8] The study of iconographic, numismatic and archaeological evidence did indeed serve to stem historical scepticism.[9]

Historical Pyrrhonism and antiquarian research: the music of the Ancients in Burney and Hawkins

Antiquarian evidence was, however, of no help in cases where there was no material testimony to support the accounts deriving from the sources. Music offers an emblematic instance of this, as may be imagined – especially as regards the music of the Ancients, where the sole evidence available to historians and scholars stemmed from literary sources. For that matter, ancient history itself – and especially that of ancient Rome – lay at the centre of the argument over historical evidence in the France of the 1720s,[10] and the numerous discussions on

---

[7]　See the excellent study by Carlo Borghero, *La certezza e la storia. Cartesianesimo, pirronismo e conoscenza storica* (Milan, 1983). The term 'Pyrrhonism' harks back to the figure of Pyrrho of Elis (c. 365-275 BC), described by his disciple Timon of Phlius. Pyrrho's philosophy hinged on the idea that sensations and opinions could not be considered either true or false. Rereading of Pyrrho's theses led to the development of scepticism, so that in speaking of 'Pyrrhonism' we are referred to the sceptical position. Note, however, that scepticism and Pyrrhonism cannot be assimilated to relativism – currently much debated – inasmuch as the latter holds that there are no absolute values, but that everyone has the right to recognize their own truth, valid for themselves. Scepticism, instead, effects an *epoché*, a suspension of judgement, in cases where it is held to be impossible to decide whether a proposition is true or not.

[8]　A. Momigliano, 'Ancient History and the Antiquarian', p. 79.

[9]　Extreme cases of this included the attempt to employ mathematical method to elaborate a system of 'certification of historical reliability': the Scottish mathematician John Craig published two interesting works in 1699, *A calculation of Credibility of Human Testimony* (*Philosophical Transactions*, XXI) and *Theologiae Christianae Principia Mathematica*. In these he used probability calculus in order to study in quantitative terms the gradual loss of reliability of oral and written traditions (see C. Borghero, *La certezza e la storia*, pp. 195-201).

[10]　Between 1722 and 1725, at the Académie Royale des Inscriptions et Belles Lettres there was a fierce dispute following the reading of the *Dissertation sur l'incertitude des quatre premiers siècles de Rome* (1722) by Jean Levesque de Pouilly; see Borghero, *La certezza e la storia*, pp. 357-390.

the nature of the music of Antiquity may be considered as having acquired a new significance between the seventeenth and eighteenth centuries in the light of that argument. Hence the writings on the subject should not be viewed merely as part of the dispute with the 'Moderns'; rather, in the attempt to define the nature and mode of ancient music, the argument should also be seen as part of the discussion on the possibility of reconstructing the practices of the Ancients with some degree of certainty.

This hypothesis is confirmed, fortunately, by Charles Burney himself in the preface to the *General History of Music*. As we know, he was initially reluctant to include the music of the Ancients in his treatment and had thought of starting with Guido d'Arezzo.[11] Thereafter he was convinced that the subject must be addressed, persuaded by the fact that in his time there was no history of music that did not start out from Greek antiquity.[12]

In the brief introduction to the *General History*, Burney feels it his duty to vindicate his own approach to the music of the Ancients, and his opening words express utter discomfort in regard to the possibility of reconstructing its history: 'concerning the music of the Greeks and Romans, about which *the learned* talk so much, it is *impossible* to speak with certainty'[13]. That this statement is not merely an aside but expresses a sort of historical 'credo' is confirmed when, shortly after, he quotes the motto of one of the leading exponents of French Pyrrhonism, François La Mothe Le Vayer (1588-1672): 'de las cosas mas seguras, la mas segura es dudar'.[14] In the second half of the seventeenth century La Mothe Le Vayer had written some important works on historical method, the most celebrated of which is the *Discours du peu de certitude qu'il y a dans l'histoire* (1668), but he was also responsible for an essay on music, *Discours sceptique sur la Musique* (1634), addressed to Mersenne. This text is a rich and lively dissertation on the impossibility of stating anything about the music of the Ancients. La Mothe Le Vayer begins by enumerating in detail the evidence for the famous *mirabilia* of ancient music, deals with the music of the spheres and all the *topoi* connected with the art of sounds, then proceeds to cite, with no particular enthusiasm, an abundant mass of authors who maintain the exact opposite to the former ones. The irony

---

[11]   As evidenced by Burney's *General Plan* of the *History* in the possession of Padre Martini and kept in the Civico Museo Bibliografico Musicale at Bologna.

[12]   With regard to the pursuit of this change of plan, we cannot underestimate the relevance of Burney's contacts with the learned Padre Martini from Bologna; see Howard Brofsky, 'Doctor Burney and Padre Martini: Writing a General History of Music', *The Musical Quarterly*, 65 (1979), pp. 313-345.

[13]   Burney, *A General History of Music*, vol. I, p. 14 (my italics).

[14]   Ibid., p. 17: 'Of all safe courses,the safest is to doubt'. This motto, which recalls a well-known Spanish proverb, appears at the end of La Mothe le Vayer's *Cinq Dialogues faits à l'imitation des anciens, par Horatius Tubero* (published posthumously in 1698).

reserved for certain *loci classici* in the reflections on the music of the Greeks is withering:[15]

> On n'avance rien à la recommandation de la Musique, qui soit plus ridicule, il me semble, que cette étendüe qu'on lui donne par tous les ordres de la Nature. Témoin la mélodie celeste qu'on veut avoir été entendue par Pythagore, qui en faisoit après leçon à ses disciples. En ces cas on pourroit esperer, que comme on a inventé depuis peu les telescopes, ou lunettes à longue vüe, qui nous ont fait voir dans le Ciel de nouvelles Etoiles qui seroient autrement invisibles: on pourroit aussi trouver la fabrique de quelque instrument Otacouste, propre à entendre cette harmonie resultante du mouvement reglé des Astres & de leurs Globes.

> [Nothing more ridiculous can be advanced in favour of Music, it seems to me, than to interpret it according to all the orders of Nature. As witness the celestial melody that is supposed to have been heard by Pythagoras, who taught it as a lesson to his disciples. In such cases, one might hope that, as telescopes or great magnifying lenses have recently been invented and have enabled us to see new stars in the heavens that would otherwise be invisible ; so one might also devise some audible instrument in order to hear that harmony that results from the orderly movement of the stars and their globes.]

Whether Burney also read this little work by La Mothe Le Vayer we do not know,[16] but his stance certainly seems to be close to that of the French sceptic, both in his attitude towards the "fables" of the Ancients and in his conception of history writing. In the section of the *General History* devoted to the 'History of Greek Music', in what regards the music of the spheres Burney is lapidary: 'it is equally to the credit and advantage of Music and Philosophy, that they have long descended from these heights, and taken their proper and separate station upon *earth*: that we no longer admit of Music that cannot be *heard*, or of Philosophy that cannot be *understood*'.[17]

It is interesting to note that, in seeking to justify his discussion of the music of the Ancients, Burney asserts that it 'has now become the business of an Antiquary more than a Musician'.[18] What does he mean by this statement? As Momigliano

---

[15]   François La Mothe Le Vayer, *Œuvres* (Geneva, 1970), vol. II, p. 247. The *Discours sceptique sur la Musique* was first published in Marin Mersennes's *Questions inouïes* (1634) in the section entitled *Questions Harmoniques*.

[16]   Burney may have viewed this text, for example, on the occasion of his visit to Padre Martini, whose library included a miscellany volume containing, among other things, the *Compendium Musicae* of Descartes, a work by Jacob Spon and the *Discours* of La Mothe Le Vayer.

[17]   Burney, *A General History of Music*, vol. I, p. 346.

[18]   Ibid., p. 16.

has shown,[19] the distinction between historians and antiquarians is often no simple matter, but at least two criteria may help to differentiate them. The first of these concerns the *form* they give their own works. A historian will arrange the material in a chronological order, an antiquarian in a largely systematic order. The second criterion comes from the type of interest informing the work. Momigliano wonderfully illustrates in a few words what he understands by 'antiquary', defining him as 'the kind of person who is interested in historical facts without being interested in history'.[20] The antiquarian is a scholarly figure who spends his life among papers and takes pleasure in research as such, he is eclectic in the full sense of the word since the objects of his study need have no connection between them, and the works he produces are brimful of the most extravagant detail and data. How different from the historian 'à la Burney'! As Burney himself says: 'I would rather be pronounced trivial than tiresome'.[21] His prime purpose in the *General History* is to entertain, *instruere* is subordinate to *delectare*, exactly as in the history of La Mothe Le Vayer, where the history writing is conceived as *opus maxime oratorium*. Burney takes pride in not making 'a vain display of erudition',[22] and in never being pedantic: pride of place in his history belongs neither to music nor to musicians but to the readers and what they expect from the historian.[23]

In the light of this exquisitely 'aesthetic' conception of the *General History*, which adopts the viewpoint of the reader, we can appreciate the character of the *Dissertation on the Music of the Ancients* placed at the head of the work. Burney states: 'I shall consider the music of the ancient Greeks under such heads only as absolutely concern Music, *according to our acceptation of the word*'.[24] His concern is not to probe a historical fact which antiquity, in any case, cannot provide for us, and clearly the exact 'nature' of ancient 'music' cannot be an important question. Burney is not interested in ancient history as such nor, therefore, in offering his

---

[19]   Arnaldo Momigliano, 'The Rise of Antiquarian Research', in his *The Classical Foundations of Modern Historiography*, pp. 54-79.

[20]   Ibid., p. 54.

[21]   Burney, *A General History of Music*, vol. I, p. 19.

[22]   Ibid. It must also be added that, as Burney himself admits, he was enabled to do this because, if need be, he could always refer more curious readers to the works of reference compiled by the 'antiquaries' and because he himself, as far as the music of the Ancients was concerned, could count on the generous assistance given him by Thomas Twining.

[23]   Indeed, Burney seems to have succeeded in his endeavours, as he appears to have gained attention and praise from Samuel Johnson – a notoriously un-musical man; see Miss Reynold's recall in her *Recollections of Dr Johnson*: 'an observation I remember to have heard him make, when expatiating in praise of Dr. Burney's history of music – "That that work evidently proved that the author understood the Philosophy of music better than any man who had ever written on the subject"' (cited in Katharine C. Balderston, 'Dr Johnson and Burney's History of Music', *PMLA*, 49/3 (1934), p. 967).

[24]   Burney, *A General History of Music*, vol. I, p. 23 (my italics).

readers a 'fully rounded' representation of it. What counts is the concept of the music 'of today' and how it is understood. This, in essence, is what he means by the opening words of his preface: 'the feeble beginnings of whatever afterwards becomes great or eminent, are interesting to mankind',[25] where it is clear that the first steps in the manifestations of this human craft are of interest to us only inasmuch as they foreshadow the great things of our own time.

The difference in Hawkins's formulation of musical history set beside Burney's can be evinced both by the structure and the nature of the 'detours' it makes: here we are dealing with a properly antiquarian work and thus, in the course of a discussion of the ancient treatises of Harmonica, we find a reference to Vitruvius leading to seven close-printed columns describing the water organ!

How does Hawkins's antiquarian interest bear on his discussion of the music of the Ancients? Firstly, I think, with regard to the diversity of a distant tradition from that of the Moderns. Hawkins recognizes the gap between the ancient concept of music and the contemporary one, but unlike Burney he is not concerned to exclude from his history those elements that may bring home a sense of that alien nature to his readers. In his work priority is not assigned to the reader but to History. Thus towards the end of his account of ancient music he states:[26]

> from the foregoing extracts a judgement may be formed, not only of the work from which they are made, but also of the manner in which the ancients, more especially the followers of Pythagoras, thought of music.

While Hawkins, too, rules out the possibility of reconstructing, based on the scant evidence at our disposal, any precise idea of how ancient music 'really was', he differs from Burney in asserting that we may, however, always try to understand how music was *conceived* by the Ancients.[27]

As we shall see in the next section, this theoretical interest of Hawkins has its importance and explains why he did not confine himself to writing a *History of Music* but dealt with the 'Science of Music'. And what is the latter if not a form of musicology *ante literam*, before *Musikwissenschaft*?

A forgotten 'Science of Music': the musicology conceived by Sir John Hawkins

Although Sir John Hawkins's history of music is well-known and often quoted, there appears to be little familiarity with its detail. To be sure, readers of today

---

[25] Ibid., p. 11.

[26] Sir John Hawkins, *A General History of the Science and Practice of Music* (Graz, 1969; facsimile reprint of the London 1875 edition), vol. I, p. 124 (book III, chap. xxvi).

[27] A similar concern for the judgment upon music of the ancient times is showed by Roger North in his *Memoires*.

may, like those before them, be daunted by its size and its lack of any index or table of the numerous chapter headings in its twenty volumes. The structure of the text is hard to make out: the author follows an arrangement that mixes the chronological plan with the systematic one, often not very effectively.[28] In general, the most discomforting element in Hawkins's work from the chronological point of view is that the author frequently reports the judgements of later writers on older theories, reconstructing disputes that arose thereafter. Classic treatment of the 'fate' of the authors clashes with historical narrative, compelling the reader to jump back and forth in time.[29] The systematic arrangement turns firstly on the distinction of musical genres and often, though not always, on the nations where these are cultivated. Then he scans the state of music in Great Britain in each epoch. Here again, this mode of proceeding may lead Hawkins astray from the topics from which he set out. For example, Book Five of the *General History* starts with the reception of the Guidonian system in England, follows the traces of sacred music a little way, then jumps to Provençal song and thence to the genres of secular music. At one point, the author diverges into a reflection on the existing connection between musical practice and the conditions of life and society in individual epochs; and this, in turn, leads him to an excursus, first on Boccaccio and then on Chaucer, as sources for understanding the way of life in the fourteenth century. Hawkins continues on this track for nearly ten pages, with extensive quotations from authors – in particular, the mid-fourteenth century *De proprietatibus rerum* by the Franciscan friar Bartholomaeus Glantville – that illustrate family structure and the tasks and conditions of men, women and children in the fourteenth and fifteenth centuries. The shift from these topics to the invention of *cantus mensurabilis* may be confusing for a reader in search of coherence, even if this method of Hawkins's, often proceeding by mere analogy or association, undeniably results in a notable wealth of documentation.

Unlike Burney, Hawkins provides a full introduction running through twenty-two densely printed pages. As we shall see, this introduction comprises a goodly part of the discussions on the arts ongoing at the time, and we will encounter many of the topics dealt with in the first part of our work. It is within this context that Hawkins addresses the problem of defining the 'Science of Music'. At the very outset of his introduction he projects us into a quite different perspective from that of Burney: his first concern, indeed, is to place his discussion of musical tradition within reflections on the faculties of the human mind solicited by the arts – which

---

[28]   A more successful instance of combining the two ways of writing history is Robert Henry's *History of Great Britain* (1771-1793), where an arrangement by themes is enclosed within the chronological plan. Henry proceeds from age to age in distinct sections dealing with political, cultural and economic history, and this arrangement is explained right from the start of the work and plainly emerges from the paragraph headings.

[29]   For example, in dealing with Johannes de Muris and *musica mensurabilis* we find ourselves discussing the errors found in it in the *Histoire de la Musique et ses Effets* (Paris, 1715) of Bonnet and Bourdelot.

received ample treatment in the first half of our work. Pleasure, imagination, beauty, imitation and expression are the first terms encountered here. Initially, Hawkins addresses the 'pleasures of the imagination', of what kind they are and which are the arts that relay them. Hawkins's references in this connection seem to be above all to James Harris (who is explicitly cited) and to Francis Hutcheson. With regard to the former, Hawkins harks back in particular to his argument that music diverges from painting and poetry in respect of the role played in them by imitation. The efficacy of painting and poetry may be ascribed to imitation, but music is a different matter.[30] Just at this point, however, Hawkins veers away from Harris's argument. For, while Harris had emphasized sympathy and association of ideas in explaining the efficacy of music, Hawkins takes up an argument of Hutchesonian kind:[31]

> in music there is little beyond itself to which we need, or indeed can, refer to heighten its charms. If we investigate the principles of harmony, we learn that they are general and universal; and of harmony itself, that the proportions in which it consists are to be found in those material forms, which are beheld with the greatest pleasure, the sphere, the cube, and the cone, for instance, and constitute what we call symmetry, beauty, and regularity; but the imagination receives no additional delight; our reason is exercised in the operation, and that faculty alone is thereby gratified.

Since the effects of music do not derive from the mimetic principle, it has no need to seek justification outside itself; the pleasure it conveys is founded in nature. And whereas in Harris this natural foundation was to be sought in the modern psychology of the mind, Hawkins prefers to remain anchored to the ancient tradition of music linked with the concept of 'harmony'.

While Hawkins's first concern is to identify the foundation of musical pleasure, his second is to define the object of his history: how to determine the knowledge that goes by the name of 'Science of Music'? And right here, in the reply to this question, we can glimpse a project of 'musicology' that antedates by a long way the 'classic' foundation of Adler.

Hawkins sites his reflection along the path traced by Sir Francis Bacon in the *Advancement of Learning* (1605). Bacon divided universal knowledge into three large kinds, each regarding a specific faculty of the mind: historical knowledge, connected with memory; poetic knowledge, connected with imagination; and philosophical knowledge, connected with reason. Historical knowledge was further divided into natural and civil; and civil history, which deals with the works and acts of mankind, was further divided into ecclesiastical and literary. Literary

---

[30]   See above p. 66 et seq.

[31]   Sir J. Hawkins, *A General History of the Science and Practice of Music*, vol. I, p. xx.

history is the branch of knowledge in which Hawkins places the 'Science of Music'.

Writing at the start of the seventeenth century, Bacon complained of how *literary history* was the historical sector least cultivated, which made history equal to 'the statue of Polyphemus, without its eye; the part that best shows the life and spirit of the person'.[32] To Bacon's way of thinking, then, literary history is the noblest and most representative part of the entire edifice under the rule of memory. Among the several tasks of that branch of knowledge, Bacon awards the highest places to what we should nowadays call 'compilative' tasks ('what particular kinds of learning and arts flourished, in what ages, and in what part of the world; their antiquities, progress, and travels on the globe; their decline, disappearance, and restoration'). Secondly, each art must be described in terms of 'its origins and occasion of invention; the manner or form of its delivery; the means of its introduction, exercise, and establishment'; then the different schools must be illustrated, the discussions narrated, but above all, Bacon specifies, 'let events be throughout coupled with their causes (which is the soul, as it were, of civil history')'.[33] Literary history, therefore, must not confine itself to narrating or reconstructing events, it must interpret them and try to investigate their causes.

As we noted, in Hawkins the 'Science of Music' is a pre-eminently historical discipline, the study of which he subdivides into four main categories:

1. writings that retrace the principles of musical science to the investigation of mathematical proportions;
2. writings addressed to the practice of music;
3. writings aiming at the physical investigation of sound;
4. writings of a literary character in which music is discussed (Dryden, Sir William Temple and Milton are among those cited).

One of the aims of the discipline, which he thinks has not received sufficient attention, is to enquire into the principles of music, as witnessing how it may be 'worthy the exercise of our rational as well as audible faculties': all of which must be directed towards the study 'of its greatest excellence, its influence on human minds'.[34] The 'Science of Music' is, then, characterized by an interest in both practice and theory, towards the rational faculties and the sense of hearing, taking account of the treatises, as of what we would now call 'literary criticism'. Strange as it may seem to the present-day reader, the *History of the Science and Practice of Music* is least of all a history of 'works of music'. For the most part, it is a history of musical science, a biographical history of musicians and composers,

---

32   Sir F. Bacon, *Of the Proficience and Advancement of Learning* (London, 1605), book II, p. 7.

33   Ibid.

34   Sir J. Hawkins, *A General History of the Science and Practice of Music*, p. xxiii.

and a compendium of a great many sources – for Hawkins often supplies indexes of the treatises he quotes, summarizes them and reproduces large extracts.

So convinced is Hawkins of the importance of musical-theoretical speculation that it underpins his praise of the art of sound. Musical encomia, he says, already overflow with tales of the effect of music on humankind, as on animals; in addition to the pleasure humans derive from this art, Hawkins desires to celebrate the satisfaction gained from studying it. The fact that it hinges on principles 'as clearly demonstrable as mathematical truth'[35] renders it superior to many other disciplines that have themselves been investigated in depth by much of humanity. Hawkins compares musical science to theology, jurisprudence, medicine and the other liberal arts, and argues that these last resemble the art of memory, which is known not to be based on natural principles but created by ourselves, 'widely differing from those which are the basis as well of musical as mathematical science'.[36] This emphasis laid on the certain and immutable basis of the art of sound leads Hawkins to criticize one of the aesthetic criteria in vogue in the eighteenth century – namely, the 'novelty' so much lauded also by Addison in the *Pleasures of Imagination*. Since music can be founded on solid principles, Hawkins wonders why 'novelty in music should be its best recommendation; or that the love of variety should so possess the generality of the hearers, as almost to leave it a question whether or no it has any principles at all'.[37]

Hawkins underlines how the principles of musical harmony afford ample room for fantasy to range and how, at least in principle, the imaginative arts and the human mind interact in a way that should enable artists to rely on the ability of the public to appreciate the value of their works. Yet at this point Hawkins shifts to a darker note, affirming the inequality among people and asserting that the effects of music are only perceptible to those[38]

> whom nature has endowed with the faculty which it is calculated to delight; and [...] a privation of that sense, which, superadded to the hearing, is ultimately affected by the harmony of musical sounds, must disable many [...] from receiving that gratification in music which others experience.

Unlike the philosophers he has evidently read, our author does not hold that all men have the same faculties. The differences among individuals that were justified by Locke, Hutcheson and Hume on the basis of experience, education and habit, Hawkins sees as a natural datum; he is perfectly aware that this is his own opinion and he supports it by the religious concept of 'blessing'. Possession, or lack of possession, of the faculty of full enjoyment of music is therefore a 'gift', and this may be the reason why, in his introduction, Hawkins appears to favour an

---

[35]   Ibid., p. xxxvii.

[36]   Ibid.

[37]   Ibid.

[38]   Ibid., p. xxxviii.

'informative' role for history, viewing the latter as a store of documents rather than as having a possibly educative function.

'Sonata' replies to Fontenelle: Charles Burney's *Essay on Musical Criticism*

Burney's work consists of four books, but it is not until the second of these that he employs the locution *General History of Music*. The first book, which covers the historical period preceding Guido d'Arezzo – a period Burney had initially decided to ignore – is titled 'Dissertation on the Music of the Ancients'. It deals with the music of the Egyptians, Jews, Greeks and Romans, and concludes with a chapter on the construction and use of the musical instruments of the Ancients. Book Two begins with *cantus firmus* and arrives at the mid-sixteenth century. Book Three, which starts the period of musical history closest to Burney's heart – from the mid-sixteenth century to the music of his time – opens surprisingly with an 'Essay on Musical Criticism' and ends with the death of Purcell. As we shall shortly see, the title 'Essay on Musical Criticism' sounds a little pretentious, consisting as it does of a mere five pages. It is, however, significant that Burney should have felt it his duty to find room for this topic. We know how in his work he insisted above all on meeting his readers' expectations and we may therefore see his reflections on criticism as witness to the extent to which these observations had their roots in the collective consciousness. The last book, too, commences with an 'Essay' on a highly topical subject – namely, the 'musicality' of national languages; whereas the remaining pages are almost entirely devoted to the opera genre and end with an account of the current state of the art in Italy, Germany, France and England.

Although, as we have seen in the previous chapters, the literature of 'musical criticism' in eighteenth-century England was fairly developed, the only source quoted by Burney on the subject is the treatise by Avison; he deals only briefly with this reference both here and in Book Four of the *General History*, where it belongs in the chronology. The main reason for such scant consideration would seem to be a divergence between Avison's musical taste and his own: note how Burney loses no opportunity to criticize Avison's opinion of Handel (too severe) and Benedetto Marcello (too generous).[39]

Though the discourse of the 'Essay on Musical Criticism' is rather tortuous and sometimes leads Burney to contradict himself, a basic idea emerges clearly: according to Burney, the critic must be familiar with practice, otherwise he who is unable to 'do' will be unable to 'judge':[40]

---

[39]   This criticism is particularly revealing of Burney's obsequious attitude towards public sensibility: we know, in fact, that in private his judgement of Handel was less kindly than he makes it seem in the *General History*; see K. S. Grant, *Dr Burney as Critic and Historian of Music*, pp. 286-290.

[40]   C. Burney, *A General History of Music*, vol. II, p. 11.

and who can judge of the originality of the composition, its fitness for the instrument, or degree of praise due to the performer, but those who have either studied composition, practised the same instrument, or heard an infinite variety of Music and great performers of the same kind?

It is noteworthy that he includes listening in the framework of musical *practice*: auditive familiarity with music, then, can do duty for the competence deriving from executive practice. And, indeed, Burney laments how the studies in musical criticism lack any works that may teach the 'ignorant lovers of Music how to listen, or to judge for themselves'[41]. His reflections on the matter, however, are not of great help. Even in specifying the ingredients of musical composition he muddles compositive elements and aesthetic criteria, placing on one and the same level 'melody, harmony, modulation, invention, grandeur, fire, pathos, taste, grace and expression'.[42]

In establishing the object of musical criticism, Burney makes a summary division between two types of pleasure. The Fine Arts, when produced by genius and passion, excite a form of enthusiasm 'beyond the reach of cold criticism',[43] but music also conveys a second, more moderate form of pleasure that appeals both to the senses and to the intellect: it is the analysis of this pleasure that constitutes the object of *musical criticism*. After what we have read in the first part of this work, it will be useful to emphasize the shallowness and imprecision of this distinction between pleasures. Of more interest, on the other hand, is the fact that Burney lays stress on pleasure. We have seen how the reflection on music in the area of philosophy focused attention largely on the *effects* of the art of sound. Physicists, doctors and philosophers are concerned with determining the *causes* of these effects and seek them in the human mind or body, accordingly as they espouse a psychological or mechanical view of the action of music.

The historian Burney and the antiquarian Hawkins show that they are not alien to this mode of thought. Indeed, the opening remarks of Hawkins's preface deal with the 'pleasures of imagination', while Burney, when he comes to define the object of musical criticism, shows that he is thinking of the *effect*, the pleasure, before the work itself. Obviously the work is present to him, but it interests him not per se, but rather in virtue of the response it arouses in the listener.

Towards the end of the 'Essay on Musical Criticism', he provides further confirmation of the foregoing, making the work of music 'speak'. He quotes Fontenelle's famous question, relayed by Rousseau in the *Dictionnaire de*

---

[41]   Ibid., p. 7 et seq. This remark of Burney's shows how he ascribed an educative function to the criticism of the arts, whereas in Hawkins, as we have seen, this was ruled out by the latter's conviction of a natural inequality among men.

[42]   Ibid., p. 8.

[43]   Ibid., p. 7.

Musique, 'Sonate, que me veux tu?' and imagines a reply by the 'Sonata' to this question, as follows:[44]

> I would have you listen with attention and delight to the ingenuity of the composition, the neatness of execution, sweetness of the melody, and the richness of the harmony, as well as to the charms of refined tones, lengthened and polished into passion.

Sonata requests that the listening be first of all empathetic, that it mark the sweetness of the tones, their charm, the passions that it excites: more than analysis, it demands attentive, involved listening.

'Unluckily for Purcell!': Charles Burney and the progressive fate of musical material

Burney's history of music is dominated by a *linear* concept of progress. Eighteenth-century histories are replete with typical titles on the model '*of the rise, progress and decay*',[45] governed by a *cyclical* idea of the advancement of human knowledge – as in Lord Bacon[46] so in Sir John Hawkins. Merely to scan the chapter titles of Burney's third and fourth volumes is to see a continuous alternation of those on the 'State of Music' and the 'Progress of Music'. The idea of decadence or 'corruption' does not appear in the index, for the simple reason that each (*musical*) progress in a certain epoch is *surpassed* by that of the next epoch: as the years go by and tastes change, genius succumbs to the passage of time. Strict application of this idea is not without consequences: the value judgements of the composers that follow one another from age to age, the contempt for ancient times, the remarks on the concept of 'taste' are all bound up with the fate of a progressive type of development.

Page after page of the *General History* shows the imprint of this vision of history, but the most significant part is that devoted to Henry Purcell since it reveals an inner conflict in Burney. On the one hand, his desire to exalt a national genius induces him (for the only time in the whole work) to abandon 'the wide range of *general history*, and assume the more minute narrative of a biographer',[47] spending a good twenty-six pages on the composer; on the other hand, he feels

---

[44]   Ibid., p. 11.

[45]   In the context of music, see for example the well-known essay by Rev. John Brown, *A Dissertation on the Rise, Union, and Power, the Progressions, Separations, and Corruptions, of Poetry and Music* (London, 1763).

[46]   On the concept of progress in Sir Francis Bacon, see the several studies by Paolo Rossi and, more in general for our period, that of David Spadafora, *The Idea of Progress in Eighteenth-Century Britain* (New Haven and London, 1990).

[47]   C. Burney, *A General History of Music*, vol. II, p. 380.

chary towards a musical production that he perceives as antiquated and ripe for retirement. Purcell falls victim to what for Burney, in the context of music, is an inevitable process. Note also how this destiny belongs *solely* to the art of sound. After setting Purcell on a par with the greatest English spirits of all time (Shakespeare, Milton, Locke, Newton), Burney writes:[48]

> Unluckily for Purcell! he built his fame with such perishable materials, that his worth and works are daily diminishing, while the reputation of our poets and philosophers is increasing by the constant study and use of their productions. And so much is our great musician's celebrity already consigned to tradition, that it will soon be as difficult to find his songs, or, at least to *hear* them, as those of his predecessors Orpheus and Amphion, with which Cerberus was lulled to sleep, or the city of Thebes constructed.

Now, anyone familiar with Burney's opinion with respect to Orpheus and Amphion ('barbarous times and more barbarous Music'[49]) will know that a statement like this sounds worse than a death sentence for the 'unlucky' Purcell!

Burney compares the history of music to a ploughed field, sown with corn one year, with potatoes the next and so on, 'but none of its productions remain';[50] the problem – as evinced by the above passage – regards music and not the other arts and disciplines owing precisely to the 'perishable materials' of which it makes use – namely, sounds. The author presses his view of the fugitive nature of sound to the point where he asserts that, if any curiosity remains as to the music of the Ancients, this is not owing to the tales told of it but to the admiration aroused by the great works of the past: were there no longer any trace of poetry, eloquence, sculpture and architecture of the Greek and Roman age, nobody would enquire into its music.[51] If the evanescent character of sound makes it impossible to know the music of the past, the mutability of taste renders ancient delights unappealing to modern ears. In reiterating the impossibility of discussing the music of the Ancients with any certainty, Burney already writes in his preface: 'for what, besides conjecture, is now left us, concerning things so transient as sound, and so evanescent as taste?'[52]

These remarks may help to account for Burney's aversion to the 'antiquarians'. Attentive as he is to the *taste* of his readers and eager to narrate history in a perspective that matches *their* expectations – such that he openly apologizes when he deviates from this course – he finds antiquarian interest hard to conceive. What is the point of attending to kinds of music no longer to be heard, to music whose sound is actually offensive to the common ear? These questions, this vision, are

---

[48] Ibid.

[49] Ibid., p. 1024.

[50] Ibid., p. 380.

[51] Ibid., vol. I, p. 336 et seq.

[52] Ibid., p. 15.

ultimately explained by the idea itself of music as entertained by Burney: 'at best, but an amusement'.[53] If delight is the sole end of music, we can hardly wonder that Burney shows no inclination whatever to furnish a 'Science of Music', which for him is a matter for scholars and pedants.

On several occasions he tries to narrate the events in musical history by analogy with political history. At one point he depicts how the ancient falls into disgrace before the modern in the crudest manner: all that is ancient is like a land open for conquest, and Moderns are free to appropriate those territories unto themselves. The example in question is of interest because it takes account of both the theoretician and the practitioner. For, in Burney's view, the theoretician is not in thrall to the precariousness of the composer: in the realm of music he assumes the role of *legislator*, whose fame often endures undiminished over time.[54]

> with Practical Musicians and Composers it is very different; the memory of these is of short duration; for however extensive their power, and splendid their reign, their empire, like that of Alexander and other rapid conquerors, acquires no permanence; but as the territories of these were divided among their captains, so the disciples or followers of great musical leaders soon appropriate to themselves the revenue and reputation of their masters, so entirely, that, when divided into small portions, they add no great profit or power to the new possessors, who generally retain and enjoy them in obscurity, till seized and appropriated by some new and more powerful conqueror.

Nevertheless we should not suppose that this distinction between 'permanent' and 'transient' leads Burney to erect a hierarchy among theoretical and practical values based on the duration of their respective fame. On the contrary, the aversion he often displays towards the writings of the musical 'legislators' shows that he does not see the durability of their fortune as a merit. For example, he feels obliged by tradition to deal at some length with Zarlino, but his annoyance with that historian emerges in every line, to the point where he confesses to being 'more frequently discouraged from the pursuit by his prolixity, than enlightened by his science: the most trivial information is involved in such crowd of words, and the suspense it occasions so great, that patience and curiosity must be invincible indeed, to support a musical enquirer through a regular perusal of all his works'.[55] Burney most often criticizes the theoreticians for their want of 'genius', however learned they may be – or, more prosaically, for being what he most dislikes: tedious. As we have seen, the author of the *General History* desires to address a vast readership and his intention is to entertain. Music is for him 'an amusement', and in this context the weight of tradition and the theoretical dimension of music – however enduring – are merely a hindrance. What counts is what pleases.

---

[53]   Ibid., p. 19.

[54]   Ibid., p. 706 et seq.

[55]   Ibid., vol. II, p. 138.

At this point I must add that, with regard to Burney's views on Purcell, I am not entirely in agreement with the interpretation of Richard Luckett in the 1980s. Luckett shows how Burney's assessment of Purcell varies in the course of his writing, and undoubtedly there are moments where Burney says that 'among Englishmen' the music of Purcell is appreciated. Luckett's conclusion concerning the ups and downs of Burney's view of Purcell is as follows:[56]

> Burney's difficulty was in being constant to his feelings or allowing them the weight they deserve, yet it is his great merit that he could not disguise what he felt. In this sense it is enlightening to view him as a 'pre-Romantic', in touch with the emotional impetus of the Romantic movement but debarred from its intellectual liberations.

In my opinion, this oscillation in the judgement should largely be ascribed to the category that underpins it. As we have seen, Burney's negative evaluations of Purcell are closely connected with a precise idea of progress in music, but he makes positive judgements whenever he sees fit to exalt the 'Englishness' of the British Orpheus. This is not merely a matter of Burney's musical sentiments, as Luckett seems to indicate, but also of 'patriotic' feeling. Nationalism must therefore be taken into account, quite as much as 'taste', when we examine the judgements expressed by these historians.

Sir John Hawkins and the non-progressive nature of taste

> In the comparison of the modern with the ancient music, it must evidently appear that that of the present day has the advantage, whether we consider it in theory or in practice.[57]

By 1776, certain points in the battle of the Ancients and the Moderns had already been settled. When Burney and Hawkins took up arms against those who maintained the superiority of the Ancients, their attack continued to fall on poor Sir William Temple, who was already long dead and whose work dated back to 1690! The Moderns had fairly swiftly reaped victory in the conflict as regarded the area of natural philosophy and mathematics, though the outcome of the clash in the domain of the fine arts was less certain.

As we can see from how Hawkins describes the topics in the 'Science of Music', his musical theory remains firmly anchored to the disciplines of physics

---

[56]   Richard Luckett, '"Or rather our musical Shakespeare": Charles Burney's Purcell', in Christopher Hogwood and Richard Luckett (eds), *Music in Eighteenth-Century England: Essays in Memory of Charles Cudworth* (Cambridge, 1983), pp. 59-78: 73.

[57]   Sir J. Hawkins, *General History of the Science and Practice of Music*, p. 917 ('Conclusion').

and mathematics, with whose progress he associates himself. At several points, he lays particular stress on the discovery of acoustics, that 'philosophy of sound' which, 'as it results from the modern discoveries in physics, the moderns only are entitled to the merit of its investigation'.[58] For Hawkins, knowledge proceeds by accumulation, and modernity advances also when there are dwarfs to stand on the shoulders of the giants (in Newtonian phrase).

Progress in the practice of music is seen to depend largely on the technical improvement of the instruments and their increasing differentiation from one another. Leaving aside the percussion instruments, which for Hawkins are not susceptible of improvement, he maintains that the Ancients were substantially acquainted with only two typologies, lyres and flutes. Among the modern instruments, on the other hand:[59]

> the instruments of the viol kind are so constructed as to reverberate and prolong that sound, which, when produced from the Lyre, must be supposed to have been wasted in the open air; the modern flutes, as far as can be judged by a comparison of them with the graphical representations of the ancient Tibiæ, have greatly the advantage; and as to pipes of other kinds, such as the Hautboy, the Bassoon, the Chalumeau, and others, these, as having the adjunct of a reed, constitute a species new and original, and are an invention unknown to the ancients.

These remarks would seem to engender an idea of linear progress similar to Burney's. How, then, can Percy Scholes – author of the only published monograph on Hawkins, as well as of the relevant entry in *Grove's Dictionary of Music and Musicians* – claim that he had 'a view in direct contrast to Burney's idea of music history as a continuous development which was reaching its zenith in his own days'?[60] This assertion of Scholes's is certainly excessive, but there is no belying the severity of Hawkins's criticism of modern authors. How is one to reconcile his impatience with the compositions of his time and the idea of a continuous progress in knowledge and technique?

But Scholes is not quite correct here, since the contrast between Burney and Hawkins lies not in a radically different 'idea of music history' so much as in the idea and evaluation of a key concept running throughout the eighteenth century: that of *taste*, a notion that affects their respective evaluations of contemporariness.

---

[58]   Ibid.; see also the introduction (p. xxii) where Sir Francis Bacon is acknowledged as one of the leading investigators of this new science.

[59]   Ibid., p. 918.

[60]   Percy Scholes, 'John Hawkins, Sir.', in S. Sadie (ed.), *The New Grove Dictionary of Music and Musicians*, vol. 11, 2nd ed. (New York, 2001), p. 166. The secondary literature on Sir John Hawkins is rather scanty: as from 1950, aside from the monograph by Scholes (*The Life and Activities of Sir John Hawkins: Musician, Magistrate and Friend of Johnson* (London, 1953)), we have only the work by Bertram H. Davis, *A Proof of Eminence: the Life of Sir John Hawkins* (Bloomington, 1973).

Something has already been said in this connection with regard to Burney, evidencing how in his *History of Music* the fortunes of composers are subject to changes in taste. Purcell is not blamed for not composing with genius, nor is he simply dubbed outdated. Taste, in Burney, alters along the path of progress, a change oriented in a teleological sense, leading to the perfection of the present day, where Handel ousts Purcell and Haydn catches up on Handel. In Hawkins's history, on the contrary, taste may act as a hindrance in the advance of the arts: even though technique and knowledge progress, public taste is able to mould musical production and performance to its own requirements. Nor is it certain that the taste of the majority tends towards improvement. From this point of view the progress described by Hawkins is better defined as 'cyclical' rather than 'linear'; for the author of the *General History of the Science and Practice of Music* allows that certain moments in past tradition have witnessed a degree of development analogous to later ones.

An example of this reading of music history can be found in the pages devoted to Franco-Flemish music. Hawkins's judgement of the great polyphony of this period is balanced between a defect and a virtue. The defect is the choice of texts to set, since many of them are held to be unsuitable 'with all the aids of melody and harmony, to excite joy, devotion, pity, or, in short, any other of those affections which are confessedly under the dominion of music'.[61] Thus if 'fine music' were only of the pathetic kind, composers like Ockeghem would have to be deemed unworthy of memory and their success ascribed to the effect of novelty they must have aroused, or to the 'ignorance of its admirers'[62]. But Hawkins's assessment is otherwise:[63]

> whoever is capable of contemplating the structure of a vocal composition in a variety of parts, will find abundant reason to admire many of those which Glareanus has been at the pains of preserving, and will discover in them a fine modulation, a close contexture and interchange of parts, different kinds of motion judiciously contrasted [...]. And such a full harmony resulting from the whole, as leaves the ear nothing to expect or wish for.

His argument concludes with the remark that Handel himself displayed a sensitivity towards the harmonic richness of those compositions.

Already in his 'Preliminary Discourse', Hawkins had identified a golden age in the domain of vocal music from 1560 onwards, with the production of madrigals; for instrumental music he cites Corelli and Geminiani. As we can see from the above-quoted passage, Hawkins distinguishes between the pleasure conveyed by the emotional qualities of the music and a second, equally valid pleasure obtained from consideration of the structural harmoniousness of the work, whose

---

[61] Sir J. Hawkins, *General History of the Science and Practice of Music*, p. 325.

[62] Ibid.

[63] Ibid.

theorization by Francis Hutcheson has been described above. In acknowledging these two possible and distinct sources of satisfaction in listening, Hawkins is also able to valorize types of music that find no favour with contemporary ears: formal attention to the structures conveyed by the concept of harmony makes it possible, as was also the case in Hutcheson's theory, to integrate the subjective dimension of judgement with an 'objective' counterpart – instead of evaluating compositions by taste alone.

Hawkins's music history does not proceed all of a piece to a final goal. While knowledge and techniques accumulate, musical production and the taste of listeners go, rather, in waves and the multiple elements of composition may find themselves in a state of perfection disconnected from one another. Hawkins saw his time as a stage of decline, and he justifies this with a somewhat 'sociological' argument: the spread of economic well-being leads to an increased desire to enjoy the pleasures society offers, so that 'in proportion as riches abound, not to be susceptible of fashionable pleasures is to be the subject of reproach'.[64] In this way people become accustomed to feign a taste that they do not actually possess but which they cannot admit to being without, on pain of collective censure. But, as long as ignorant persons continued to be a minority of consumers of works of art, they relied on the judgement of a majority who were capable of exercising critical competence; now that the former are in the majority they pique themselves on having their own opinions, and the result is that taste becomes severed from the knowledge of art. Hawkins's criticism of modern symphonies is a harsh one:

> Music of this kind, constructed without art or elegance, awakens no passion: the general uproar of a modern symphony or overture neither engages attention, nor interrupts conversation; and many persons, in the total absence of thought, flatter themselves that they are merry.

Shortly after this, he underlines a couple of features that make these compositions ill-suited to reflection: their tempi are too rapid, their execution too complicated. The listener's attention is thus shifted from the composition itself to the skill of the performer, dissipating the lasting effects of the music on the person. Here, too, we return to a topic already discussed in the first part of this work, regarding the value ascribed by philosophers and writers to the fact that the effects of music do not evanesce when the sound ceases. Unfortunately, Hawkins does not press on further with his argument, but confines himself to saying that the best test for comparing the symphonies of his time with the music of Corelli, Handel and Purcell remains 'the different effects of each'.[65] Before concluding this paragraph, however, we must add that the closing words of Sir John Hawkins's *General History* – here quoted entire – are full of sanguine hopes for the future:[66]

---

[64]   Ibid., p. 919.

[65]   Ibid.

[66]   Ibid.

notwithstanding these evils, it does not appear that the science itself sustained any loss; on the contrary, it is certain that the art of combining musical sounds is in general better understood at this time than ever. We may therefore indulge a hope that the sober reflection on the nature of harmony, and its immediate reference to those principles on which all our ideas of beauty, symmetry, order and magnificence are founded; on the infinitely various modifications of which it is capable; its influence on the human affections; and, above all, those nameless delights which the imaginative faculty receives from the artful disposition and succession of concordant sounds, will terminate in a thorough conviction of the vanity and emptiness of that music with which we now are pleased, and produce a change in the public taste, that, whenever it takes place, can hardly fail to be for the better.

It would therefore be difficult, not to say reductive, to relegate Hawkins among the detractors of modernity. While Burney chronicles the development of music from ancient barbarism to the perfection of the modern age, Hawkins's history treads a stonier path, where music attains peaks of excellence and periods of crisis supervene in which the listeners' taste and critical capability diverge: for, in the face of fashions and changes in taste, he asserts that the competent judge – and remember that Hawkins was himself a judge by profession, in the strict sense of the word – must found his opinion on the immutable principles of the nature of music.[67]

The histories of music: cultural collocation of a literary genre

Having examined the concepts that underpin the reflections and assessments on music of the two historians, it will be useful to conclude with some remarks on the literary genre to which their works belong: 'general history'. The eighteenth century saw the birth of the first 'histories of music' – as their titles proclaim. However, that does not mean that the previous tradition was devoid of historical reflection on music. The histories of Burney and Hawkins, in their construction, were able to turn the solid foundations of pre-existing traditions to good advantage. The philosophical thinking on the nature of sound and of musical pleasure and the idea of 'taste' represents a fundamental horizon for the conception of the two *Histories*, as does the literary dispute between the Ancients and Moderns or the debate on historical scepticism.

---

[67] Though he makes frequent mention of these principles, Hawkins's statements on the matter are somewhat general; it is fairly clear, however, that his view is very close to that, for example, of Hutcheson: the foundations of music rest, on the one hand, on mathematics (here and there Hawkins also writes 'on geometry'), on the other hand, on natural philosophy, and these disciplines explain why music exerts an effect on the human mind.

A second horizon to take into account, in which the new music history writers were able to find matter for reflection for their works, is the treatise on music. Its Renaissance version comprised every form of musical knowledge regarding the 'Science of Music': the historical-anthropological dimension found expression in the pages devoted to the invention of music or in the chapters *de inventoribus*. In the case of Malcolm we have seen how, earlier in the eighteenth century, the treatise could still try to summarize all these aspects. But there is an increasing separation of genres that deal with individual aspects of musical knowledge, as witnessed by the *Essay* of Charles Avison. The histories of music can also be read in the light of the breakdown of the old universal and encyclopaedic musical knowledge on which the treatise genre was modelled, and thus as a response to the need to discuss the ancient topics in more detail and according to new criteria.

To collocate the genesis of music history we must also consider the historiographic tradition as well as that of philosophy and music. In an article of 2001,[68] Franco Alberto Gallo investigated this intellectual tradition as a context in which to approach the *Historia dell'origine dei Sassoni* (1697) and the *Historia musica* (1695) of Giovanni Bontempi, recalling in this connection the distinction made at the time between *historia civilis* and *historia naturalis*. His work, together with what has already been said here on our two historians, will help us to collocate the *General Histories* within this broader classification of historical learning. In order to describe the ramifications of the tree of historical knowledge and the possible collocation of the reflection on music within it, we shall at this point make use of the detailed picture drawn by Sir Francis Bacon in 1605 in *Of the Proficience and Advancement of Learning*, which we already encountered in dealing with Hawkins's 'Preliminary Discourse' to the *General History* and which had a determining influence on seventeenth- and eighteenth-century British culture.[69]

In order to consider the emerging histories of music, in a time warp running from the end of the seventeenth through the eighteenth centuries, with a view to their cultural collocation, we need to bear in mind the areas of knowledge into which music entered in the seventeenth century. With the gradual substitution/ integration of the system of liberal arts – divided into trivium and quadrivium – with the projection of encyclopaedias of knowledge arranged according to the faculties of the human mind (for example, in the Baconian system, memory, imagination and reason), the term 'music' begins to find more areas of collocation, alongside the traditional one which sites it among the various mathematics.

In Bacon's *Advancement of Learning*, as we saw, the encyclopaedia of knowledge is ordered on three primary axes: historical knowledge, under the faculty of memory; poetic knowledge, connected with the imagination; and philosophical knowledge, under the head of reason. Figures 4.1 to 4.3 show a

---

68   F. A. Gallo, 'Historia civilis e Cultural heritage', *Il Saggiatore musicale*, 8 (2001), pp. 15-20.

69   See pp. 139-140 above.

reduced version of the tree conceived by Bacon, aiming to evidence the areas of knowledge where reflections on music may find a place. Immediately apparent is a parallelism between the areas in which music can be discussed under the aegis of memory and reason; and by the same token, within historical knowledge – and we shall see how – music can be found in natural history, in civil history, and under the head of philosophical knowledge it fits into both natural philosophy and the philosophy of man.

History divides mainly into two subgenres: natural and civil. In both of these the term *history* may hark back to the still cogent concept of 'history' as a diachronic process and a form of narrative, to an idea of 'history' as description and testimony. *Civil History*, for example, encompasses narratives like *De Bello Gallico*, as well as the simple public registers and acts and antiquarian evidence. Now, music, under a different head, may be incorporated in both *Natural* and *Civil History*.

In a *Natural History* compiled by Bacon himself, the *Sylva Sylvarum*, 'music' makes frequent appearances, especially in the second and third chapters. The Lord Chancellor commences his treatise on the art of sound with the following words:[70]

> Music, in the practice, hath been well pursued, and in good variety; but in theory, and especially in the yielding of the causes of the practice, very weakly; being reduced into certain mystical subtilities of no use and not much truth. We shall, therefore, after our manner, join the contemplative and active part together.

Much of what Bacon subsequently says can be collocated in the segment of natural philosophy studied in the seventeenth century under the heading of *acoustics*. The first fourteen paragraphs, from which the investigation of the nature of sound starts out, involve topics familiar to the discussion on music: consonance and dissonance, harmony, the capacity of musical sounds to influence the human spirit and the reason why we evince pleasure or displeasure on listening to musical sounds. The need to provide fuller explanations of the pleasure (or displeasure) of listening and music's capacity to act on persons leads to a more detailed enquiry into the propagation and quality of sound, backed by numerous experiments. The integration between the experimental dimension ('active part') and theoretical dimension ('contemplative part') belongs in Bacon's project to reform knowledge, which is to lead to results 'as shall not vanish in the fume of subtle, sublime or delectable speculation, but such as shall be operative to the endowment and benefit of man's life'.[71]

---

[70] Sir Francis Bacon, *Sylva Sylvarum* (London, 1626), p. 35.

[71] Sir F. Bacon, *Of the Proficience and Advancement of Learning*, book II, p. 10. For an in-depth study of the Baconian project, see the classic work by Paolo Rossi, *Francis Bacon: from Magic to Science* (Chicago, 1968).

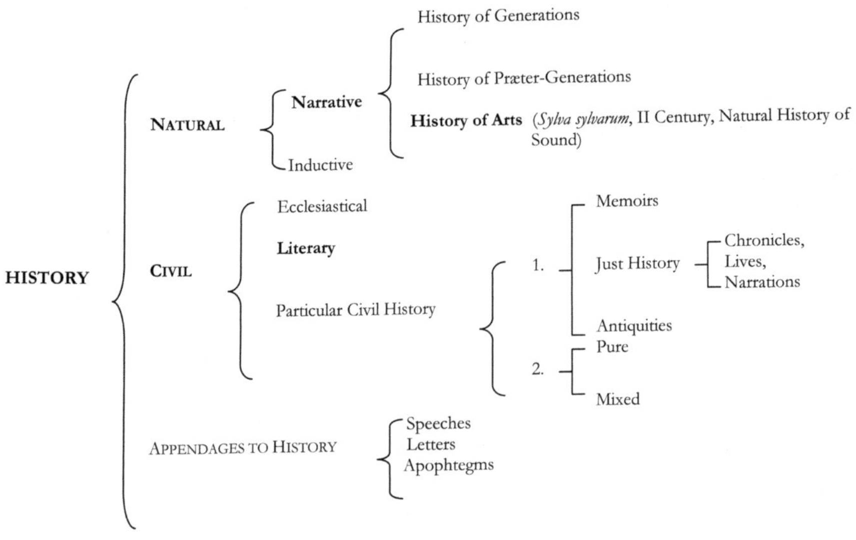

Figure 4.1   Sir Francis Bacon, General distribution of human knowledge – Memory

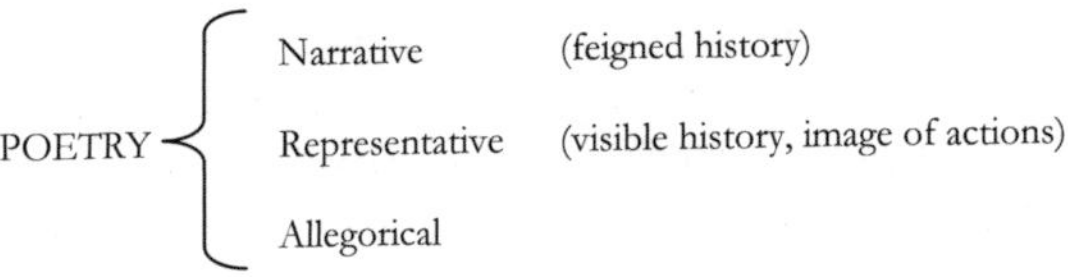

Figure 4.2   Sir Francis Bacon, General distribution of human knowledge – Imagination

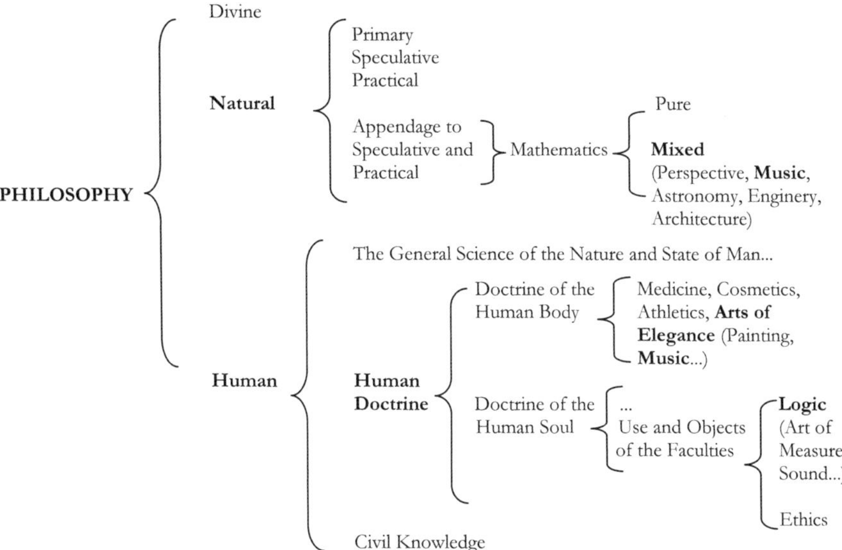

Figure 4.3   Sir Francis Bacon, General distribution of human knowledge –
Reason

The main topics of the particular branch of *Civil History* denominated *Literary History* have already been described in the section dealing with Hawkins's concept of 'Science of Music'.[72] Bacon had hoped for the development of this new genre of history. It must treat of the state of culture from age to age and everything that had influenced it. The aim of Literary History is of particular importance, since 'it will make learned men wise in the use and administration of learning',[73] Although Bacon does not go into detail on the eventual contents of such history, the general reference to a history of culture made it possible to conceive of a history-based discussion of music within this context. As we have seen, the cue was taken up by Sir John Hawkins, who explicitly sets his own *General History* within this branch of the encyclopaedia of knowledge.[74] The Lord Chancellor had evidenced how, although no history had addressed the subject in general, certain particular sciences had already moved in this direction, compiling 'some small memorials of the schools, authors, and books; and so likewise some barren relations touching

---

[72]   See pp. 139-140 above.

[73]   Sir F. Bacon, *Of the Proficience and Advancement of Learning*, book II, p. 7 et seq.

[74]   Here I must disagree with F. A. Gallo's analysis in his article 'Historia civilis e Cultural heritage', where he classes the histories of Burney and Hawkins under *Historia naturalis*.

the inventions of arts and usages'.[75] And, except for the adjective 'small', this description corresponds fully to what Hawkins (to a great extent) and Burney (to a lesser extent) envisaged. Both of them review the main authors – writers, composers, performers – of whom we have evidence, and cite and summarize their works. Of the two texts, that of Hawkins, whose title bears the dual heading 'Science and Practice of Music, is the one that conveys the more complete view of the areas of knowledge with which music was in contact, for it sets up a historical discussion of music understood both as part of a *Natural Philosophy* and as part of a *Human Philosophy*. The interplay of devices and ideas deriving from philosophy, from historical learning, from the reflections of writers of treatises on music, from the new systematization of knowledge ongoing since the seventeenth century – all this has enabled music to be conceived as a discipline in a new way, but without isolating it from the rest of the *studia humanitatis*. In eighteenth-century Britain, music is still part of a 'natural and human philosophy', whose central interest remains focused on man.

Conclusions

I would like to conclude with some remarks that concern not only this chapter but the whole work. William Weber, who has devoted several detailed studies to the epoch with which we are dealing, detects the birth of the musical canon in the England of the eighteenth century. In his analysis of the formation of this canon he writes:[76]

> a performed canon began to arise in early eighteenth-century England because of a weakening, indeed a crisis, in its literary counterpart, and that it emerged on its own ground and on its own terms. The fact that the two canons were moving in different directions was fundamental: while an emergent musical one was only now defining itself, the literary one was being recast in its perimeters and its authority.

It is of interest to site the histories of music as genre at the intersection of these two canons that proceed along apparently diverging paths. What Weber identifies as a crisis in the literary-musical canon has also been mentioned here, at the beginning of Chapter 3, and can be identified in the crisis of the genre of treatise on music. Evidently, the eighteenth century saw the need to find new ways of literary relation with musical culture. What I would suggest is that the birth of modern histories of music is intimately connected with this context: crisis of an ancient way of treating musical knowledge and birth of a musical canon.

---

[75]   Ibid.

[76]   W. Weber, 'The Intellectual Origins of Musical Canon in Eighteenth-Century England', p. 491.

The above-cited case of Burney's consideration of Purcell seems to me to witness how, from an intellectual point of view, the theoretical justification of an already existing canon from an executive standpoint was not an established fact (for, as we know, theory usually lags behind practice). Burney feels obliged to dwell at some length on Purcell, compares him with Shakespeare, and acknowledges his importance: yet, as regards Purcell's compositions, he denies the very possibility of a musical canon, stating that musical material is not on a par with the other arts – not so much, or not merely, because its nature is ephemeral per se, but because musical taste seems more prone to changes than other arts. An idea of progress and taste as manifested by Burney would appear to militate against justifying the existence of a musical canon. Yet, at the same time, histories of music are a form of 'celebration' of this very canon: they preserve the composers and their works from oblivion, and they select which works to mention and which not. In this sense I think that the two histories by Hawkins and Burney stand at an interesting crossroads in musical culture: precisely because their works are not entirely consistent: in virtue of their small incongruences, the cracks in their apparently smooth surface, we can glimpse the formation of a cultural change of particular importance for musicology.

It is not for reasons of chronology that I have placed the discussion of the two histories at the end of this work. As I trust will by now be clear, to understand them requires an approach not confined to the musicological horizon. For while it is true that 'historians must come to recognize music as a vital aspect of general history' and that music 'must be approached in terms of its own traditions', as Weber writes with regard to current music history,[77] music historians too – as is ever more frequently the case – must recognize that music is an active part of a culture with which it shares an entire history.

This study has concentrated on the link between literature, philosophy and music in order to trace a mutual exchange of ideas that appears highly significant. Moreover, the literature examined provides evidence for an aspect of intellectual investigation in the eighteenth century that in our culture seems at times to be disappearing and that has to do with the very aim of the humanistic disciplines. As I hope I have made clear, the centre-stage of most of the investigations dealt with is occupied, not so much by individual objects or disciplines, but by a full-scale conception of man. Their objective may be moral, instructive or more generally recreational, but there is always a clear idea of 'who' is being addressed and what is the sense of the work vis-à-vis human society. This anthropological kind of interest seems to me one of the aspects of eighteenth-century culture that – even in an age of increasing specialization like our own – we should strive to keep alive.

---

[77] William Weber, 'Beyond *Zeitgeist*: Recent Work in Music History', *The Journal of Modern History*, 66/2 (1994), pp. 321-345: 344 et seq.

Bibliography

Ancient sources

Aristotle, *Poetics*, in *Aristotle on Poetry and Style*, trans. G. M. A. Grube (New York: Liberal Arts Press, 1958).

——, *Politics*, ed. H. Rackham (London and Cambridge, MA, 1959).

——, *Problems*, ed. W. S. Hett (London and Cambridge, MA, 1961).

Epictetus, *The Discourses, as reported by Arrian, the Manual, and Fragments*, trans. W. A. Oldfather (London and Cambridge, MA: Harvard University Press, 1959-1961).

Horace, *The Satires and Epistles of Horace: A Modern English Verse Translation*, trans. Smith Palmer Bovie (Chicago: University of Chicago Press, 2002 [1959]).

Primary sources

Addison, Joseph, *The Works of the Right Honourable Joseph Addison*, ed. Richard Hurd (6 vols, London: G. Bell & Sons, 1889).

Alison, Archibald, *Essays on the Nature and Principles of Taste* (Edinburgh, 1790).

Armstrong, John, *The Art of Preserving Health* (London, 1744).

——, *Sketches: or Essays on Various Subjects* (London, 1758.)

Avison, Charles, *An Essay on Musical Expression* (London, 1752); anastatic reprint of the edition of 1753 (New York: Broude, 1967); also *Charles Avison's Essay on Musical Expression: with related writings by William Hayes and Charles Avison*, ed. Pierre Dubois (Burlington: Ashgate, 2004).

Bacon, Francis, Sir, *Of the Proficience and Advancement of Learning* (London, 1605).

——, *Sylva Sylvarum* (London, 1626),

——, *The Wisedome of the Ancients*, trans. Sir Arthur George (London, 1619).

Batteux, Charles, *Les Beaux Arts réduits à un même principe* (Paris, 1746).

Beattie, James, *An Essay on Poetry and Music, as they affect the Mind* (Edinburgh, 1776); reprinted in *The Philosophical and Critical Works of James Beattie*, Vol. I, *Essays*, ed. B. Fabian (Hildesheim and New York: Olms, 1975).

Berkeley, George, *The Works of George Berkeley Bishop of Cloyne*, Vol. VIII 'Letters', ed. A. A. Luce and T. E. Jessop (London: Thomas Nelson and Sons, 1964[2] [1956]).

Bisse, Thomas, *Musick the Delight of the Sons of Men. A Sermon Preached at the Cathedral Church of Hereford, at the Anniversary Meeting of the Three Choirs, Gloucester, Worcester, Hereford, September 7, 1726* (London, 1726).

Blair, Hugh, *Lectures on Rethoric and Belles Lettres* (London, 1783).

Bonnet, Pierre and Bourdelot, Pierre, *Histoire de la Musique et ses Effets* (Paris, 1715).

Brocklesby, Richard, *Reflections on Antient and Modern Musick* (London, 1749).

Brown, John, Rev., *A Dissertation on the Rise, Union, and Power, the Progressions, Separations, and Corruptions, of Poetry and Music* (London, 1763).

Browne, Richard, *Medicina Musica; or, a Mechanical Essay on the Effects of Singing, Musick, and Dancing, on Human Bodies* (London, 1729).

Burke, Edmund, *A Philosophical Enquiry into the Origin of our Ideas of the Sublime and Beautiful* (London, 1757).

Burney, Charles, *A general History of Music, from the earliest Ages to the present Period* (London, 1776-1789); with critical and historical notes by Frank Mercer (2 vols, New York: Dover [1935] 1957).

Coleire, Richard, *The Antiquity and Usefulness of Instrumental Musick in the Service of God* (London, 1738).

Collier, Jeremy, *A Short View of the Immorality, and Profaneness of the English Stage* (London, 1698); anastatic reprint of the edition of 1730 (Hildesheim: Georg Olms Verlag, 1969).

Cooper, John Gilbert, *Letters concerning taste* (London, 1755).

Dennis, John, *The Impartial Critick: or, some Observations upon a Late Book, entituled, A Short View of Tragedy, written by Mr Rymer* (London, 1693).

——, *The Usefulness of the Stage* (London, 1698).

——, *An Essay on the Opera's after the Italian Manner, which are about to be establish'd on the English Stage: with some Reflections upon the Damage which they may bring to the Publick* (London, 1706).

——, *An Essay upon Publick Spirit* (London, 1711).

Descartes, René, *Compendium Musicae*, (Trajecti ad Rhenum, 1650); *Abrégé de musique*, ed. F. De Buzon (Paris: PUF, 1987).

Donaldson, John, *Principles of Taste* (Edinburgh, 1786).

Du Bos, Jean-Baptiste, *Critical Reflections on Poetry, Painting and Music, with an Inquiry into the Rise and Progress of the Theatrical Entertainments of the Ancients*, trans. Thomas Nugent (London, 1748).

Eastcott, Richard, *Sketches of the origin, progress and effects of music, with an account of the ancient bards and minstrels* (Bath, 1793).

Euterpe; or Remarks on the Use and Abuse of Music as a part of Modern Education (London, 1778).

Ferguson, Adam, *Principles of Moral and Political Science* (Edinburgh: W. Creech; London: Printed for A. Strahan and T. Cadell, 1792).

Gerard, Alexander, *Essay on Taste* (Edinburgh, 1759); ed. W. J. Hipple Jr. (New York: Delmar, 1978; reprint of the third edition, London, 1780).

Goldsmith, Oliver, *The Bee, being Essays on the Most Interesting Subjects* (London, 1759).

Gregory, John, *A comparative View of the State and Faculties of Man with those of the animal World* (London, 1765).

Harper, John, *The natural Efficacy of Musick to prepare the Mind for good Impressions: A Sermon* (London, 1730).

Harris, James, *Three Treatises* (London, 1744); in *The Works of James Harris* (2 vols, Bristol: Thoemmes Press, 2003; facsimile of the London: F. Wingrave, 1801 edition).

Hartley, David, *Observations Upon Man, his Frame, his Duty and his Expectations* (London, 1749).

Hawkins, John, Sir, *An account of the institution and progress of the Academy of Ancient Music* (London, 1770).

——, *A General History of the Science and Practice of Music* (London, 1776); facsimile (Graz: Akademische Druck, 1969; reprint of the London 1875 edition).

Hayes, William, *Remarks on the Essay on Musical Expression* (London, 1753).

——, *Anecdotes of the five music-meetings, on account of the charitable foundations at Church Langton* (Oxford, 1768).

Henry, Robert, *History of Great Britain* (London, 1771-1793).

Holden, John, *An Essay towards a Rational System of Music* (Glasgow, 1770).

Home, Henry, Lord Kames, *Elements of Criticism* (Edinburgh, 1762); in *Collected Works of Henry Home, Lord Kames*, ed. J. V. Price (13 vols, London: Routledge/ Thoemmes Press, 1993), vol. I.

Hume, David, *A Treatise of Human Nature* (London, 1739); ed. T. H. Green and T. H. Grose (Aalen: Scientia Verlag, 1964; reprint of the London 1886 edition).

Hutcheson, Francis, *An Inquiry into the Original of our Ideas of Beauty and Virtue* (London, 1725); in *Collected Works of Francis Hutcheson*, ed. Bernard Fabian (7 vols, Hildesheim: Olms, 1971).

Jackson, William, *Thirty Letters on Various Subjects* (London, 1783).

Jacob, Hildebrand, *Of the sister Arts, an Essay* (London, 1734).

Jones, William, Rev., *Letters from a Tutor to his pupils* (London, 1780).

——, *Phisiological Disquisitions* (London, 1781).

——, *The Nature and Excellence of Music. A Sermon Preached at the Opening of a New Organ, in the Parish Church of Nayland in Suffolk; on Sunday, July the 29th, 1787* (London, 1787).

Jones, William, Sir, *Essay on the arts commonly called imitative* (Oxford, 1772); in *The Collected Works of Sir William Jones*, ed. Garland Cannon (13 vols, Richmond: Curzon Press, 1993).

——, *On the Musical modes of the Hindus: written in 1784, and since much enlarged* (Calcutta: 1792); in *The Collected Works of Sir William Jones*, ed. Garland Cannon (13 vols, Richmond: Curzon Press, 1993).

Knight, Richard Payne, *An analitical Inquiry into the Principles of Taste* (London, 1805).

La Mothe le Vayer, François, *Œuvres* (2 vols, Geneva: Slatkine, 1970; reprint of the Dresden 1756-1759 edition).

Lampe, John Frederick, *The Art of Musick* (London, 1740).

Locke, John, *An Essay Concerning Human Understanding* (London, 1690), ed. P.H. Nidditch (Oxford: Oxford University Press, 1975).

Malcom, Alexander, Rev., *A Treatise of Musick, Speculative, Practical and Historical* (Edinburgh, 1721).

Mason, John, *An Essay on the Power of Numbers, and the Principle of Harmony in Poetical Compositions* (London, 1749).

Mayne, Zachary, *Two dissertations concerning sense and the imagination* (London, 1728).

Naish, Thomas, *A Sermon Preach'd at the Cathedral Church of Sarum, November the 30th, 1726, being the Anniversary Day appointed for the Meeting of the Society of Lovers of Musick* (London, 1726).

Newton, Sir Isaac, *Opticks* (London, 1704); reprinted (New York: Dover, 1952).

North, Roger, *The Musicall Grammarian*, MS, 1728; published as *Roger North's The Musicall Grammarian 1728*, ed. J. C. Kassler and M. Chan (Cambridge: Cambridge University Press, 1990, 2006),

——, *Theory of Sounds shewing, the genesis, propagation, effects and augmentation of them reduced to a specific inquiry into the cripticks of harmony and discord, with eikons annexed exposing them to ocular inspection*, MS, 1726 and 1728, BL Add MS 32535.

Payne, Thomas, *A Defence of Church-Musick, A Sermon Preach'd In The Cathedral-Church Of Hereford, At The Anniversary Meeting Of The Three Choirs* (Oxford, 1738).

Pepusch, Johann Christopher, *A Treatise on Harmony* (London, 1731).

Raguenet, François, *Paralèle des Italiens et des François, en ce qui regarde la musique et les opéra* (Paris, 1702); reprinted (Geneva: Minkoff Reprints, 1976).

Reid, Thomas, *Lectures on the Fine Arts*, MS, 1774; printed in *Thomas Reid's Lectures on the Fine Arts*, ed. Peter Kivy (The Hague: Martinus Nijhoff, 1973).

——, *An Inquiry into the Human Mind on the Principles of Common Sense* (Edinburgh, 1764); ed. Derek R. Brookes (Edinburgh: Edinburgh University Press, 1997).

——, *Thomas Reid On Logic, Rhetoric and the Fine Arts*, ed. Alexander Brodie (Edinburgh: Edinburgh University Press, 2005).

Reynolds, Joshua Sir, *Seven Discourses Delivered in the Royal Academy by the President* (London, 1778); printed in *Discourses on Art*, ed. Robert R. Wark (New Haven and London: Yale University Press, 1997).

Robertson, Thomas, Rev., *An Inquiry into the Fine Arts* (London, 1784).

Rymer, Thomas, *A Short View of Tragedy; It's Original, Excellency, and Corruption* (London, 1693).

Shaftesbury, Anthony Ashley Cooper, third Earl of, *Characteristicks of Man, manners, Opinions, and Times* (London, 1714); reprinted in *Characteristics of Men, Manners, Opinions, Times*, ed. L. Klein (Cambridge: Cambridge University Press, 1999); also ed. D. den Uyl (3 vols, Indianapolis: Liberty Fund, 2001), vol. III.

Smith, Adam, *Essays on Philosophical Subjects* (London, 1795); reprinted in ed. W. P. D. Wightman and J. C. Bryce (Indianapolis: Liberty Fund, 1982; reprint of the 1980 Oxford University Press edition); also *Essais esthétiques. L'imitation dans les arts et autres texts*, foreword by D. Deleule (Paris: Vrin, 1997).

Smith, Robert, *Harmonics, or the Philosophy of Musical Sounds* (London, 1759).

*Some Observations on Dr Brown's Dissertation on the Rise, Union, & of Poetry and Musick, in a Letter to Dr B****** (London, 1764).

Steele, Richard, *Town-Talk in a Letter to a Lady in the Country* (London, 1715-1716).

——, *Chit-Chat in a Letter to a Lady in the Country* (London, 1715-1716).

——, *Richard Steele's Periodical Journalism 1714-1716*, ed. Rae Blanchard (Oxford: Clarendon Press, 1959).

Sterne, Laurence, *The Life and Opinions of Tristram Shandy, Gentleman* (London, 1759-1767); reprinted ed. M. and J. New (London: Penguin, 1997).

Stiles, Francis, Sir, *An Explanation of the Modes or Tones in the Ancient Greek Music* (London, 1761).

The Spectator (London, 1711-1712).

Turnbull, George, *Observations upon Liberal Education* (London, 1742).

Twining, Thomas, Rev., *Aristotle's Treatise on Poetry, Translated: with Notes on the Translation, and on the Original; and Two Dissertations, on Poetical, and Musical Imitation* (London, 1789).

Webb, Daniel, *Observations on the correspondance between Poetry and Music* (London, 1769).

Wotton, William, *Reflections upon Ancient and Modern learning* (London, 1694).

Secondary literature

Abrams, Meyer Howard, *The Mirror and the Lamp: Romantic Theory and the Critical Tradition* (Oxford: Oxford University Press, 1953).

Adler, Guido, *Methode der Musikgeschichte* (Leipzig: Breitkopf & Härtel, 1919).

Aldridge, Alfred Owen, 'Shaftesbury and the Classics', in Karl Bosl (ed.), *Gesellschaft, Kultur, Literatur: Rezeption und Originalität im Wachsen einer europäischen Literatur und Geistigkeit* (Stuttgart: Hiersemann, 1975): 241-258.

Allan, David, *Virtue, Learning and the Scottish Enlightenment* (Edinburgh: Edinburgh University Press, 1993).

Allen, Richard C., *David Hartley on Human Nature* (Albany: State University of New York Press, 1999).

Allen, Warren Dwight, *Philosophies of Music History* (New York: Dover, 1962 [1939]).

Anceschi, Luciano, *Autonomia ed eteronomia dell'arte. Saggio di fenomenologia delle poetiche* (Milan: Garzanti, 1992 [1936]).

——, *Da Bacone a Kant* (Bologna: il Mulino, 1959).

Anderson, Howard Peter and Shea, John S. (eds), *Studies on Criticism and Aesthetics, 1660-1800: Essays in Honor of Samuel Holt Monk* (Minneapolis: University of Minneapolis Press, 1967).

Arregni, Jorge V. and Arnau, Pablo, 'Shaftesbury: Father and Critic of Modern Aesthetics', *British Journal of Aesthetics*, 34 (1994): 350-62.

Asfour, Amal and Williamson, Paul, 'Splendid Impositions: Gainsborough, Berkeley, Hume', *Eighteenth-Century Studies*, 31/4 (1998): 403-432.

Balderston, Katharine C., 'Dr Johnson and Burney's History of Music', *PMLA*, 49/3 (1934): 966-968.

Barber, W. H., et al. (eds), *The Age of Enlightenment. Studies Presented to Theodore Bestermann* (Edinburgh and London: Oliver & Boyd, 1967).

Barnouw, Jeffrey, 'Of the Sublime: To John Dennis', *Comparative Literature*, 35/1 (1983): 21-42.

Barry, Kevin, *Language, Music and the Sign. A Study in Aesthetics, Poetics and Poetic Practice from Collins to Coleridge* (Cambridge: Cambridge University Press, 1987).

Bate, Walter Jackson, *From Classic to Romantic: Premises of Taste in Eighteenth-Century England* (Cambridge: Harvard University Press, 1949).

——, 'The Sympathetic Imagination in Eighteenth-Century English Criticism', *Journal of English Literary History*, 12/2 (1945): 144-164.

Baldwin, Anna and Hutton, Sarah (eds), *Platonism and the English Imagination* (Cambridge: Cambridge University Press, 1994).

Betz, Sigmund A. E., 'The Operatic Criticism of the *Tatler* and the *Spectator*', *Musical Quarterly*, 31 (1945): 318-330.

Bevilacqua, Vincent M., 'Classical Rhetorical Influences in the Development of Eighteenth-Century British Aesthetic Criticism', *Transactions of the American Philological Association*, 106 (1976): 11-28.

Bien, Günther (ed.), *Die Frage nach dem Glück* (Stuttgart and Bad Cannstatt: Frommann- Holzboog, 1978).

Bollino, Fernando, 'Derive della mimesis. Il nesso imitazione-espressione fra Batteux e Kant', *Studi di Estetica*, 11/12 (1995): 85-136.

Bonds, Mark Evan, *Wordless Rhetoric. Musical Form and the Metaphor of the Oration* (Cambridge, MA and London: Harvard University Press, 1991).

Borghero, Carlo, *La certezza e la storia. Cartesianesimo, pirronismo e conoscenza storica* (Milan: Franco Angeli, 1983).

Bour, Isabelle, 'Ut pictura musica? Signe et sens dans l'esthétique musicale britannique au XVIIIe siècle', *Bulletin de la Société d'études anglo-américaines des XVIIe et XVIIIe siècles*, 40 (1995): 115-129.

Bouveresse-Quilliot, Renée, *Esthétique, psychologie et musique: l'esthétique expérimentale et son origine philosophique chez David Hume* (Paris: Vrin, 1995).

Bowen Oberg, Barbara, 'David Hartley and the Association of Ideas', *Journal of the History of Ideas*, 37 (1976): 441-454.

Boyd, John D., *The Function of Mimesis and its Decline* (Harvard: Harvard University Press, 1968).

Brett, Raymond L., *The Third Earl of Shaftesbury* (London: Hutchinson's University Library, 1951).

Brewer, John, *The Pleasures of the Imagination: English Culture in the Eighteenth Century* (Chicago: The University of Chicago Press, 1997).

Broadie, Alexander (ed.), *The Cambridge Companion to the Scottish Enlightenment* (Cambridge: Cambridge University Press, 2003).

Brofsky, Howard, 'Doctor Burney and Padre Martini: Writing a General History of Music', *The Musical Quarterly*, 65 (1979): 313-345.

Brook, Barry S., Downes, Edward O. D. and Solkema, Sherman Van (eds), *Perspectives in Musicology* (New York: Norton, 1972).

Brown, Leslie Ellen, 'Thomas Reid and the Perception of Music: Sense vs. Reason', *International Review of the Aesthetics and Sociology of Music*, 20/2 (1989): 121-140.

Brugère, Fabienne and Malherbe, Michel (eds), *Shaftesbury: Philosophie et politesse* (Paris: Champion, 2000).

Buelow, George J., 'Originality, Genius, Plagiarism in English Criticism of the Eighteenth Century', *International Review of the Aesthetics and Sociology of Music*, 21/2 (1990): 117-128.

——, 'Music, Rhetoric, and the Concept of the Affections: A Selective Bibliography', *Notes*, 30/2 (1973): 250-259.

Bullit, John – Bate, Walter Jackson, 'Distinctions between Fancy and Imagination in Eighteenth-Century English Criticism', *Modern Language Notes*, 60/1 (1945): 8-15.

Burrows, Donald (ed.), The Cambridge Companion to Handel (Cambridge: The Cambridge University Press, 1997).

Burrows, Donald and Dunhill, Rosemary, *Music and Theatre in Handel's World: The Family Papers of James Harris, 1732-1780* (Oxford: Oxford University Press, 2002).

Bushnell, Rebecca, 'Experience, Truth, and Natural History in Early English Gardening Books', in D. R. Kelly and D. H. Sacks (eds), *The Historical Imagination in Early Modern Britain. History, Rhetoric, and Fiction, 1500-1800* (Cambridge: Cambridge University Press, 1997): 179-209.

Camic, Charles, 'Experience and Ideas: Education for Universalism in Eighteenth-Century Scotland', *Comparative Studies in Society and History*, 25/1 (1983): 50-82.

Campa, Cecilia, *La repubblica dei suoni. Estetica e filosofia del linguaggio musicale nel Settecento* (Naples: Liguori, 2004).

Cant, R. G., 'Scottish Universities and Scottish Society in the Eighteenth Century', *Studies on Voltaire and the Eighteenth Century*, 58 (1967): 1953-66.

Cappelletto, Chiara and Franzini, Elio, *Estetica dell'espressione* (Florence: Le Monnier, 2005).

Carabelli, Giancarlo and Zanardi, Paola, *Il Gentleman filosofo, nuovi saggi su Shaftesbury* (Padua: il Poligrafo, 2003).

Carey, Daniel, Locke, *Shaftesbury, and Hutcheson : Contesting Diversity in the Enlightenment and Beyond* (Cambridge: Cambridge University Press, 2006).

Carter, Jennifer J. and Pittock, Joan H. (eds.), *Aberdeen and the Enlightenment* (Aberdeen: Aberdeen University Press, 1987).

Casini, Paolo, *Filosofia e fisica da Newton a Kant* (Turin: Loescher, 1978).

——, *Introduzione all'illuminismo. Da Newton a Rousseau* (Rome and Bari: Laterza, 1973).

——, *L'universo macchina* (Bari: Laterza, 1969).

Cassirer, Ernst, *The Philosophy of the Enlightenment* (Princeton: Princeton University Press, 1951).

——, *The Platonic Renaissance in England* (London – Edinburgh: Nelson, 1953).

Charrak, André, *Musique et philosophie à l'âge classique* (Paris: PUF, 1998).

——, *Raison et perception. Fonder l'harmonie au XVIIIe siècle* (Paris: Vrin, 2001).

——, *Empirisme et théorie de la connaissance. Réflexion et fondement des sciences au XVIIIe siècle* (Paris: Vrin, 2009).

Chitnis, Anand C., *The Scottish Enlightenment: A Social History* (London: Croom Helm, 1976).

Christensen, Thomas, 'Eighteenth-Century Science and the "Corps Sonore": The Scientific Background to Rameau's "Principle of Harmony"', *Journal of Music Theory*, 31 (1987): 23-50.

——, *Rameau and Musical Thought in the Enlightenment* (Cambridge: Cambridge University Press, 1993).

Coley, Awen A. M., 'The Science of Man: Experimental Routes to Happiness in Duclos and Rousseau', *Studies on Voltaire and the Eighteenth Century*, 8 (2000): 235-327.

Conrad, Stephen A., *Citizenship and Common Sense* (New York, Garland, 1987).

Cocking, John M., *Imagination: A Study in the History of Ideas* (London: Routledge, 1991).

Dahlhaus, Carl, *Foundations of Music History* (Cambridge: Cambridge University Press, 1983).

Daiches, David, *The Paradox of Scottish Culture. The Eighteenth Century Experience* (London: Oxford University Press, 1964).

D'Angelo, Paolo and Velotti, Stefano (eds), *Il 'non so che'. Storia di una idea estetica* (Palermo: Aesthetica, 1997).

Darenberg, Karl H., *Studien zur englischen Musikaesthetik des 18. Jahrhunderts* (Hamburg: de Gruyter, 1960).

Davie, George, *The Scotch Metaphysics* (London e New York: Routledge, 2001).

Davis, Bertram H., *A Proof of Eminence: The Life of Sir John Hawkins* (Bloomington: Indiana University Press, 1973).

Deleule, Didier, 'Adam Smith et la difficulté surmontée', in Adam Smith, *Essais Esthétiques* (Paris: Vrin, 1997): 15-33.

De Palézieux, Nikolaus, *Die Lehre vom Ausdruck in der englischen Musikæsthetik des 18. Jahrhunderts* (Hamburg: Wagner, 1981).

DeWitt Thorpe, Clarence, 'Addison's Theory of Imagination as "Perceptive Response"', *Papers of the Michigan Academy of Science, Arts and Letters*, 21 (1936): 509-530.

——, 'Addison and Hutcheson on the Imagination', *English Literary History*, 2/3 (1935): 215-234.

Dickie, George, *The Century of Taste: The Philosophical Odyssey of Taste in the Eighteenth Century* (Oxford: Oxford University Press, 1996).

Dixon, Thomas, *From Passions to Emotions. The Creation of a Secular Psychological Category* (New York, 2003).

Downing, A. Thomas, *Music and the origins of language* (Cambridge: Cambridge University Press, 1995).

Draper, John W., 'Aristotelian "Mimesis" in Eighteenth Century England', *Publications of the Modern Language Association of America*, 36/3 (1921): 372-400.

Drummond, Pippa, 'The Royal Society of musicians in the Eighteenth-Century', *Music & Letters*, 59 (1978): 268-289.

Dubois, Pierre (ed.), *Normes et transgression au XVIIIe siècle* (Paris: Presses de l'Université de Paris-Sorbonne, 2002).

——, *La conquête du mystère musical en Grande-Bretagne au siècle des Lumières* (Lyon : Presses Universitaires de Lyon, 2009).

Dunhill, Rosemary, *Händel and the Harris Circle* (Winchester: Hampshire County Council, 1995).

Eccles, Mary Hyde, *The Thrales of Streatham Park* (Cambridge, MA, and London: Harvard University Press, 1977).

Ehrard, Jean, *L'idée de nature en France dans la première moitié du XVIIIe siècle* (2 vols, Chambéry: Imprimeries réunies, 1963).

Emerson, Roger, 'The Philosophical Society of Edinburgh 1737-1747', *The British Journal for the History of Science*, 12 (1979): 154-191.

——, 'The Philosophical Society of Edinburgh 1748-1768', *The British Journal for the History of Science*, 14 (1981): 133-75.

——, 'The Social Composition of Enlightened Scotland: the Select Society of Edinburgh, 1754-1764', *Studies on Voltaire and the Eighteenth Century*, 114 (1973): 291-329.

——, 'Natural Philosophy and the Problem of the Scottish Enlightenment', *History of Science*, 26 (1988): 333-66.

Eraw, Willem, 'Canon Formation: Some More Reflections on Lydia Goehr's Imaginary Museum of Musical Works', *Acta Musicologica*, 70 (1998): 109-115.

Farmer, Henry George, *Music Making in the Olden Days. The Story of the Aberdeen Concerts, 1748-1801* (London: Peters-Hinrichsen Edition, 1950).

Fawcett, Trevor, *Musical Life in Eighteenth-Century England* (Norwich: University of East Anglia, 1979).

Fiske, Roger, *English Theatre Music in the Eighteenth Century* (London: Oxford University Press, 1973).

Flynn, Philip, 'Scottish Aesthetics and the Search for a Standard of Taste', *Dalhousie Review*, 60 (1980): 5-19.

Formigari, Lia, *L'estetica del gusto nel Settecento inglese* (Florence: Sansoni, 1962).

——, 'Sulla genesi del concetto di espressione', *Revue internationale de philosophie*, 16 (1962): 101-115.

Fortune, Nigel (ed.), *Music and Theatre: Essays in Honour of Winton Dean* (Cambridge: Cambridge University Press, 1987).

Fox, Christopher (ed.), *Psychology and Literature in the Eighteenth Century* (New York: AMS Press, 1987).

Franzini, Elio, *L'estetica del Settecento* (Bologna: il Mulino, 1995).

Friesen, John, 'Hutchinsonianism and the Newtonian Enlightenment', *Centaurus*, 48 (2006): 40-49.

Fubini, Enrico, *Musica e cultura del Settecento europeo* (Turin: EDT, 1986).

Gallo, Franco Alberto, 'Historia civilis e Cultural heritage', *Il Saggiatore musicale*, 8 (2001): 15-20.

——, *Musica e storia tra Medio Evo e Età moderna* (Bologna: il Mulino, 1986).

Garin, Eugenio, *L'illuminismo inglese* (Milan: Bocca, 1941).

Gatti, Andrea, 'Il gentile Platone d'Europa'. *Quattro saggi su Lord Shaftesbury* (Udine: Campanotto, 2000).

Gerhard, Anselm, *London und der Klassizismus in der Musik. Die Idee der 'absoluten Musik' und Muzio Clementis Klavierwerke* (Stuttgart-Weimar: Metzler, 2002).

Gibson, Elizabeth, *The Royal Academy of Music 1719-28: the Institution and its Directors* (New York and London: Garland, 1989).

Goehr, Lydia, *The Imaginary Museum of Musical Works. An Essay in the Philosophy of Music* (Oxford: Clarendon, 1992).

Goldberg, M. A., 'Wit and the Imagination in Eighteenth-Century Aesthetics', *The Journal of Aesthetics and Art Criticism*, 16 (1958): 503-509.

Goldgar, Anne, *Impolite Learning. Conduct and Community in the Republic of Letters 1680-1750* (New Haven and London: Yale University Press, 1995).

Goldgar, Bernard A., *Walpole and the Wits: The Relations of Politics to Literature, 1722-42* (Lincoln: University of Nebraska, 1976).

Gouk, Penelope, 'Acoustics in the early Royal Society, 1660-1680', *Notes and Records of the Royal Society*, 36 (1982): p. 155-175.

——, *Music, Science and Natural Magic in Seventeenth-Century England* (New Haven and London: Yale University Press, 1999).

——, 'Some English Theories of Hearing in the Seventeenth Century: before and after Descartes', in C. Burnett, M. Fend and P. Gouk (eds), *The Second Sense: Studies in Hearing and Musical Judgment from Antiquity to the Seventeenth Century* (London: Warburg Institute, 1991): 95-113.

——, 'Music's Pathological and Therapeutic Effects on the Body Politic: Doctor John Gregory's Views', in Penelope Gouk and Helen Hills (eds), *Representing Emotions: New Connections in the Histories of Art, Music and Medicine* (Aldershot: Ashgate, 2005): 191-207.

Gozza, Paolo and Serravezza, Antonio, *Estetica* e *Musica. L'origine di un incontro* (Bologna: Clueb, 2004).

Grant, Kerry S., *Dr Burney as Critic and Historian of Music* (Ann Arbor, MI: UMI Research Press, 1983).

Grattan-Flood, William H., 'Handel and the Earl of Egmont', *The Musical Times*, 65 (1924): 1016-1017.

Grave, Selwyn Alfred, *The Scottish Philosophy of Common Sense* (Oxford: Clarendon Press, 1960).

Griffin, Martin I. J., *Latitudinarianism in the Seventeenth-Century Church of England* (Leiden: Brill, 1992).

Hadot, Pierre, *Philosophy as a Way of Life. Spiritual Exercises from Socrates to Foucault*, ed. A. I. Davidson (Oxford: Blackwell, 1995).

Halliwell, Stephen, *The Aesthetics of Mimesis. Ancient Texts and Modern Problems* (Princeton and Oxford: Princeton University Press, 2002).

Harris, Ellen T., 'With Eyes on the East and Ears in the West: Handel's Orientalist Operas', *Journal of Interdisciplinary History*, 36 (2006): 419-443.

Hegar, Elisabeth, *Die Anfänge der neueren Musikgeschichtsschreibung um 1770 bei Gebert, Burney und Hawkins* (Strasburg: Heitz, 1932).

Heninger, Simeon K. Jr, *Touches of Sweet Harmony. Pythagorean Cosmology and Renaissance Poetics* (San Marino, CA: The Huntington Library, 1974).

Hipple, Walter John, *The Beautiful, the Sublime and the Picturesque in Eighteenth-Century British Aesthetic Theory* (Carbondale: Southern Illinois Press, 1957).

Hogwood, Christopher and Luckett, Richard (eds), *Music in Eighteenth-Century England: Essays in Memory of Charles Cudworth* (Cambridge: Cambridge University Press, 1983).

Horsley, Phyllis Margaret, 'Charles Avison: the man and his milieu', *Music and Letters*, 55 (1974): 5-23.

Howell, Wilbur Samuel, *Eighteenth-Century British Logic and Rhetoric* (Princeton: Princeton University Press, 1971).

Hume, Robert D. and Milhous, Judith, 'J. F. Lampe and English Opera at the Little Haymarket in 1732-33', *Music & Letters*, 78 (1997): 502-531.

Hunter, Jean Paul, *Before Novels: The Cultural Context of Eighteenth Century English Fiction* (New York: Norton & Co., 1990).

Hutton, James, 'Some English Poems in Praise of Music', in Rita Guerlac (ed.), *Essays on Renaissance Poetry* (Ithaca and London: Cornell University Press, 1980).

Innocenti Manolescu, Beth, 'Traditions of Rhetoric, Criticism, and Argument in Kames's "Elements of Criticism"', *Rhetoric Review*, 22/3 (2003): 225-242.

Jackson, Wallace, 'Affective Values in Early Eighteenth-Century Aesthetics', *The Journal of Aesthetics and Art Criticism*, 27 (1968): 87-92.

Jacob, M. C., *Cultural Meaning of the Scientific Revolution* (New York: Knopf, 1988).

——, *The Newtonians and the English Revolution, 1689-1720* (Ithaca: Cornell University Press, 1976).

Jacobi, Erwin R., 'Harmonic Theory in England after the Time of Rameau', *Journal of Music Theory*, 1 (1957): 126-146.

Jauss, Hans Robert, *Literaturgeschichte als Provokation der Litteraturwissenschaft* (Frankfurt am Main: Suhrkamp, 1967).

——, *Ästhetische Erfahrung und literarische Hermeneutik* (Frankfurt am Main: Suhrkamp, 1982.

Jauss, Steven A., 'Associationism and Taste Theory in Archibald Alison's *Essays*', *The Journal of Aesthetics and Arts Criticism*, 64 (2006): 415-428.

Johnson, David, *Music and Society in Lowland Scotland in the Eighteenth Century* (Edinburgh: Mercat Press, 2003^2 [1972]).

Jones, Catherine, 'James Beattie and the Ethics of Music', *British Journal for Eighteenth-Century Studies*, 30 (2007): 55-71.

Jones, Peter (ed.), *Philosophy and Science in the Scottish Enlightenment* (Edinburgh: John Donald, 1988).

—— (ed.), *The 'Science of Man' in the Scottish Enlightenment* (Edinburgh: Edinburgh University Press, 1989).

Jones, Richard F., 'Science and Criticism in the Neo-Classical Age of English Literature', *Journal of the History of Ideas*, 1/4 (1940): 381-412.

Jones, Robert W., *Gender and the Formation of Taste in Eighteenth-Century Britain: The Analysis of Beauty* (Cambridge: Cambridge University Press, 1998).

Kallich, Martin, 'The Association of Ideas and Critical Theory: Hobbes, Locke and Addison', *English Literary History*, 12 (1945): 290-315.

——, 'The Meaning of Archibald Alison's *Essays on Taste*', *Philological Quarterly*, 27 (1948): 314-324.

——, *The Association of Ideas and Critical Theory in Eighteenth-Century England* (The Hague: Mouton, 1970).

Kassler, Jamie C., 'Burney's Sketch of a Plan for a Public Music-School', *The Musical Quarterly*, 58/2 (1972): 210-234.

——, *Inner Music: Hobbes, Hooke and North on Internal Character* (London: The Athlone Press, 1995).

——, *The Honourable Roger North, 1651-1734. On Life, Morality, Law and Tradition* (Farnham and Burlington: Ashgate, 2009).

——, 'The Systematic Writings on Music of William Jones (1726-1800)', *Journal of the American Musicological Society*, 26 (1973): 92-107.

——, *The Science of Music in Britain, 1714-1830: A Catalogue of Writings, Lectures and Inventions* (2 vols, New York and London: Garland, 1979).

Kelly, Donald R. and Sacks, David H. (eds), *The Historical Imagination in Early-Modern Britain* (Cambridge: Cambridge University Press, 1997).

Kelly, Michael (ed.), *Encyclopedia of Aesthetics* (York and Oxford: Oxford University Press, 1998).

Kivy, Peter, 'Reid's Philosophy of Art', in Terence Cuneo and René van Woudenberg (eds), *The Cambridge Companion to Thomas Reid* (Cambridge: Cambridge University Press, 2004): 267-288.

——, 'The "Sense" of Beauty and the Sense of "Art": Hutcheson's Place in the History and Practice of Aesthetics', *The Journal of Aesthetics and Art Criticism*, 53/4 (1995): 349-357.

——, *The Seventh Sense. Francis Hutcheson and Eighteenth-Century British Aesthetics* (New York: Oxford University Press, 1976).

Klein, Hannelore, *There is no disputing about taste. Untersuchungen zum englischen Geschmacksbegriff im 18. Jahrhundert* (Münster: Aschendorff, 1967).

Klein, Lawrence E., *Shaftesbury and the Culture of Politeness: Moral Discourse and Cultural Politics in Early Eighteenth-Century England* (Cambridge: Cambridge University Press, 1994).

Kloth, Karen, *James Beatties ästhetische Theorien. Ihre Zusammenhänge mit der Aberdeener Schulphilosophie* (Munich: Fink, 1974).

Knabe, Peter-Eckhard, Mortier, Roland and Moureau, François (eds), *L'Aube de la modernité 1680-1760* (Amsterdam and Philadelphia: John Benjamins Publishing, 2002).

Knepler, Georg, *Geschichte als Weg zum Musikverständnis: Beiträge zur Theorie, Methode und der Musikgeschichte* (Cologne: Hans Gerig, 1977).

Knif, Henrik, *Gentlemen and Spectators: Studies in Journals, Opera and the Social Scene in Late Stuart London* (Helsinki: Finnish Historical Society, 1995).

Korsmeyér, Caroline Wilker, 'The Two Beauties : A Perspective on Hutcheson's Aesthetics', *Journal of Aesthetics and Art Criticism*, 38 (1979/80): 145-151.

Koselleck, Reinhart, *Futures Past: On the Semantics of Historical Time*, trans. Keith Tribe (New York: Columbia University Press, 2004).

Kristeller, Paul Oskar, 'The Modern System of the Arts: A Study in the History of Aesthetics I & II', *Journal of the History of Ideas*, 12 (1951): 496-527; 13 (1952): 17-46; reprinted in Paul Oskar Kristeller, *Renaissance Thought and the Arts: Collected Essays* (Princeton, NJ: Princeton University Press, 1990).

Kümmel, Werner Friedrich, *Geschichte und Musikgeschichte: die Musik der Neuzeit in Geschichtsschreibung und Geschichtsauffassung des deutschen Kulturbereichs von der Aufklärung bis zu J. G. Droysen und Jacob Burckhardt* (Marburg: Görich & Weiershäuser, 1967).

Langwill, Lyndesay G., 'J. F. Lampe: a Forgotten Contemporary of Handel', *The Musical Times*, 76 (1935): 604 sg.

Larson, Roger B., 'Charles Avison's "Stiles in Musical Expression"', *Music & Letters*, 63/3-4 (1982): 261-275.

La Rue, Steven C., *Handel and his Singers: The Creation of the Royal Academy Operas, 1720-1728* (Oxford: Clarendon, 1995).

Le Huray, Peter, *Music and the Reformation in England* (New York: Oxford University Press, 1967).

Leppert, Richard, *Music and Image: Domesticity, Ideology and Socio-Cultural Formation in Eighteenth-Century England* (Cambridge: Cambridge University Press, 1988).

Levine, Joseph M., *Humanism and History: Origins of Modern English Historiography* (Ithaca: Cornell University Press, 1987).

Lindgren, Lowell, '*Camilla* and *The Beggar's Opera*', *Philological Quarterly*, 59 (1980): 44-61.

Lipking, Lawrence, *The Ordering of the Arts in Eighteenth-Century England* (Princeton: Princeton University Press, 1970).

Loftis, John, 'Richard Steele's Censorium', *The Huntington Library Quarterly*, 14 (1950): 43-66.

Longo, Antonio, 'Charles Avison estetico della musica', *Rivista Italiana di Musicologia*, 27 (1992): 183-204.

Lowerre, Kathryn, 'Dramatick Opera and the Theatrical Reform: Dennis's *Rinaldo and Armida* and Motteux's *The Island Princess*', *Theatre Notebook*, 59 (2005): 23-40.

——, *Music and Musicians on the London Stage, 1695-1705* (Farnham and Burlington: Ashgate, 2009).

Luckett, Richard, '"Or rather our musical Shakespeare": Charles Burney's Purcell', in Christopher Hogwood and Richard Luckett (eds), *Music in Eighteenth-Century England: Essays in Memory of Charles Cudworth* (Cambridge: Cambridge University Press, 1983), pp. 59-78.

Lund, Roger D., 'Wit, Judgment, and the Misprisions of Similitude', *Journal of the History of Ideas*, 65/1 (2004): 53-74.

MacDonald, Wilbert L., *Pope and his Critics: A Study in Eighteenth-Century Personalities* (London: Dent, 1951).

MacKerness, Eric Donald, *A Social History of English Music* (London and Toronto: Routledge & Kegan Paul, 1974).

MacLean, K., *John Locke and English Literature of the 18th Century* (New Haven: Yale University Press, 1936).

Maillard, Michel, 'Histoire et association d'idées dans l'esthétique de la fin du XVIIIe siècle et du début du XIXe siècle en Ecosse', *Bulletin de la Société d'études Anglo-Americaines des XVIIe et XVIIIe siècles*, 25 (1987): 103-114.

Malek, James, *The Arts Compared: An Aspect of Eighteenth Century British Aesthetics* (Detroit: Wayne State University Press, 1974).

——, 'Thomas Twining's Analysis of Poetry and Music as Imitative Arts', *Modern Philology*, 68/3 (1971): 260-268.

——, 'Adam Smith's Contribution to Eighteenth-Century British Aesthetics, *The Journal of Aesthetics and Art Criticism*, 31/3 (1972): 49-54.

Manns, James, *Reid and his French Disciples* (Leiden: Brill, 1994).

Marquard, Odo, *Der angeklagte und der entlastete Mensch in der Philosophie des 18. Jahrhunderts, in Abschied vom Prinzipiellen* (Stuttgart, 1981): 39-66; in English as *Farewell to Matters of Principle*, trans. R. Wallace (Oxford: Oxford University Press, 1989).

Mathieson, William Law, *Scotland and the Union. A History of Scotland from 1695 to 1747* (Glasgow: James Maclehose & Sons, 1905).

——, The Awakening of Scotland. A History from 1747 to 1797 (Glasgow: James Maclehose & Sons, 1910).

Mattick, Paul (ed.), *Eighteenth-Century Aesthetics and the Reconstruction of Art* (Cambridge: Cambridge University Press, 1993).

Maurer, Maurer, 'Alexander Malcom in America', *Music & Letters*, 33 (1952): 226-231.

McElroy, Davis D., *Scotland's Age of Improvement: A Survey of Eighteenth-Century Literary Clubs and Societies* (Washington: Washington State University Press, 1969).

McGeary, Thomas, 'Shaftesbury, Handel, and Italian Opera', *Händel-Jahrbuch*, 32 (1986): 99-104.

——, 'Shaftesbury on Opera, Spectacle and Liberty', *Music & Letters*, 74 (1993): 530-541.

McKendrick, Neil, Brewer, John and Plumb, John H. (eds), *The Birth of a Consumer Society: The Commercialization of Eighteenth-Century England* (London: Europa Publications, 1982).

McVeigh, Simon, 'Music and the Lock Hospital in the 18th Century', *The Musical Times*, 129 (1988): 235-40.

Mercier, Roger, *La réhabilitation de la nature humaine (1700-1750)* (Villemomble: La Balance, 1960).

Michael, Emily, 'Francis Hutcheson on Aesthetic Perception and Aesthetic Pleasure', *British Journal of Aesthetics*, 24 (1984): 241-55.

Migliorini, Ermanno, *Studi sul pensiero estetico di Francis Hutcheson* (Padua: Liviana, 1974).

Miller, Leta E., 'Rameau and the Royal Society of London', *Music & Letters*, 66 (1985): 19-33.

Momigliano, Arnaldo, 'Ancient History and the Antiquarian', *Journal of the Warburg and Courtauld Institutes*, 13 (1950): 285-315.

——, *The Classical Foundations of Modern Historiography* (Berkeley: University of California Press, 1990, 'Sather Classical Lectures').

——, *Contributo allo studio degli studi classici* (Rome: Edizioni di Storia e Letteratura, 1955).

——, *Ottavo contributo allo studio degli studi classici* (Rome: Edizioni di Storia e Letteratura, 1987).

Montgomery, Franz, 'Early Criticism of Italian Opera in England', *Musical Quarterly*, 15 (1929): 415-425.

Montgomery, Robert, 'Addison and Hutcheson', in Charles Fox (ed.), *Psychology and Literature in the Eighteenth Century* (New York: AMS Press, 1987): 149-166.

Moravia, Sergio, *La scienza dell'uomo nel Settecento* (Rome and Bari, Laterza, 2000²).

——, 'Dall'"homme machine" all'"homme sensible". Meccanicismo, animismo e vitalismo nel secolo XVIII', *Belfagor*, 29 (1974): 633-48.

Morillo, John, 'John Dennis: Enthusiastic Passions, Cultural Memory, and Literary Theory', *Eighteenth-Century Studies*, 34/1 (2000): 21-41.

Mulsow, Martin and Rohls, Jan (eds), *Socinianism and Arminianism: Antitrinitarians, Calvinists, and Cultural Exchange in Seventeenth-Century Europe* (Leiden and Boston: Brill, 2005).

Neubauer, John, *The Emancipation of Music from Language* (New Haven and London: Yale University Press, 1986).

Oberti, Elisa, 'Charles Avison e l'estetica musicale', *Rivista di estetica*, 3 (1958): 206-228.

Okie, Laird, *Augustan Historical Writing. Histories of England in the English Enlightenment* (Lanham, MD: Lanham University Press, 1991).

Omasreiter, Ria, *Naturwissenschaft und Literaturkritik im England des 18. Jahrhunderts* (Nuremberg: H. Carl, 1971).

Ottenberg, June C., 'Musical Currents of the Scottish Enlightenment', *Journal of the Aesthetics and Sociology of Music*, 9 (1978): 99-109.

Pacchi, Arrigo, *Cartesio in Inghilterra* (Bari: Laterza, 1973).

Pfeiffer, Helmut, Jauss, Hans-Robert and Gaillard, Françoise (eds), *Art social et art industriel. Funktionen der Kunst im Zeitalter des Industrialismus* (Munich: Fink, 1987).

Phillips, Mark Salber, 'Historiography and Genre; a More Modest Proposal', *Storia della Storiografia*, 24 (1993): 119-132.

——, 'Reconsiderations on History and Antiquarianism: Arnaldo Momigliano and the Historiography of Eighteenth-Century Britain', *Journal of the History of Ideas*, 57/2 (1996): 297-316.

——, *Society and Sentiment: Genres of Historical Writing in Britain, 1740-1820* (Princeton: Princeton University Press, 2000).

Phillipson, Nicholas, 'James Beattie and the Defence of Common Sense', in Bernhard Fabian (ed.), *Festschrift für Rainer Gruenter* (Heidelberg: Winter, 1978): 145-158.

Phillipson, Nicholas and Mitchison, Rosalind (eds), *Scotland in the Age of Improvement* (Edinburgh: Edinburgh University Press, 1970).

Plumb, John Harold, *The Commercialisation of Leisure in Eighteenth-Century England* (Reading: University of Reading, 1973).

Porter, Roy and Teich, Mikulas (eds), *The Enlightenment in National Context* (Cambridge: Cambridge University Press, 1981).

Powers, Harlod S. (ed.), *Studies in Music History: Essays for Oliver Strunk* (Princeton: Princeton Univesity Press, 1968).

Pritchard, Brian W., 'Provincial Music Meetings of the Ashley Family', *Galpin Society Journal*, 22 (1969): 58-77.

Probyn, Clive, *The Sociable Humanist: the Life and Works of James Harris 1709-80. Provincial and Metropolitan Culture in Eighteenth-Century England* (Oxford: Clarendon Press, 1991).

Ralph, Cohen (ed.), *Studies in Eighteenth-Century British Art and Aesthetics* (Los Angeles and London: University of California Press, 1985).

Rand, Benjamin (ed.), *The Life, Unpublished Letters, and Philosophical Regimen of Anthony, Earl of Shaftesbury* (London: Swan Sonnenschein, 1900; reprinted London: Thoemmes Continuum, 1994).

Restaino, Franco, *Scetticismo e senso comune. La filosofia scozzese da Hume a Reid* (Bari: Laterza, 1974).

Robertson, J. Charles, Review of *Thomas Reid's Lectures on the Fine Arts*, *Canadian Philosophical Review*, 14 (1975): 710-714.

Rohr, Deborah, *The Careers of British Musicians, 1750-1850* (Cambridge: Cambridge University Press, 2001).

Rossi, Mario Manlio, *L'estetica dell'empirismo inglese* (Florence: Sansoni, 1944).

Rossi, Paolo, *Francis Bacon: from Magic to Science* (Chicago: University of Chicago Press, 1968).

——, *The Birth of Modern Science* (Oxford: Blackwell, 2001).

Rousseau, George, '"Brainomania": Brain, Mind and Soul in the Long Eighteenth-Century', *Journal for Eighteenth-Century Studies*, 30 (2007): 161-191.

Rousseau, G. S., 'Science and the Discovery of the Imagination in Enlightened England', *Eighteenth-Century Studies*, 3 (1969): 108-135.

Roux, Louis (ed.), *Le Char ailé du Temps – Temps, mémoire, histoire en Grande-Bretagne aux XVIIe et XVIIIe siecle* (Saint-Étienne: Publications de l'Université de Saint-Étienne, 2003).

Rumbold, Valerie, 'Music Aspires to Letters: Charles Burney, Queeney Thrale and the Streatham Circle', *Music & Letters*, 74/1 (1993): 24-38.

Russo, Luigi (ed.), *Il Gusto. Storia di un'idea estetica* (Palermo: Aesthetica, 2000).

Sadie, Stanley and Hicks, Anthony (eds), *Handel Tercentenary Collection* (London: Macmillan, 1987).

Sadie, Stanley (ed.), *The New Grove Dictionary of Music and Musicians* (2nd ed., New York: Macmillan, 2001).

Santucci, Antonio (ed.), *Eredità dell'illuminismo: studi di cultura europea fra Settecento e Ottocento* (Bologna: il Mulino, 1979).

—— (ed.), *Filosofia e cultura nel Settecento britannico* (2 vols, Bologna: il Mulino, 2000).

——, *Sistema e ricerca in David Hume* (Bari: Laterza, 1969).

Scholes, Percy, *The Life and Activities of Sir John Hawkins: Musician, Magistrate and Friend of Johnson* (London: Oxford University Press, 1953).

Schueller, Herbert M., 'Correspondences between Music and the Sister Arts, according to 18th Century Aesthetic Theory', *The Journal of Aesthetics and Art Criticism*, 11/4 (1953): 334-359.

——, '"Imitation" and "Expression" in British Music Criticism in the 18th Century', *The Musical Quarterly*, 34 (1948): 544-566.

——, 'The Pleasures of Music: Speculation in British Music Criticism, 1750-1800', *The Journal of Aesthetics and Art Criticism*, 8/3 (1950): 155-171.

——, 'The Quarrel of the Ancients and the Moderns', *Music & Letters*, 41/4 (1960): 313-330.

——, 'The Use and Decorum of Music as Described in British Literature, 1700 to 1780', *Journal of the History of Ideas*, 13/1 (1952): 73-93.

Seidel, Wilhelm, 'Der *Essay* von Adam Smith über die Musik [Einführung und Text]', *Musiktheorie*, 15 (2000): 195-204.

——, 'La musica va annoverata tra le arti mimetiche? L'estetica dell'imitazione riveduta da Adam Smith', *Il Saggiatore Musicale*, 3 (1996): 259-272.

Semi, Maria (ed.), *Il suono eloquente* (Palermo: Aesthetica Preprint, 2008).

——, 'Musica e perfezionamento dell'uomo: John Gregory e l'Inghilterra del Settecento', *Intersezioni. Rivista di Storia delle Idee*, 28/2 (2008): 209-234.

Siegfried, Susan L., 'Engaging the Audience: Sexual Economies of Vision in Joseph Wright', *Representations*, 68 (1999): 34-58.

Smith, Andrew Cannon, *Theories of the Nature and Standard of Taste in England 1700-1790* (Chicago: The University of Chicago Libraries, 1937).

Smith, Ruth, *Handel's Oratorios and Eighteenth-Century Thought* (Cambridge: Cambridge University Press, 1995).

Sörbom Göran, 'Aristotle on Music as Representation', *The Journal of Aesthetics and Art Criticism*, 52/1 (1994): 37-46.

Spadafora, David, *The Idea of Progress in Eighteenth-Century Britain* (New Haven and London: Yale University Press, 1990).

Spitzer, Leo, *Classical and Christian Ideas of World Harmony* (Baltimore and London: Johns Hopkins University Press, 1963).

Starobinski, Jean, *The Living Eye*, trans A. Goldhammer (Cambridge, MA and London: Harvard University Press, 1989).

Steinwachs, Burkhart, *Epochenbewusstsein und Kunsterfahrung: Studie zur geschichtsphilosophischen Ästhetik an der Wende vom 18. zum 19. Jahrhundert in Frankreich und Deutschland* (Munich: Fink, 1986).

Stevenson, Robert, 'Hawkins, Burney, and Boswell', *The Musical Quarterly*, 36 (1950): 67-82.

Stewart, Alexander M., 'Berkeley and the Rankenian Club', *Hermathena*, 139 (1985): 25-45.

Stolnitz, Jerome, 'Locke and the Categories of Value in Eighteenth-Century British Aesthetic Theory', *Philosophy*, 38 (1963): 40-51.

Stone, Reppard, 'An Evaluative Study of Alexander Malcom's *Treatise of Musick: Speculative, Practical and Historical*' (PhD Dissertation, Catholic University of America, Washington D.C., 1974).

Strasser, Mark, 'Hutcheson on Aesthetic Perception', *Philosophia*, 21 (1991/92): 107-118.

Summers, David, *The Judgement of Sense: Renaissance Naturalism and the Rise of Aesthetics* (Cambridge: Cambridge University Press, 1987).

Sweet, Rosemary, 'Antiquaries and Antiquities in Eighteenth-Century England', *Eighteenth-Century Studies*, 34/2 (2001): 181-206.

Thomson, Herbert F., 'Adam Smith's Philosophy of Science', *The Quarterly Journal of Economics*, 79/2 (1965): 212-233.

Todorov, Tzvetan, *The Defence of the Enlightenment* (London: Atlantic Books, 2009).

——, *Theories of the Symbol* (Ithaca: Cornell University Press, 1992).

Tolley, Thomas, *Painting the Cannon's Roar: Music, the Visual Arts and the Rise of an Attentive Public in the Age of Haydn, c.1750 to c.1810* (Aldershot: Ashgate, 2001).

——, 'Music in the Circle of Sir William Jones: A Contribution to the History of Haydn's Early Reputation', *Music & Letters*, 73 (1992): 525-550.

Townsend, Dabney, *Hume's Aesthetic Theory: Taste and Sentiments* (London: Routledge, 2001).

——, 'Shaftesbury's Aesthetic Theory', *The Journal of Aesthetics and Art Criticism*, 41/2 (1982): 205-213.

——, 'The Aesthetics of Joseph Priestley', *The Journal of Aesthetics and Art Criticism*, 51 (1993): 561-571.

——, 'Thomas Reid and the Theory of Taste', *The Journal of Aesthetics and Art Criticism*, 61 (2003): 341-51.

Treitler, Leo, *Music and the Historical Imagination* (Harvard: Harvard University Press, 1989).

Trevor-Roper, Hugh, 'The Scottish Enlightenment', *Studies on Voltaire and the Eighteenth Century*, 58 (1967): 1635-1658.

Trottein, Serge (ed.), *L'esthétique naît-elle au XVIIIe siècle?* (Paris: PUF, 2000).

Turco, Luigi, *Dal sistema al senso comune. Studi sul newtonismo e gli illuministi britannici* (Bologna: il Mulino, 1974).

—— (ed.), *Filosofia, scienza e politica nel Settecento britannico* (Padua: Il Poligrafo, 2003).

——, *Hutcheson, Hume, senso morale e simpatia* (Bologna: CLUEB, 2007).

Ulman, Lewis H. (ed.), *The Minutes of the Aberdeen Philosophical Society, 1758-1773* (Aberdeen: University of Aberdeen Press, 1990).

Vendrix, Philippe, *Aux origines d'une discipline historique. La Musique et son Histoire en France aux XVIIe et XVIIIe siècles* (Geneva: Droz, 1993).

Viano, Carlo Augusto, *John Locke. Dal razionalismo all'illuminismo* (Turin: Einaudi, 1960).

Yolton, John W., Price, John V. and Stephens John (eds.), *Dictionary of Eighteenth-Century British Philosophers* (Bristol: Thoemmes Press, 1999).

Wasserman, Earl R. (ed.), *Aspects of the Eighteenth Century* (Baltimore: Johns Hopkins University Press, 1965).

Weber, William, 'Beyond *Zeitgeist*: Recent Work in Music History', *The Journal of Modern History*, 66/2 (1994): 321-345.

——, *The Rise of Musical Classics in Eighteenth-Century England: A Study in Canon, Ritual, and Ideology* (Oxford: Clarendon, 1992).

——, 'The Intellectual Origins of Musical Canon in Eighteenth-Century England', *Journal of the American Musicological Society*, 47/3 (1994): 488-520.

White, Harry, '"If It's Baroque, Don't Fix It": Reflections on Lydia Goehr's "Work Concept" and the Historical Integrity of Musical Composition', *Acta Musicologica*, 69 (1997): 94-104.

Wilbert, Jerome D., 'Poetry and Music as Observed by Daniel Webb', *Studies on Voltaire and the Eighteenth-Century*, 193 (1980): 1730-1735.

Winn, James Anderson, *Unsuspected Eloquence: A History of the Relations between Poetry and Music* (New Haven, CT: Yale University Press, 1985).

Wiora, Walter, 'Musikgeschichte und Universalgeschichte', *Acta Musicologica*, 33 (1961): 84-104.

—— (ed.), *Die Ausbreitung des Historismus über der Musik* (Regensburg: Bosse, 1968).

——, *Ideen zur Geschichte der Musik* (Darmstadt: Wissenschaftliche Buchgesellschaft, 1980).

Wollenberg, Susan and McVeigh, Simon (eds), *Concert Life in Eighteenth-Century Britain* (Aldershot and Burlington: Ashgate, 2004).

Wood, Paul B., *The Aberdeen Enlightenment. The Arts Curriculum in the Eighteenth Century* (Aberdeen: Aberdeen University Press, 1993).

Woodfield, Ian, *Opera and Drama in Eighteenth-Century London. The King's Theatre, Garrick and the Business of Performance* (Cambridge: Cambridge University Press, 2001).

Woolf, Daniel, *The Idea of History in Early Stuart England: Erudition, Ideology, and 'The Light of Truth' from the Accession of James I to the Civil War* (Toronto: Toronto University Press, 1990).

Wroth, Warwick, *The London Pleasure Gardens of the Eighteenth Century* (London: Macmillan, 1896; facsimile reprint 1979).

Youngren, William H., 'Addison and the Birth of Eighteenth-Century Aesthetics', *Modern Philology*, 79 (1982): 267-283.

Zeitz, Lisa, 'Addison's "Imagination" Papers and the Design Argument', *English Studies*, 73 (1992): 493-502.

Index

References to figures are in **bold**.

Aberdeen Philosophical Society 86
acoustics 9, 13, 122, 148, 153
    laws of 21
Addison, Joseph 24, 123
    on opera 28, 46-50
    Pleasures of the Imagination 27, 29,
        59, 123, 141
    self-assessment 30
    on taste 49, 50
Adler, Guido 106-7
aesthetic evaluation, Sterne on 9-11 *see*
    also beauty
aesthetic experience 57
aesthetics
    literature on 16
    morality, historical connection 16
    origins of term 16
Allen, Richard 79
Allen, Warren Dwight, *Philosophies of*
    Music History 19, 105
antiquarians
    Burney on 145-6
    historians, distinction 136
Aristotle
    on movement 81, 103
    on music 91
    on tragedy 39
    works
        Nichomachean Ethics 63, 64, 81
        Physics 63
        Poetics 41, 89
        Politics 91-2
        Problems 90, 91
        Rhetoric 81
Arsinoe, criticism of 37
art
    definitions 63

as mind 65
    nature, relationship 64-5
    and self-improvement 63-4
arts, the
    Harris on 65-6
    imitative, Smith on 94-5, 102
    Shaftesbury on 35-6
    and substitution 70
    as work 64
association principle 79, 95
    Beattie on 85-6
    Kames on 72, 73
    Webb on 78
Avison, Charles
    on consistency 127-8
    on musical expression 83-4, 102,
        124-5, 127-8, 129
    on musical imitation 124
    works
        An Essay on Musical Expression
        13, 19, 83, 105, 121-3, 152
        Concerti 128

Bacon, Francis 22
    on literary history 140
    tree of knowledge 1, 139-40, 152-5
        music in 153, 155
    works
        Advancement of Learning 1, 119,
        139, 152
        De sapientia veterum 20
        Orpheus sive Philosophia 20
Baumgarten, Alexander G., *Aesthetica* 16
Beattie, James
    on association principle 85-6
    Essay on Poetry and Music 84-5, 98
    on expression principle 86

on instrumental music 85-6
on musical imitation 99
beauty
    absolute 59-60
    and harmony 33, 60
    Hutcheson on 61-2
    Jones on 11
    kinds of 59
    nature of 61
    relative 59
biography, and improvement 8
Bisse, Thomas 12
Bonds, Mark Evan 18
Bontempi, Giovanni
    Historia dell'origine de Sassoni 152
    Historia musica 152
Broadie, Alexander 6
Brocklesby, Richard, *Reflections on Antient
    and Modern Musick* 79
Brook, Taylor, *Philosophical Transactions*
    120
Browne, Richard, *Medicina Musica* 79
Burney, Charles 13, 19
    on ancient music 135, 136-7
    on antiquarians 145-6
    General History of Music 93, 131, 134,
        136, 142, 146, 149
        Essay on musical Criticism 122,
            142-4
    linear progression 144
    on listening 143
    on Purcell 144-5, 147, 157

Camilla, Addisons' critique 47-8
Cassirer, Ernst 1
Censorium project 51-4
Chan, Mary 13
Cheselden, William 2
Chrysippus 6, 7
Collier, Jeremy
    *A Short View of the Immorality, and
        Profaneness of the English Stage*
        37, 40
    on music 41-2
consonance 114
    definition 113
Cooper, Anthony Ashley *see* Shaftesbury,
    Earl of

critics
    and music 9
    and opera 37-46
    role 36, 111

de Palézieux, Nikolaus, *Die Lehre vom
    Ausdruck* 14
Dennis, John 24
    on music 41
    opera, critique of 42-3, 44
    on pleasure 40
    on tragedy 39-40
    works
        An Essay upon Publick Spirit 44
        The Impartial Critick 37, 38-9
        The Usefulness of the Stage 37, 40
Descartes, René, *Compendium Musicae*
    115
Diderot, Denis, *Encyclopédie* 61
dissonance, and variety 60
Du Bos, Jean-Baptiste, *Réflexions critiques
    sur la poésie et sur la peinture* 68-9
Dubois, Pierre 15, 122

emotion
    and movement 80
    and music 74, 75, 85
        in *Tristram Shandy* 11
    passion, distinction 73
    and sound 75, 76, 79-80
    sympathetic 73-4
        and instrumental music 74
Epictetus 33
    on the soul 35
Epicurus 6, 7
eudaimonia, search for 23, 58
expression principle 84
    Beattie on 86

Franco-Flemish music, Hawkins on 149

Gallo, Franco Alberto 152
Garth, John 121
gaze, reflected 2
genius, Reynolds on 2-3
Glantville, Bartholomaeus, *De
    proprietatibus rerum* 138
Goehr, Lydia, the 'work' concept 16-17

Goldsmith, Oliver, *Present State of Polite Learning* 8
Gouk, Penelope 13, 15
Grimaldi, Nicola 37
Guido d'Arezzo 134, 142

Hadot, Pierre, *La philosophie comme méthode de vie* 6
Halliwell, Stephen 19
happiness *see eudaimonia*
harmony
    and beauty 33, 60
    concept 24, 32-3
    internal sense of 59
    and motion 75
    and taste 33
Harris, James
    on the arts 65-6
    on listening 67-8
    works
        Concerning Happiness 63
        Dialogue concerning Art 63
        Discourse on Music, Painting and Poetry 19, 63, 65, 125
Hartley, David, *Observations Upon Man* 78, 79
Hawkins, John, Sir 13, 19
    on ancient music 137
    on ancient/modern music 147-8
    on Franco-Flemish music 149
    General History of the Science and Practice of Music 131, 137-42, 149, 152, 155
        content 140-1
        Harris, citation of 139
        hope for future 150-1
        individual responses 141
        'Science of Music', categories 140
        structure 138
    symphonies, criticism of 150
hearing 13
    and movement 114
    sense of 120, 140
    Shaftesbury on 36
    and sight 68, 114
    and the theatre, Horace on 38, 45
    see also listening
historians, antiquarians, distinction 136

Holder, William, *Natural Grounds and Principles of Harmony* 113
Hooke, Robert, *Curious Dissertation* 113
Horace
    Epistle to Augustus 37-8, 45
    on hearing and the theatre 38, 45
Horizontabhebung concept 132
human typologies, and musical instruments 30-1
Hume, David 3, 87
    cause-effect relation 96
    on time 101
    Treatise on Human Nature 17-18, 72-3, 96, 101
Hunter, Paul J., on the novel 3
Hutcheson, Francis 15, 19, 150
    on beauty 61-2
    Inquiry into the Original 23, 58, 60

imitation, in the arts, Smith on 94-5
    musical *see* musical imitation
instrumental music 149
    Beattie on 85-6
    criticism of 74
    Kames on 76-7
    and passions 117
    Smith on 100-1
    and sympathetic emotion 74
    transitoriness 74
    Twining on 92-3
    vocal music, difference 81-2, 90

Jones, Peter, *Science of Man in the Scottish Enlightenment* 6
Jones, William, Sir 19, 78
    on beauty 11
    on listening 12
    on music 12, 70, 71
    works
        Essay on the Arts 69
        Letters from a Tutor to his Pupils 11
        'On Taste' 11

Kames, Lord 19
    on association principle 73
    Elements of Criticism 17, 72, 75, 76, 77, 82

on imitation 75-6
on instrumental music 76-7
on opera 77
Kassler, Jamie C. 13, 15
Kivy, Peter 14
knowledge, Bacon's tree of 1, 139-40,
        152-5
Koselleck, Reinhart 57
Kristeller, Paul O. 59
Kümmel, Werner Friedrich, *Geschichte
        und Musikgeschichte* 19, 106

La Mothe Le Vayer, François
        on ancient music 134-5
        Discours du peu de certitude 134
        Discours sceptique sur la Musique 134
Lampe, John Frederick
        on musical composition 119, 120-1
        on sound 120
        works
                Amelia 118
                The art of Musick 105, 118-21
language, Reid on 87-8
liberty, and music 45-6
listening
        Burney on 143
        Harris on 67-8
        Jones on 12
        and taste 31, 54
        see also hearing
literary history, Bacon on 140
Locke, John 2
        Essay on Human Understanding 25,
                112
        theory of mind 25, 112, 118
Luckett, Richard 147

Malcolm, Alexander
        on ancient/modern music 116
        on sound 112-13
        Treatise of Musick 105, 109-18
                ode 110
manners, concern for 7
Marcus Aurelius 34, 35
Marquard, Odo 57
mathematics, and music 9
Meier, Georg Friedrich, *Äesthetik* 16
Mersenne, Marin 120

mind
        art as 65
        cognitive processes 1
        Locke's theory of 25, 112, 118
        and music 115-18
Molyneux, problem of 2
Momigliano, Arnaldo 20, 105, 132-3,
        135-6
morality, and music 82
motion, and harmony 75
movement
        Aristotelian 81, 103
        and emotion 80
        and hearing 114
        and sight 114
        see also vibration theory
Mure, William 3
music
        aesthetics, studies 14-15
        ancient
                Burney on 135, 136-7
                Hawkins on 137
                La Mothe Le Vayer on 134-5
                modern
                        comparison 115
                        Hawkins on 147-8
                        Malcolm on 116-17
                and polyphony 116
                Twining on 90-1
                Wotton on 115-16
        Aristotle on 91
        as art 71
        in Bacon's tree of knowledge 153, 155
        canon, origins 156-7
        'classic' idea 16
        Collier on 41-2
        and the critics 9
        Dennis on 41
        effects, Twining on 89
        elevation of status 8-9
        and emotion 74, 75, 85
                in *Tristram Shandy* 11
        as fine art 71
        genres 97
        Jones on 12, 70, 71
        and liberty 45-6
        listening to 30-1
        and mathematics 9

and mind 115-18
  modern, and polyphony 116
  and morality 82
  and passions 97, 100, 102, 103, 117
  and philosophy 12-13, 156
  and pleasure 24, 115
  and poetry 67, 68-9, 69-70, 84, 85, 125-6
  progress in 144, 148
    and taste 149, 157
  as science 71
  sermons on 11-12
  social dimension 128
  and sympathy 19, 60-1, 62, 67, 70, 71
  and text 12, 28-9
  and thought 102
  and time 18
  and vibration principle 79
  writings on (1713-1830) 13, 24
  see also instrumental music; vocal
    music
music history
  and historiographic tradition 152
  as literary genre 151
  political history, analogy 146
  purpose 107
  treatises on 152
musical composition, Lampe on 119, 120-1
musical expression 19, 83-9
  Avison on 83-4, 102, 124-5, 127-8, 129
  definition 83-4
  Reid on 88
musical imitation 14, 16, 19, 28, 66, 83
  Avison on 124, 126
  Beattie on 99
  Kames on 75-6
  Smith on 97-8, 99
  Twining on 90
  vocal music 97
musical instruments, and human typologies
  30-1
musicology 20

natural philosophy, and the Orpheus myth
  21
nature, art, relationship 64-5
Neubauer, John, *The Emancipation of
  Music from Language* 14
Newcastle Music Society 121

Newton, Isaac, Sir
  Opticks 78
  sensorium 52
North, Francis, *Philosophical Essay of
  Music* 113
North, Roger 13
novel, the, Hunter on 3

Ockeghem, Johannes 149
opera
  Addison on 28, 46-50
  alternatives to 50-1
  and the critics 37-46
  Dennis' critique of 42-3, 44
  Kames on 77
  Shaftesbury on 44-6
Orpheus myth 20-1
  and natural philosophy 21

passion, emotion, distinction 73
passions
  and instrumental music 117
  and music 97, 100, 102, 103
Pepusch, Christopher, *Treatise on
  Harmony* 121
perception, sensation, distinction 87
Perrault, Claude 111, 112
Phillips, Mark Salber 3-4, 7-8
philosophy
  ancient 6-7
  and music 12-13
  philosophical discourse, distinction 6
  Shaftesbury on 7
Plato, *Republic* 42
pleasure
  Dennis on 40
  and music 115
poetry, and music 67, 68-9, 69-70, 84, 85,
  125-6
Poisson, Nicolas, *Elucidationes Physicae*
  111
Polybius, *Histories* 41
polyphony
  and ancient music 116
  and modern music 116
Purcell, Henry, Burney on 144-5, 147, 157
Pyrrhonism 133-7
  French 134

quadrivium 8

Raguenet, François, *Paralèle des Italiens
    et des François* 44-5
Rameau, Jean-Philippe, *Traité de
    l'harmonie* 120
Reid, Thomas 86-7
    on language 87-8
    on musical expression 88
    works
        Inquiry into the Human Mind 87
        Lectures on the Fine Arts 88
resonance, sympathetic 114
Reynolds, Joshua, Sir, on genius 2-3
Rymer, Thomas, *A Short View of Tragedy* 37

Sauveur, Joseph 120
Scholes, Percy 148
Schueller, Herbert 14
'Science of Man' 1
Scruton, Roger 14
sculpture 27-8
self-improvement, and art 63-4
sensation, perception, distinction 87
sermons, on music 11-12
Shaftesbury, Earl of (Anthony Ashley
        Cooper) 7
    on the arts 35-6
    on critics' role 36
    on harmony 32
    on hearing 36
    on opera 44-6
    on philosophy 7
    on the soliloquy 31
    works
        A Letter concerning Design 45
        *Characteristics of Men, Manners,
            Opinions, Times*, frontispiece
            34, 45
        Soliloquy 35, 111
        The Moralists 32, 64
 sight
    and hearing 68, 114
    and movement 114
Sirens myth 21-2
Smith, Adam 87
    on the imitative arts 94-5, 102
    on instrumental music 100-1

on musical imitation 97-8, 99
on wonder 94, 95-6
works
    History of Astronomy 93, 95, 101
    Of the Nature of that Imitation 17,
        93, 94
    Theory of Moral Sentiments 4, 17,
        100
    Wealth of Nations 17
Smith, Ruth 11, 15
social dimension, of music 128
soliloquy, Shaftesbury on 31
soul, the, Epictetus on 35
sound
    and emotion 75, 76, 79-80
    identification of 112
    Lampe on 120
    Malcolm on 112-13
spiritual exercises 6
Starobinski, Jean, *Le voile de Poppée* 2
Steele, Richard
    Censorium 51-3
    opera, alternative to 50-1
    on taste 51, 53
Sterne, Laurence, on aesthetic evaluation
        9-11
Stoicism 33-4
substitution, and the arts 70
sympathy
    meaning 62
    and music 19, 60-1, 62, 67, 70, 71, 77-8
symphonies, Hawkins' criticism of 150

taste 20, 49
    Addison on 49, 50
    changes in 145, 148-9, 150, 151, 157
    coarse 38
    diversity 61
    feigning 150
    good 26, 45
    and harmony 33
    Jones on 11
    and judgement 116, 147
    and listening 31, 54
    musical 142, 157
    natural 33
    and progress in music 149, 157
    Steele on 51, 53

Temple, William, Sir 115, 147
text, and music 12, 28-9
thought, and music 102
time, Hume on 101
Town-Talk in a Letter to a Lady in the Country 50, 51
tragedy
    Aristotle on 39
    chorus, function 39-40
    Dennis on 39-40
    task of 40
trivium 8
Twining, Thomas
    on ancient music 90-1
    on effects of music 89
    on instrumental music 92-3
    on musical imitation 90
    On the Different Senses of the Word Imitative 89

variety, and dissonance 60
Vendrix, Philippe 106
vibration theory 78-9, 83
    and music 79
    see also movement

vocal music 76, 149
    instrumental music, difference 81-2, 90
    musical imitation 97
Vossius, Isaac 115

Wallis, John 120
Webb, Daniel 77-83
    on association principle 78
    Observations on the Correspondence between Poetry and Music 18, 78
Weber, William 15-16, 109
    on the musical canon 156
wit, judgement, distinction 25-6
wonder 96-7
    Smith on 94, 95-6
Wotton, William
    Ancient and Modern Music 115
    on ancient music 115-16
Wright, Joseph
    A Philosopher Giving a Lecture 4
    An Experiment on a Bird 4, **5**
    The Blacksmith's Shop 4

Zarlino, Gioseffo 146